One Heart, Many Voices: A Biographical History of the American Balkan Scene

Hayna Cohen

Copyright © 2014 by Hasina Cohen
All rights reserved.
Cover illustration by Susan Reagel
ISBN: 978-1496152732

In memory of Anne Dhu McLucas,
beloved mentor and friend.
I honor you with every breath.

For Mark, Dena, Rachel, Eva, Peter, and Briget.
Thank you for the gift of your stories.

Contents

Acknowledgements	7
Preface	9
Introduction	11
1. Mark Levy	21
2. Dena Bjornlie	47
3. Rachel MacFarlane	75
4. Eva Salina Primack	95
5. Peter Jaques	132
6. Briget Boyle	155
Conclusion	182
Glossary	191
References	195
Appendix	199

Acknowledgements

I began writing this book at the age of twenty and penned the final words at twenty-seven. In essence, it constitutes the interior lattice of my second decade. Thus, acknowledgement is due not only to those who guided my work, but to all whose patient affection kept me rooted in the earthly realm.

In both categories, I offer heartfelt gratitude to my late advisor, Anne Dhu McLucas, who was first to suggest that my thesis had greater ethnographic and literary potential. I miss your wit, your wisdom, your wide-open enthusiasm, and the way you referred to my colorful phrasing as "a bit purple." Gratitude also goes to Mark Levy and Carol Silverman, my first Balkan music instructors: thank you for opening the world to me. I hope you will consider this book a testament to your endeavors.

I am deeply indebted to the East European Folklife Center, which labors tirelessly to cultivate the shared ground between so many diverse people's dreams. Though I have given it considerable effort, there really is no way to capture the magic of Balkan Camp—magic that I am certain will long resound.

Blessings on the memory of Mirjana Laušević, whose book, *Balkan Fascination*, is an infinite source of inspiration for me. Your legacy is evident in the warmth that fills Scene members' voices whenever they speak your name.

With this book, I honor my eight original interviewees, who nourished me to the core with their sensitivity, insight, and a host of gentle life lessons. By inviting me to journey through your hearts and minds and trusting me to formulate my own impressions, you rooted my sense of responsibility while encouraging me to take ownership of my work. It is my great hope that our friendship will endure.

As it traded private for public existence, my manuscript benefited from the expertise of three skilled artists and wordsmiths. In this category, I acknowledge Kimberlee Wollter: my editor, an avid folk dancer, and the first person to whom I entrusted my manuscript in full; Kirsten Healey, whose extraordinary generosity saved me the trouble of learning to navigate InDesign; and Susan Reagel, whose cover illustration exquisitely conveys the heart of my inquiry.

On a personal level, I am immensely grateful to my family, Warren, Leslie, Naomi, and Maria, for their incredible willingness to support me throughout the writing process. There is truly no way that I could have followed my muse without you. Here as well I owe a great deal to my beloved surrogate families. SueSue, Phil, and Grace; Ellie, John, Navah, Naomi, and Reuben Reed; Tracy, Pukha, Bodhi, and Lila; Hattie, JC, Maggie, and Joey; Christi, Kuriakose, and Anya Mae; and Amanda, Nathan, Nola, and Finn: over the past five years, you have helped me to grow in joy, curiosity, and wonder.

Thanks also to Bob Glynn, Shea Pedersen, Lauren Visconti, Giovanna Coto, Emily West, Tina Dreisbach, Leigh Ann Starcevich, Mary Goldman, Beth Leonard, Anita Dilles, Marcella Ovalle, Tatevik Simonian, and Leah Flippen: near or far, your care, counsel, and friendship could sustain me for several lifetimes.

A deep bow to Deborah Nixdorf, Peter Eschwey, Emily Barry, and Therese Waterhous for empowering me to inhabit a place of integrity as this path opens to the next.

Finally, I want to express my profound gratitude and respect for the American Balkan community. Differences in experience, opinion, and aesthetic aside, the love members harbor for one another is fierce. I am continuously humbled by your knowledge, by your devotion to craft, and by your passion for Balkan music and dance. Each and every one of you is inscribed in these pages; this book is my love for you made manifest.

Preface

The seed for this project was sown in 2006, when I participated as a vocalist in the University of Oregon East European Folk Ensemble (EEFE) and then in a Balkan fusion band with a self-professed Led Zeppelin aesthetic. With the EEFE, I sang monophonic and diaphonic Bulgarian, Macedonian, Romanian, Serbian, Albanian, and Balkan Romani folk songs, either a cappella or accompanied by a band that juxtaposed Bulgarian *gajda* and *tambura* with violin, trumpet, drum kit, accordion, and clarinet. I heard the instructor classify portions of our repertoire as "village style" or "arranged," and I learned to associate a polyphonic texture with the efforts of twentieth-century socialist governments to modernize and westernize rural folk traditions. I appreciated the leap required to add a banjo to our instrumental assemblage, and I pondered lyrics that offered tantalizing vignettes of village life, in which courtship, the harvest, and five centuries of Ottoman rule[1] resound from the core of what I envisioned as a tumultuous yet idyllic existence. At the end of the term, I was captivated by the complexity of playing in partnership with a body of folk dancers, reveling in the sense that I had transcended space and time.

The fusion band shattered my reverie. Performing at a local bar with nary a folk dancer in sight, I was caught between savoring our unique sound and fretting that I was both encroaching upon and publicly misrepresenting a venerable tradition. The result was a sort of paralysis, as I grew reluctant to act from what I now perceived as a position of inherent pretension. Still, I was unwilling to accept that in honoring my desire to sing Balkan music I need dishonor the music itself, and I reasoned that only through deeper and more mindful engagement could I hope to comprehend its role in my life.

---

[1] The Balkans fell under Ottoman dominion from the late 14th to the late 19th centuries. In Bulgaria, this was a period of cultural isolation, forced religious conversion, oppressive taxation, and obligatory military service. Scales and instruments derived from Turkish and Arabic music are now integral to Balkan folk tradition, and songs about resistance fighters and the capture of Slavic women are still sung today.

During my second year with the EEFE, I was surprised to discover that I was benefitting from the work of a national organization founded by Americans who had been playing Balkan folk music and dancing Balkan folk dances for decades. My initial concept of what I heard termed the American Balkan Scene amounted to a litany of names, which specified from whom my instructor and his vocal coach had learned the songs they presented. This litany was peppered with repeated reference to the Balkan Music and Dance Workshops (in standard parlance, Balkan Camp) as the primary context of transmission. Privileged to attend Balkan Camp in the summer of 2007, I witnessed these names walk into the flesh, suddenly and breathtakingly embodied as my teachers and fellow students.

Beyond introducing me to a sizeable contingent of the Scene population, my experience at Camp convinced me that I was not alone in my concerns about tradition and representation, traces of which I discerned as American instructors verbally deferred to native Balkan instructors they had earlier performed beside, as the authenticity of various sounds and styles was contested, and as enthusiasts of all backgrounds shared moments of communion and conflict in the classroom and on the dance floor. Contemplating examples of tension, I noted clear patterning based on age; the prospect of generational transition proved to be a dominant theme as I attended a second Camp session and began to invest in the Scene.

In short, this book represents a formal attempt to address questions I asked as I immersed myself in the study and performance of Balkan music through progressive involvement with a community of like-minded individuals operating out of the United States. Given the degree to which I became embedded in the world I describe, my greatest challenge has been to delineate the boundaries of my inquiry. This is the subject of a two-part Introduction, in which I summarize my research methodology before reviewing published resources.

Introduction

In March 2007, I began to think seriously about what was originally an undergraduate thesis project. At the time, I knew that I wanted to investigate the politics of performing Balkan music as an American Balkan musician, though my familiarity with this topic was sufficiently limited that I approached it with neither focal point nor conceptual framework. Uncertain of how to formulate a research strategy, I lacked even basic assurance that relevant material could be found. Having completed two terms in the University of Oregon EEFE, what I did know was twofold: 1) within the American cultural landscape existed a quantity of individuals who shared my passion for Balkan folk music, and 2) a significant proportion of these individuals congregated each summer in Mendocino, California for an intensive weeklong workshop. As I submitted my application, I told myself that—if viable—my inquiry would take shape at Balkan Camp.

I am pleased to report that my audacity was rewarded. Prior to Camp, I was driven by compelling yet vague curiosity. Following a single Camp session, I harbored nascent awareness of the scope and activity of the American Balkan Scene, rooted in firsthand interaction with affiliated musicians and dancers. My conversations with my fellow attendees were similarly integral to my bibliography. As she helped me unpack, a cabinmate asked whether I had read the book *Balkan Fascination*.[1] "It's about Americans and Balkan music," she explained. "The author did a lot of her research here." Exhilarated by this unexpected validation, I prepared for the week ahead, intent on absorbing anything and everything I could.

Brimming with song and fully inspired, I returned from Camp and took stock of my resources. First, I purchased a copy of *Balkan Fascination*, which provided an historical overview of Balkan Camp and the Scene, laying the groundwork for the more intimate chronicle I now wished to produce. Next, I consulted the Balkan Camp roster, sending a barrage of emails to a dozen

---

[1] Lauševič 2007.

attendees to inquire whether they might consent to be interviewed. Most accepted promptly, eager to expound on a facet of their lives often neglected in daily conversation. I conducted my first interview in late July; by March 2008, I had collected the musical histories of eight Scene members, though I was ultimately obliged to narrow my focus to six. Each interview encompassed on average two two-hour sessions, with preliminary and follow-up questions distributed via email. The majority of these sessions were held over the phone, recorded by means of a simple adaptor. Four were conducted in person—one (Mark Levy) at the University of Oregon, and three (Dena Bjornlie, Eva Salina Primack, and Briget Boyle) in California. Each interviewee was granted multiple opportunities to review my work, occasioning additional phone conversations as I continued to write and revise.

More than a tool for gathering information, the interview process left a deep impression on my research ethic. Approaching my interviewees as complex individuals, I strove to build relationships characterized by mutual respect, generating a level of trust that enhanced the humanity and ethnographic value of my project while strengthening my commitment to representational integrity. The benefits were equally personal. Although our early interactions were framed by the interview as both method and context, it seems blasphemous to refer to these individuals as my subjects; rather, the standard ethnographic dichotomy is fundamentally destabilized by the reality that I have come to consider them honored friends.

To avoid the danger of a musical ethnography fashioned entirely from verbal exchange, I made a point to attend pertinent concerts. In September 2007, I traveled to the San Francisco Bay Area for a performance by Brass Menažeri, an intergenerational ensemble that figures prominently in Chapters 3, 5, and 6. That December, I celebrated New Year's Eve at the Ashkenaz Music and Dance Community Center in Berkeley, California, where Brass Menažeri was joined by vocalist Eva Salina Primack, the voice of Chapter 4. Several days later, I attended a showing of *The Rusalka Cycle*, an innovative musical theater production detailed in Chapter 6. In February 2008,

Introduction

Eva came to Eugene, Oregon on tour with American Balkan brass band Slavic Soul Party! After sharing the bill with Slavic Soul Party! at a San Francisco nightclub, Brass Menažeri retraced its route, performing in Eugene the following month.

In addition to my role as a spectator, I sought to deepen my relationship with Balkan folk music as a musician. In November 2007, I was invited to sing with Kef,[2] a spirited ensemble formed approximately two years before from the ranks of the EEFE. Like the more widely acclaimed Brass Menažeri and Slavic Soul Party!, Kef encapsulates the dynamic present of the Scene, playing for folk dancers while courting young listeners at greater proximity to the mainstream. As a member of Kef, my passion for Balkan music soared, and I gained an intuitive appreciation for topics with immediate bearing on my work.

The relevance of my personal narrative is a function of the process by which this project was conceived. Instead of asserting a central idea and endeavoring to support it through research, I embraced my research as the raw material from which my inquiry would develop. As the rise of a new generation had piqued my interest at Balkan Camp, I formulated my interview questions with attention to generational transition. In conversing with my interviewees, however, I came to regard today's Scene as an entity more fully defined by intergenerationality and broadened my inquiry to give equal weight to both generational demographics. Another shift transpired as I prepared to write. Though I had already resolved to proceed without a conceptual framework, I had maintained that I would compose a traditional thesis paper, in which fragments of evidence advance an analytical argument. In sifting through the stories contained in my interview transcriptions, however, I grew uncomfortable with the idea of obliging them to conform to an academic model. To honor the integrity of each story, I now understood,

[2] For more information about Kef and to hear musical samples (recorded after I left the group), see www.balkanmusic.org.

I would have to allow it to speak for itself, and I decided to structure my document as a series of narrated biographies.

Two caveats are in order. First, this project is not built on a representative sample of the Scene. As previously stated, I solicited potential interviewees after observing and interacting with them at Mendocino Balkan Camp, which I attended as a musician. Accordingly, not one is exclusively a folk dancer, and most reside and make music on the West Coast. Second, I make no claim to ethnographic objectivity. Having established a participant population, I employed what I knew of each individual to craft variations on a stock set of interview questions. Yet for me the ideal of objectivity betokens oversimplification. Hardly monolithic, community materializes at the interface of members' experiences and perceptions, and my questions conveyed a concern for honest detail that elicited frank disclosure.

Herein lies the essence of my approach. In research as well as in writing, I choose to celebrate the chaos of interaction and interpretation. I choose to celebrate conflicting views as a source of creative tension. I choose to leave scaffolding exposed and cadences unresolved, inviting a diversity of conclusions. And perhaps in my commitment to honoring idiosyncrasy and bias in all perspectives including my own, I will illuminate a methodology capable of producing an account more human than commonly known.

My work on this project has been informed by a number of published resources, the majority of which I encountered as an ethnomusicology student at the University of Oregon.

Useful in thinking, talking, and writing about what contemporary ethnomusicologists call "music-culture" is *Subcultural Sounds: Micromusics of the West*, in which Wesleyan professor Mark Slobin develops a set of three categories to "lay out the musical interplay—the cultural counterpoint—between individual, community, small group, state, and industry" in the face of global exchange.[3] The category "superculture" refers to

---

[3] Slobin 1987, 14.

Introduction

the "overarching" mode of musical performance, transmission, and consumption within a given region.[4] Experience of the superculture is contingent on factors that range from ethnicity and socio-economic background to age and aesthetic, opening the door to any number of "subcultures" characterized by common investment in a specific body of repertoire and practice. Whether diasporic or affinity based, elements of a superculture or subculture in turn harbor the capacity to become "intercultural," a quality[5] that invokes "the far-flung, expansive reach of musical forces that cross frontiers."[6] With the acknowledgment that all three are fundamentally entwined, this final category is critical to my depiction of the American Balkan Scene.

My impression of Balkan music-culture largely derives from the work of American ethnomusicologists.[7] The following texts exhibit an emphasis on Bulgaria that mirrors the country's status as the historical focus of western research.

Written by University of California, Los Angeles (UCLA) ethnomusicologist Timothy Rice, *Music in Bulgaria: Experiencing Music, Expressing Culture* offers an overview of the origin, structure, and function of traditional and contemporary Bulgarian genres and styles, among them those discussed by my interviewees. Of greater relevance to this project is Rice's *May it Fill Your Soul: Experiencing Bulgarian Music*, an in situ account of the music-cultural histories of *gajda* player Kostadin Varimezov and vocalist Todora Varimezova that incorporates Rice's reflections on his role as ethnographer. Biographical, theoretical, and personal narratives similarly interweave throughout my book.

---

[4] Ibid., 29.

[5] Slobin's usage is actually more noun than adjective, referring both to an inflated superculture that spans multiple geo-cultural areas and to beliefs and practices carried across geo-cultural lines through human migration or a desire to cultivate cultural affinity beyond the dictates of birth.

[6] Ibid., 61.

[7] This bias is a reflection of the texts made available to me as an undergraduate music major at a public university with a small ethnomusicology program. I see now that I could have been more proactive in procuring translated texts, either directly from my professors or from other university libraries.

16   Introduction

Built on a comparable premise is *Listen, Daughter, and Remember Well*, in which ethnomusicologist Martha Forsyth revisits her conversations with elderly Bulgarian vocalist Línka Gékova Gérgova. At once a loving portrait of an individual musician, an intimate chronicle of music and ritual in an early twentieth-century village, and a treasury of song, this book is a perpetual source of inspiration for me, as it is for many Scene members.

I owe much of my awareness of the politics of music in the Balkans to Donna Buchanan, a University of Illinois ethnomusicology professor who examines the strategies Bulgarian musicians have historically employed to negotiate social, economic, and cultural change. Centered on the communist and post-communist transitions, her oeuvre encompasses numerous articles[8] and an acclaimed book, *Performing Democracy: Bulgarian Music and Musicians in Transition*. The latter assists in charting the process through which communist officials transfigured Bulgarian folk tradition by constructing collective vocal and instrumental ensembles to perform polyphonic arrangements of village music.[9] Aversion toward the resultant aesthetic supplied ideological impetus for the genesis of the American Balkan Scene.

Finally, I note the work of Carol Silverman, a prominent folklorist, anthropologist, ethnomusicologist, and founding Scene member. In writing that probes the post-communist marketing of Bulgarian women's choral singing[10] and the vital yet

[8] These articles includes "Dispelling the Mystery: The Commodification of Women and Musical Tradition in the Marketing of Le Mystère des Voix Bulgares" and "Metaphors of Power, Metaphors of Truth: The Politics of Music Professionalism in Bulgarian Folk Orchestras."
[9] Prior to the twentieth century, folk music in Bulgaria was dominated by individual musicians and small musical groupings that mirrored the context and function in which they arose. Solo instrumental repertoire was performed by shepherds or other male laborers, while women sang a cappella in the course of agricultural work or with instrumental accompaniment in the village square. Around mid-century, the socialist government began recruiting talented villagers to perform with urban orchestral and vocal ensembles built on a western classical model. This effort sparked the foundation of conservatories designed to educate future generations of music professionals and led to the propagation of standardized techniques and new emphasis on virtuosity. The most celebrated ensembles later toured Western Europe and the United States, where their music was promoted as authentic folk tradition and the cultural wellspring of a modern western socialist state.
[10] See "'Move Over Madonna': Gender, Representation, and the 'Mystery' of

Introduction   17

often uncredited influence of Balkan Rom (or "Gypsy")
musicians,[11] Silverman challenges a common proclivity to
romanticize Balkan music-culture by calling attention to entrenched social and political inequalities. Her commitment
to tangible activism[12] is a key aspiration of my interviewees.

The sole book with an explicit connection to my inquiry is
the aforementioned *Balkan Fascination: Creating an Alternative
Music Culture in America*. A brief summary acquaints us
with trends intended to frame my account as it unfolds.

In a sweeping analysis sparked by a chance encounter[13]
shortly after her relocation to the United States, Bosnian-born
ethnomusicologist Mirjana Laušević identifies what she terms
"the Balkan music and dance scene" as an outgrowth of the
International Folk Dance Movement, itself a product of turn-
of-the-century settlement efforts to promote harmony among
immigrant groups. Later adopted by public educators as a
means to instill Old World values into the hearts and minds
of America's youth,[14] folk dance curricula were typified by
pervasive disregard for the provenance of individual dances, and musical accompaniment borrowed from western

Bulgarian Voices" in *Over the Wall/After the Fall: Post-Communist Cultures through
an East-West Gaze.*
[11] See "Music and Marginality: Roma (Gypsies) of Bulgaria and Macedonia" in
Retuning Culture: Musical Changes in Central and Eastern Europe.
[12] Carol discusses her work with Romani musicians in the Spring/Summer 2001 issue
of the East European Folklife Center's *Kef Times.*
[13] Mirjana Laušević encountered the Scene at New York's annual Golden Festival,
which she was astonished to learn was primarily attended by Americans as opposed
to ex-patriots like herself. Scene members report a similar response from native
Balkan individuals upon indicating familiarity with Balkan folk music and dance.
[14] Embraced by school and church officials, organized folk dance activity acquired
a moralistic and preservationist tone. Laušević (2007, 127) writes: "If the common
perception was that there was, on one side, American culture whose values are determined by commercialism and, thus, are ever-changing and shallow and, on the other
side, Old World folk cultures that were stable, tried and true, historically proven, rich
and deep, it was obvious that the latter needed to be saved and embraced in order to
give depth and stability to American culture." This view is echoed by Scene members
who prioritize musical genres and ways of performing that they deem traditional, at
times in direct opposition to the attitudes of native musicians who wish to teach and
perform newer styles.

18   Introduction

classical tradition[15] was "most often provided on a piano."[16]

During the 1930s, institutional initiative gave way to a
grassroots phenomenon driven by recreational folk dancers who
gathered to share "the joy found in participation."[17] Over the next
several decades, this phenomenon "grew to such prominence that
one would not be surprised to find that there was some sort of
folk dance program in just about any city, large town, or college
campus in the country."[18] If this period saw the release of the
first international folk dance recordings,[19] however, these attest
to continued reliance on western classical instruments and were
again employed with little thought to geo-cultural correlation.[20]

In the 1950s, a new breed of "teacher-ethnographers" began
traveling to study folk dances in their native surroundings,
prompting the fragmentation of the International Folk Dance
Movement into regionally specific contingents.[21] Dancers drawn
to Balkan material were further inspired by the North American
tours of Soviet and Soviet-model folk troupes, which triggered
a mushrooming of performance ensembles[22] in cities across the
United States.[23] American enthusiasm was accompanied by an
upsurge in the number and variety of recordings[24] available to the

---

[15] Ibid., 121 – 122.
[16] Ibid., 116.
[17] Ibid., 138.
[18] Ibid., 169.
[19] These recordings were the contribution of pioneering dance instructor Michael
Herman, whose first album featured "Mexican, Lithuanian, Danish, Czech, Swiss,
Estonian, and Polish dances" (Laušević 2007, 160) performed by the Herman
Orchestra. With fellow instructor David Rosenberg, Herman went on to found the
Folk Dancer label on Sonart Records, which ultimately released some 300 recordings
(Laušević 2007, 160). Herman and his wife Mary Ann were also responsible for
organizing the first folk dance camp in 1940 (Laušević 2007, 161 – 162).
[20] Ibid., 161.
[21] Ibid., 183.
[22] Designed to rally domestic (and later, international) support for the modern
socialist state, these ensembles presented elaborate choreographies and polyphonic
arrangements of village repertoire as organic outgrowths of village tradition. Laušević
(2007, 197) explains: "It is interesting and somewhat ironic that such highly polished
and nationalized presentations of the 'folk' constructed by the socialist states would
be adopted and perpetuated among Americans as true representations of peasant
cultures."
[23] Ibid., 197.
[24] As Laušević (2007, 201) describes, "These included imported records (brought

Introduction

folk dance population, leading some to develop "an avid interest" in Balkan folk music.[25] It is from the lattermost trend that Lauševič derives the birth of what I refer to as the American Balkan Scene.

Before opening these pages to my interviewees, whose narratives build on Lauševič's findings, I discuss two books that shaped my approach to "doing" and "writing" ethnomusicology by establishing a precedent for what I initially feared was an overly unconventional research design.

Influenced by parallel movements in anthropology and folklore,[26] contributors to *Shadows in the Field: New Perspectives for Fieldwork in Ethnomusicology* call for a methodology that favors the experience of fieldwork over the act of representation.[27] More than a mode of data acquisition, co-editor Timothy Cooley sees fieldwork as "an inherently valuable and extraordinarily human activity with the capacity of integrating scholar, scholarship, and life,"[28] and urges the ethnomusicologist to cultivate awareness of his or her role as the center of signification. "By creating a reflexive image of ourselves as ethnographers and the nature of our 'being in the world,' we believe we stand to achieve better intercultural understanding as we begin to recognize our own shadows among those we study,"[29] he states.

This goal is also addressed in *Writing Ethnographic Fieldnotes*, in which Robert Emerson, Rachel Fretz, and Linda Shaw outline a procedure for generating what they term an "ethnographic story." "Structurally, in a text which presents a logical

back from Balkan travels or acquired through shops serving ethnic communities), commercial recordings made by Americans of native musicians in the Balkans, and pirated recordings (mostly reprints of releases originally put out by record labels in the Balkans)." Production and distribution were facilitated by a fledging folk dance music industry built around labels such as Worldtone Records, Balkan Records, Folkways, and Folkraft.

[25] Ibid., 202.

[26] Examples include the work of Richard Bauman and Victor Turner, in addition to the seminal article "Folklore's Crisis" by Barbara Kirshenblatt-Gimblett.

[27] Barz and Cooley 1997, 3.

[28] Ibid., 5.

[29] Ibid., 4.

argument, the author sets forth a formal thesis or proposition in the introduction as a stance to be argued, and then develops each analytic point with evidence logically following from and clearly supporting the propositional thesis," they suggest. Against this, "an ethnographic story proceeds through an intellectual examination of evidence to eventually reach its contributing central idea,"[30] using quotations "not as illustrations and examples of points that have already been made, but as building blocks for constructing and telling the story in the first place."[31] This produces "a distinctly dialogic text"[32] that enables the ethnographer to more fully honor each individual's perspective. It is with this very commitment that I introduce my first interviewee.

[30] Emerson, Fretz, and Shaw 1995, 202 – 203.
[31] Ibid., 203.
[32] Ibid., 212.

1

Mark Levy

We begin our journey with Mark Levy, who became in-terested in Balkan folk music as a folk dancer in the late 1960s. By virtue of his pioneering efforts to provide live music for folk dance events, Mark is credited as the founder of the Mendocino Balkan Music and Dance Workshops, which fed the rise of the American Balkan Scene. His narrative furnishes a framework for subsequent chapters, illuminating key themes and trends.

I met Mark during my freshman year at the University of Oregon, when I took an introductory ethnomusicology course he had taught since the early 1990s. Like many such classes, this surveyed the music of three regions, one of which was the Balkans. At the time, my experience of Balkan music encompassed a single album gifted to me by a family friend who knew one of the musicians from their student days at the University of California, Santa Cruz. When Mark opened the term with a bleat from his gajda, I recognized the sound and approached him to inquire whether he had heard of the band Medna Usta. His response alluded to a friendship of several decades. Though it left me profoundly bewildered, I now commemorate this exchange as my first encounter with the Scene.

Even as a child, Mark Levy appreciated the power of music to engage individuals in the experience of community. "I played piano as a young person, but I found it to be very isolating," he states. "This did not become fully apparent to me until the eighth grade, when I started playing clarinet and joined the band. It was just such a different thing, and I was kind of a loner, so it was great for me socially." A novice when the school year began, he was assigned to "the very last chair" of the clarinet section. By spring, he had been named section leader. "I progressed rather swiftly, and it gave me a lot of acknowledgement," he allows. Soon, Mark was playing first chair in the Chicago All City Band, which performed at Orchestra Hall, a venue he describes as "the Carnegie Hall of Chicago." As college approached, his teacher encouraged him to pursue a career as a clarinetist. He chose to study medicine.

In 1964, Mark enrolled at the University of Chicago, where his resolve to become a physician was eroded by music classes. Attempting to establish himself in the music department, he faced an immediate hurdle. Despite his rapid advance as a young clarinetist, his preliminary audition was rejected by the university symphony. "There are only two clarinets in an orchestra anyway," he notes. "But it felt like a blow at the time." Loath to relinquish the opportunity to participate in an ensemble, he re-auditioned on the violin, an instrument he had picked up in high school. This time he was accepted, and here he lingered, hoping for a chance to fill the next available clarinet position. His eventual triumph did little to mitigate a mounting disillusionment with the world of western classical music, in which even collaboration now seemed to him a privilege apportioned by talent.

Meanwhile, Mark had become aware of a mysterious campus subculture composed of students and community members who congregated to folk dance. Though he was initially baffled by their zeal, folk dancing would prove to be the mechanism of his transformation. "I kept encountering it here and there, but I didn't really buy it," he recounts:

I went on a weeklong ski trip with the University of Chicago Ski Club, which was led by Steve and Nahoma Sachs, two prominent Chicago folk dance teachers. Whenever we got out at a rest stop, Steve would lead a dance line, and I just thought it was the silliest thing. And then I had a girlfriend who danced, but really I had no interest in it. One evening during my junior year—it must have been 1967—I was walking through the student union, and I looked into a room, and there was the Sunday evening folk dance group. They were doing one of the Israeli favorites, though of course I didn't know that at the time. Maybe it was because I kept seeing it, but finally I said, "Okay, let's give this a shot!" And that was it! People talk about being "bitten"; I went in that night, and I never stopped.

Pretty soon I was dancing literally every night of the week, and some nights there would be several hundred people. It was amazing!

In *Balkan Fascination*, Mirjana Laušević designates the mid-twentieth century as a turning point in the history of the International Folk Dance Movement, citing new interest in regional specialization that produced an array of subsidiary scenes. This was already underway when Mark arrived at the University of Chicago, where one night each week was devoted to Israeli dances, another to English and Scottish country dances, a third to Balkan dances, and so forth. Empowered to distinguish stylistic patterns, dancers perpetuated this approach, tailoring their attendance to reflect personal preference for material of particular regions. "I realized pretty quickly that there was a certain kind of dance that I really liked," Mark affirms. "I think at first it was Macedonia—Macedonian stuff really intrigued me, and that was what I wanted to focus on."

After a year with the University of Chicago folk dancers, Mark auditioned for Balkanske Igre,[1] a performance group modeled on a series of Soviet and Balkan folk troupes that had toured the United States after World War II. "Balkanske Igre performed highly choreographed dances from Bulgaria and the former Yugoslavia for members of local ethnic communities," he explains. "Some of the dancers had Balkan heritage, but most of them were American, and they asked me to join them." In addition to a boost in quality and rigor, membership in Balkanske Igre brought a major shift in Mark's experience of musical accompaniment. At the University of Chicago, he danced to standard folk dance albums. "Live music wasn't even a thought," he states. In contrast, Balkanske Igre incorporated live music into a number of its productions, enlisting dancers to perform on whatever instruments they had at hand. "By the time I joined, somebody played *tapan*, and somebody else had a *gajda* that didn't work," Mark recalls. "And then a man named David

---

[1] Still active today, Balkanske Igre is a primary force behind the Chicago Spring Festival, a celebration of East European and Mediterranean music and dance held annually since 1976. For more information, see www.balkanskiigri.com.

Golber started playing clarinet with us, and somebody else played accordion." Lacking instructors, these individuals learned to play by following along with available recordings, assisting each other in a manner depicted to Laušević as "the deaf leading the deaf."[2]

Mirroring his development as a folk dancer, Mark demonstrated persistent reluctance to engage Balkan folk music. "I listened to a lot of Balkan music, but I was mainly into the dance," he remarks. "I dabbled—I think I tried *frula* a little bit. I was still playing classical clarinet, but for a long time I wasn't trying to play Balkan stuff. It's weird, looking back." Though I agree with Mark that his early disinclination to play Balkan clarinet is worthy of mention, for me it represents the logical extension of his musical background. Alienated by the impression that membership in a symphony orchestra was a privilege to be won, Mark's attraction to folk dancing was in part a response to its inherent inclusivity. At issue, then, was the prospect of playing "community music" on an instrument he associated with talent and competition, an argument from which I distill the concept of *approach*. Had Mark sought to play Balkan clarinet upon first exposure to Balkan music, he would have *approached* it as a classical musician. By *approaching* Balkan clarinet through dance and, as we are about to see, through academic ethnomusicology, this association was largely expunged. I revisit the concept of *approach* throughout this book, treating it as an indicator of generational identity at the level of the American Balkan Scene.

In 1968, Mark enrolled in an ethnomusicology class taught by visiting professor Anthony Seeger,[3] whom he credits with jumpstarting the University of Chicago ethnomusicology program, now among the foremost in the country. Seeger's class was instrumental for Mark, enlightening him to the fact that a career

---

[2] Laušević 2007, 206 – 207.
[3] Anthony Seeger is the nephew of Pete, Mike, and Peggy Seeger and the grandson of Charles Seeger, all prominent members of a family at the forefront of American folk music, musicology, and ethnomusicology. He is the author of *Why Suyá Sing: A Musical Anthropology of an Amazonian People*. Champaign: University of Illinois Press, 2004 and served as Director of Smithsonian Folkways Recordings from 1988 to 2000.

in music need not imply a career in classical performance. "I thought, 'I've got to do that!'" he exclaims. "I'd had no idea that folk music could be a legitimate academic pursuit." With graduation in sight, he began researching ethnomusicology programs and was thrilled to discover that UCLA and the State University of New York (SUNY) Binghamton boasted native Balkan professors. "At UCLA, there was Boris Kremenliev from Bulgaria, and then at SUNY Binghamton there was Sam Chianis, who studies Greek music," he explains.[4] Denied admittance by his first choice, UCLA, he accepted an invitation to study under Chianis in New York.

A proponent of participant-observation technique, Sam Chianis encouraged Mark to renew his focus on musical activity. "My first Balkan clarinet was Greek!" he laughs, deeming this ironic given his later preference for Bulgarian and Macedonian music coupled with folk dancers' propensity to consider Greek repertoire only peripherally Balkan. Having at last determined to play, he made rapid progress, though he attributes this as much to his folk dance experience as to his experience as a clarinetist. To recreate the sense of community he had enjoyed in Chicago, he started an international folk dance group[5] on the SUNY Binghamton campus and, with Chianis and several other students, assembled "a miniature folk dance band." Due in part to the reality that Chianis operated as "a one-person ethno department," however, Mark's efforts bore little fruit, and he grew starved for people whose passion for Balkan folk music and dance was commensurate with his own. Toward the end of his first term, Chianis advised Mark to reapply to UCLA, urging him to move to Los Angeles regardless of admission.

[4] Boris Kremenliev contributed to the proposal for UCLA's Institute for Ethnomusicology in 1959, paving the way for the foundation of the Department of Ethnomusicology in 1988. He is the author of *Bulgarian-Macedonian Folk Music* (1952), among the first such resources in English.
Sam (or Sotorios) Chianis received his PhD in ethnomusicology from UCLA and in 1976 "became the first ethnomusicologist in the entire SUNY system" (www.ethnomusic.ucla.edu/archive/previous-site/biochianis.htm).
[5] An email to the Binghamton Student Association confirmed that this group is no longer active.

Beyond the comparative vitality of the UCLA ethnomusicology program, Chianis directed Mark to Los Angeles out of recognition that it had emerged as a hub of interest in Balkan folk dance and—increasingly—music.[6] "Chianis thought Binghamton wasn't a good place for me, and he told me about the Balkan music and dance scene in LA," Mark relates:

I was looking through these catalogues at the SUNY Binghamton career office, trying to find some way to get to LA, and I kept being attracted to special education because I thought it would be great to help people. One program involved a twelve-month training period at Cal State LA—it was to be an orientation and mobility instructor for visually impaired kids, teaching them daily living skills like how to get around with a cane. It just seemed like something concrete, as opposed to all of the cerebral library work that I had been doing. So I got into the program, and that was my way of getting to LA!

Three days after his arrival in Los Angeles, Mark attended Balkan night at The Intersection,[7] perhaps the most beloved of a constellation of recreational folk dance cafes scattered across the city. "I was used to East Coast folk dancing, which was held on college campuses or community centers, and in LA they had all these cafes," he states:

At The Intersection, Wednesday night was Balkan night, and they also had Greek night, Hungarian night, and so on—Greek was totally separate from Balkan! Balkan didn't mean Greek, it meant South Slavic—mainly Bulgarian, Macedonian, Serbian, and Croatian.

It was at Balkan night that Mark encountered a member of the AMAN Folk Ensemble, a Balkan and Middle Eastern[8]

---

[6] For an invaluable resource on folk dance history in the Los Angeles area, see www.phantomranch.net/folkdanc, a website curated by prominent dancer Dick Oakes.
[7] The Intersection was active from 1964 to 1984. Since 1991, former Intersection dancers have hosted a series of reunion gatherings, held first at the cafe's original location and later at regional festivals and community centers. An article memorializing founder Athan Karras can be viewed online in the Spring 2010 *Kef Times*.
[8] AMAN was originally termed a "Balkan and Oriental" ensemble, a description

performance group founded on the UCLA campus in 1963. Acclaimed for artistic excellence rooted in careful ethnographic research, AMAN had been conceived "for the purpose of preserving and presenting America's multicultural heritage as it is expressed through music, song, and dance,"[9] a settlement-era goal it worked to advance through the intricate choreography, elaborate costuming, and live accompaniment of the Soviet paradigm. Though the ensemble dissolved in 2004,[10] its reputation endures, and alumni rank among today's leading American Balkan musicians and dancers.

Overlap between the recreational and performing folk dance spheres proved critical for Mark, granting him entry into AMAN and a position within the burgeoning Los Angeles Balkan scene. "I met this guy, and I must have said that I was playing some Balkan clarinet because he told me about AMAN and said that I should come to the next rehearsal," he explains. "It turned out they didn't need anybody in the orchestra, so I became a dancer. And then an opening emerged, so I did both. It was nuts!" Delighted by the opportunity to perform with AMAN, Mark was quickly discouraged by what he felt to be a homogenous musical aesthetic. "The music was decent, but we were doing everything with the same instruments—accordion, clarinet, upright bass, western flute, and guitar," he recalls. "I'm very indebted to AMAN, but it got old." A hallmark of the International Folk Dance Movement, western instrumentation was more immediately a practical matter, as Balkan village instruments were a rarity in the United States at the time, and there was an even greater shortage of Americans who knew how to play them. Yet for Mark the idea of folk music performed on village instruments had begun to hold irresistible appeal. "Of the few recordings I had, what I was nuts about was *gajda* and *zurla*; I used to just lie on the

later altered to reflect changing views surrounding the negative implications of Orientalism as detailed in a noted book by Edward Said.

[9] http://www.phantomranch.net/folkdanc/perform/aman.htm.

[10] In recent years, former AMAN members Mady Taylor and Ian Price have organized the monthly Café AMAN, a folk dance cooperative with an emphasis on Balkan repertoire. For more information, see www.phantomranch.net/folkdanc/coffeehs/cafe_aman.htm.

floor between two speakers and listen to *zurla* music," he states.

In 1970, Mark was given a *gajda* by fellow AMAN member Ian Price. As if procuring an instrument had not presented sufficient challenge, it was now that his true struggle commenced. In making the transition from classical to Balkan clarinet, he had benefitted from familiarity with the instrument. No such foundation was available as he strove to acquaint himself with the *gajda*. Added to this was a more formidable obstacle. "There were absolutely zero teachers!" he exclaims. "Somebody said to me, 'I think you put your hands here, and you blow in here,' but that was it. Learning to play was about listening to recordings and just trying to figure it out." Though he was at times discouraged, Mark has since embraced this process as helping him to become a mindful and resourceful musician. "I actually really appreciate it now," he affirms. "There's something about that kind of learning that's very valuable."

As soon as he could produce a decent sound, Mark attempted to incorporate his *gajda* into the AMAN orchestra. "It was just me, and it was kind of all mushed together—*gajda*, accordion, and clarinet," he describes. "Nobody played *gŭdulka* or anything like that."[11] Change came in 1971, when folk dancer and *gŭdulka* player Lauren Brody[12] visited from New York. "She said, 'You play *gajda*? I play *gŭdulka*! Why don't we try playing together?'" Mark narrates. "I knew four or five tunes, she knew four or five tunes, and we had a couple of tunes in common. So we played together, and it was amazing. I had to find a way to do it again." This was far less remote a possibility than he could have imagined. In airing his vision, Mark discovered that he was one of a handful of AMAN musicians beginning to experiment with Bulgarian and Macedonian village instruments, most using models the

[11] Mark later informed me that there had been some use of *gajda* and *kaval* before he joined the group. AMAN's first official accompaniment was provided by a group of *tamburica* musicians under the name Hajduks.

[12] Lauren Brody maintains the informative website Song of the Crooked Dance, which draws on her analysis of the early Bulgarian recording industry. Brody also compiled and annotated several collections of Bulgarian folk music, including the *Lost Treasures* series. She became interested in Bulgarian music as a teenager in New York and was later sponsored by the socialist government to conduct post-graduate research at the State Music Conservatory in Sofia. An interview with Brody appears in the Summer 2006 *Kef Times*.

ensemble had acquired in the course of overseas research:

> There was this fellow, Stuart Brotman—he had recently gone to Bulgaria and returned with a *gŭdulka*. And then Chris Yeseta, who's Croatian-American—he started playing Macedonian *tambura*. Ed Ledell played *tapan*, and Stewart Mennin, who played clarinet in AMAN—he was also playing *gajda*. And then Dave Shochat, who was a western flute player and a dancer in AMAN—he picked up a *kaval*.

Anticipating a fruitful alliance, Mark and his fellow folk instrument enthusiasts began getting together to exchange information and to play. While AMAN remained their chief performance context, however, such activity could offer little more than outside diversion. "Even when some of us were playing Balkan instruments, we were given little opportunity to play them in AMAN, where Balkan music was played on clarinet and accordion," Mark notes. "Anyway, we had started listening to this other kind of music." Recordings of an iconic group introduced the AMAN musicians to what they would come to know as the Bulgarian *bitov*, or "village" ensemble.[13] "The musicians on these recordings were Kostadin Varimezov—the most famous Bulgarian *gajda* player—and he played with the most famous *gŭdulka*, *kaval*, *tambura*, and *tapan* players,"[14] Mark explains:

> I didn't know this then, but these were musicians from the Radio Sofia orchestra who had been asked by the State to create a village foundation for the radio sound, and I just thought it was the best thing I had ever heard! In the radio, they were playing polyphonic arrangements of village folk songs, but they were all villagers, and there were a number of recordings that they made together to

---

[13] *Bitov* does not translate to "village" per se, though Scene members often use the terms somewhat interchangeably. Rather, *bitov* refers to a group of traditional village instruments made to play together in a configuration once championed as the village foundation of government-driven choral and orchestral collectives.

[14] Kostadin Varimezov (1918 – 2002) was born in Strandža and later served as a professional folk musician with the Bulgarian National Radio Folk Orchestra. Varimezov and his wife Todora are primary subjects of Timothy Rice's book *May it Fill Your Soul: Experiencing Bulgarian Music*.

create the monophonic or heterophonic *bitov* style. They called themselves Strandžanskata Grupa—the Group from Strandža.[15]

Ignorant of the ideological framework distinguishing the State-sponsored radio orchestra from the smaller, purportedly more populist *bitov* ensemble, Mark contends that his gravitation towards Bulgarian *bitov* music "wasn't any kind of righteous political stance" but rather an honest, "gut-level" response. "There was just something that really spoke to me about the *gajda-gŭdulka-kaval-tambura-tapan* sound," he avows. Whatever the draw, identification with a specific tradition gave Mark and his fellow musicians a musical raison d'être—a sonic template for the formation of their own ensemble. "Stuart Brotman, Stewart Mennin, Chris Yeseta, Ed Ledell, Dave Shochat, and me," he recites. "It's so funny, though. It was actually while I was in Palo Alto completing my residency for the special education program that it all came together—this band called Pitu Guli."[16]

Mark developed his passion for Bulgarian *bitov* music on the basis of its aesthetic. "None of us even knew the word *bitov* then; even after we were playing *bitov* music, we didn't know it!" he laughs. "We heard it from Marcus Moskoff—he was the first American I knew who went to Bulgaria and really seriously studied there. He played *gŭdulka* and *gajda*, and he came back with the word." This chronology is significant on two major levels. *Balkan Fascination* author Mirjana Laušević deems travel a catalyst in the rise of a national Balkan contingent due in part

---

[15] As summarized by Timothy Rice (2004, 63 – 64), "Communist ideology is based on nineteenth-century ideas about the evolution and progress of humankind." Government officials sought "to imbue traditional music with the aesthetic forms and values and positive symbolic meanings of classical music" by creating polyphonic arrangements of village songs in a manner at once exotic and recognizable to the western ear.
Strandžanskata Grupa was co-founded in 1956 by Kostadin Varimezov (*gajda*) and Stoyan Veličov (*kaval*). Other members included Neno Ivanov (*gŭdulka*), Yordan Tzvetkov (*tambura*), and Ognyan (Jimmy) Vassilev (*tapan*).
[16] Somewhat ironically, Pitu Guli (1865 – 1903) was a Macedonian revolutionary who became a national hero when he led a rebel squad against the Ottoman Empire.

to its role in expanding dancers' musical consciousness. Still, if Mark's experience is any indication, early travelers trafficked in recordings alone; back home, live music was restricted to professional folk troupes such as AMAN and was performed on instruments of western origin. Then, in the summer of 1971, Mark made his first trip to the Balkans, a journey that established him as a primary architect of what would become the American Balkan Scene. Like several emerging young leaders in the folk dance community,[17] he planned his itinerary to coincide with the second quinquennial folk festival in Koprivštica, Bulgaria,[18] intending to visit smaller festivals in Bulgaria and Macedonia prior to the Koprivštica weekend. "I landed in London and took a boat to Amsterdam," he recounts:

> In Amsterdam, I bought an old car and drove to Macedonia. I had heard about this festival called Sveti Naum, which happens every July at a church on Lake Ohrid, so there was this huge rush to get there. Being there was amazing—I was totally blown.

Hoping to benefit from his time overseas, the directors of AMAN had charged Mark with a series of errands, the fulfillment of which enabled him to situate his experience of Balkan music within the fabric of village life. In his words:

> On the way to Lake Ohrid, I stopped in Istria, which is this peninsula across the Adriatic from Italy. I was supposed to buy a pair of *sopile* for AMAN. You have to hear Istrian music—it's not like any other Balkan music. The *sopila* is in the *zurna* family, and they play in very condensed parallel thirds. So right off the bat I had some introduction to local culture. Next, I had to get some Bosnian *opanci* in Jajce, which is in the middle of Bosnia. I drove really fast through Croatia and Bosnia, and all of the villagers were in what we would

---

[17] According to Mark, these young dancers included Stephen Kotansky, Yves Moreau, Bob Liebman, and Larry Weiner, each of whom was in the Balkans on an independent venture.

[18] Founded in 1965 to celebrate Bulgarian music and dance, the National Festival of Bulgarian Folklore in Koprivštica attracts some 18,000 performers from across Bulgaria.

call costumes; a lot has changed since the early '70s. In Bosnia, I gave a ride to these young guys, and we stopped at a café and they sang *ganga*! I have a recording of that. I was blown, really. A lot of this had been totally theoretical for me—it was on recordings and in textbooks or whatever. But here were these guys singing *ganga*![19]

From Bosnia, Mark made his way to Macedonia, where he joined his fellow travelers at Sveti Naum. Coming from Los Angeles, where the only Balkan musicians he knew were American novices like himself, he found the festival a veritable musical heaven. "There were all these *gajda* and *zurla* players at a huge *sabor* around this old church," he describes. "I saw a live Macedonian *gajda* player there for the first time. He wasn't very good—this really old guy—but I was completely blown!"

Leaving Lake Ohrid, Mark and his companions congregated in Oteševo, where they participated in "an intensive weeklong dance workshop" led by celebrated folk dancer and *gajda* player Pece Atanasovski.[20] Though the workshop was designed to focus on dance, Mark was chiefly thrilled to spend a week with one of his model *gajda* players "from the recordings." His admiration was not lost on Atanasovski. "Pece saw how interested I was, and he offered to give me lessons after the workshop," he states. "I had to pass up going to Smotra Folklora,[21] which was this huge, pan-Yugoslav festival in Zagreb—it was so hard for me to decide what to do! But I got to have these daily private lessons with Pece Atanasovski, the most famous Macedonian *gajda* player." As Mark's first formal instructor, Atanasovski

[19] See Glossary for an explanation of *ganga* and other terms.
[20] Petar (Pece) Atanasovski (1927 – 1996) launched his career as a dancer with the State-run Tanec ensemble and later worked with ethnomusicologist Živko Firfov to engineer the Macedonian *izvorno* style, roughly equivalent to Bulgarian *bitov*. As Mark relates, "It was also this totally invented thing. They had a Bulgarian model, but they created their own sound—Radio Skopje. It was Macedonian *gajda*, *kaval*, *tambura*, *tapan*, and singers—a village derived style." In 1972, Atanasovski toured North America as a performer and teacher, and many of the dances he taught became standards. His seminars were attended by music and dance enthusiasts from the United States, Europe, and Asia.
[21] Held annually since 1966, Smotra Folklora was founded to showcase and preserve traditional culture through collaboration with folklorists and other cultural experts. For more information, see http://www.msf.hr/Smotra/en/en-index.html.

acquainted him with the stylistic nuance of traditional *gajda* playing in Macedonia. "I learned so much from him!" he exclaims:

> He was a great teacher, and I taped every lesson. I was staying at a campground, so I would go back and slow everything down—half speed, quarter speed, sometimes even eighth speed—to get the ornaments. And then I ordered an instrument from him, which I still play today.

In early August, Mark made his way to Bulgaria, where he was reunited with his fellow Americans at the Koprivštica festival. "I have some funny memories of Koprivštica," he remarks:

> You know what I did? On the second day, I used the same tape that I had recorded the first day on—I taped over it! Isn't that tragic? I taped over this fantastic *gajda* player. I felt bad about it for years. The state that I was in, though—it was just so overwhelming, and there was so much sensory input. The best way to meet musicians was to talk to them while they were warming up backstage. They were so friendly! I had tried to teach myself Bulgarian before I left, but I really hadn't gotten very far. I had all of these *Teach Yourself Bulgarian* books put out by the military, so I learned handy phrases like, "Where is the nearest landing field?" and, "Is this field mined?" So my language was almost nonexistent. But I saw—I just *saw*. I saw *gajda* players, *zurla* players, and even all of this clarinet and accordion stuff.

The language barrier aside, Mark experienced many fruitful interactions with Koprivštica performers, who pointed him in the direction of musicians and instrument makers throughout Bulgaria. "I ended up going on a pilgrimage of sorts," he reflects:

> I went to visit this legendary instrument maker in Strandža, Slavi Ivanov. He made *gajda* and *kaval*, and just about every Bulgarian ensemble musician had one of his instruments. I ordered a bunch of instruments from him. Then I went to Gabrovo, which is where the most famous *gŭdulka* maker lived. That was the main thing—I was *obsessed* with these instruments, and I wanted to bring back as many of them as possible. It was tricky, but

there was this governmental organization called the Slavianski Komitet—the Slavistics Committee—and they were so helpful in terms of shipping stuff! I bought zillions of books, records, and instruments, and they didn't even charge me to ship them! That would never happen today. But really, my first trip was a collecting trip. Hardly anyone in the folk dance community had folk instruments at the time, and this was the first time that I could get a hold of them and see how people actually played them.[22]

Having identified Mark's initial journey to the Balkans as the fulcrum wedding his personal development to the birth of the American Balkan Scene, I take a moment to elucidate the underlying processes. If travel precipitated the rise of a national Balkan contingent by stoking interest in Balkan folk music, even professional folk troupes aiming to transcend the international folk dance model were limited by a dearth of knowledge and resources. Enter Mark, who returned from the Balkans bearing a treasure trove of folk instruments and playing techniques and hungering to bring all he had witnessed to life among Balkan music and dance enthusiasts in Los Angeles and beyond. The lattermost impulse was particularly compelling; whether performed by *bitov* ensemble or clarinet and accordion, a summer spent hearing live music in the Balkans had turned his distaste for the comparatively homogeneous AMAN aesthetic to outright dislike. "That trip is what ruined me," he explains. "That's when I got really disillusioned with AMAN, though I stayed with them for years afterwards. Seeing the music and dance in villages and at weddings and things—it was the real stuff." Now, far exceeding his previous efforts to integrate village instruments into the AMAN orchestra, Mark mobilized the members of Pitu Guli to launch a live music revolution. He tells the story as follows:

When I got home, I embarked on this fervent mission to have live Balkan music at Balkan folk dance events. I mean, I had just been in the Balkans, and people weren't dancing to recordings

[22] An agent of the socialist government, the Slavianski Komitet was invested in supporting activities that promoted traditional culture abroad.

there, now were they? We played around LA and Santa Barbara, and then Northern California. Most people went crazy over it, but some people hated it because we played each song for more than the two minutes and forty-six seconds it was on the recording. People would say, "You didn't play it like the recording, and we didn't get to do step three!" But there was also a large contingent of people who loved it. I remember at one event we played a *pravo* for two hours and twenty minutes, just stringing together all of the tunes in that meter that we knew. People really got into that, and it was like my few experiences in the village—dances last for more than two minutes and forty-six seconds in the village!

The live music revolution did more than awaken folk dancers to the intimate partnership between Balkan music and dance. Central to any definition of the American Balkan Scene is the notion that affiliated musicians and dancers engage in regular exchange, coming together in various configurations across the country to make merry and to collaborate. Despite inherent overlap, however, such collaboration remained the exception until Pitu Guli awakened the recreational Balkan folk dance population to the joy of interacting with musicians, sparking new interest in musical activity in a cycle that continues today. Yet if Pitu Guli was effective in fostering a sense of cohesion among American Balkan musicians and dancers up and down the California coast, what of the mechanism by which that cohesion was extended to other sectors of the national Balkan contingent? The answer is Balkan Camp (or more properly, the annual Balkan Music and Dance Workshops), also attributable to Mark. In the following section, I illuminate three streams of influence that converged to give rise to the first Balkan Camp in Mendocino, California: 1) the UCLA Balkan Ensemble, 2) the Sweet's Mill Balkan folk dance workshops, and 3) a series of weekend folk dance retreats at Camp Mattole.

At the vanguard of academic ethnomusicology, UCLA had a reputation for hosting international musical luminaries as

36   One Heart, Many Voices

guest artists and visiting professors. These renowned individuals drew a coterie of fans from the institution and its environs. "There were always people hanging around the ethno building because there were these visiting musicians from all across the world; students, people from AMAN, and a lot of community members—they'd just hang out there," Mark recalls. With his arrival in Los Angeles, Mark followed suit, cultivating a connection to the UCLA ethnomusicology program that carried him beneath the formalities of university admission. "I got to know people in the ethno program, and I got to know the Bulgarian professor, and eventually I got in that way," he states.

In 1972, Mark began graduate studies in ethnomusicology at UCLA. That fall, he was asked to direct the Balkan Ensemble,[23] which operated on a model reminiscent of AMAN. "It had been taught like, 'Whatever instrument you have, bring it, and we'll all play together!'" he describes. Eager to share what he had learned overseas, Mark transformed the ensemble, introducing students to the fundamentals of playing Bulgarian *bitov* music on village instruments. "Class was one evening a week, and we took over the music building," he explains:

> There was a room of *gajda*, a room of *kaval*, a room of *gŭdulka*, etc. I had all of my Pitu Guli friends helping to teach, and some of the better singers from AMAN came to teach singing. We weren't picky about who registered; there were some UCLA ethno students and a lot of AMAN people who were also ethno students. The Balinese man who taught Balinese *gamelan* came and played *tapan*, and Dick Crum came to learn *kaval*! And then we'd give a

---

[23] As stated on the UCLA Department of Ethnomusicology website, "The Music of the Balkans Ensemble began in 1960 – 61 as part of an academic course, Music 129, Music of the Balkans, taught by Boris Kremenliev. The course included 'performance on representative instruments' as a requirement. During the 1964 – 65 academic year, the course Music 45B/145B (Music and Dance of the Balkans) was offered for the first time. The course was divided into two sections: instrumental and vocal" (http://www.ethnomusic.ucla.edu/index.php?option=com_content&view=article&id=1402:balkan-ensemble&catid=93&Itemid=226). Mark's leadership came during what was considered Kremenliev's term.

performance at the end of every term. Looking back, it was like a mini Balkan Camp—we camped out in the music building![24]

As leader of the UCLA Balkan Ensemble, Mark honed his skill as an instructor while disseminating information about the Bulgarian *bitov* tradition to a shifting mosaic of students and folk dancers. Feeding on the energy of the live music revolution, the second stream in the birth of the Balkan Music and Dance Workshops reintroduced him to the California folk dance circuit in a more explicit educational capacity. In the early 1970s, Pitu Guli was hired to perform for a series of weekend folk dance retreats at Sweet's Mill,[25] a former logging camp located east of Fresno in the Sierra Nevada foothills. "It was so funky there!" Mark laughs. "You brought your own food, and you brought your own tent. And it was total hippiedom! Those were fantastic weekends—there were maybe fifty or sixty people there, and it was just us playing." Inspired by Pitu Guli, proprietors Virgil and Edith Byxbe asked Mark if the ensemble would be willing to lead a weeklong Balkan music and dance workshop in the summer of 1974 for credit through University of California, Santa Cruz (UCSC) extension. "It sounded so scary, but I said, 'Yeah,' and we did it!" Mark recounts:

---

[24] Among the most beloved folk dance instructors the Scene has known, Dick Crum (1928 – 2005) taught Balkan dance at folk dance camps across the United States and Canada and released a collection of Yugoslav folk songs. According to fellow dancer Dick Oakes, Crum spoke numerous Slavic languages, with functional ability in at least ten more. Remembered for careful attention to cultural nuance and context, he also delighted in elaborate choreography, focusing on the joy of dance as recreation. The Dick Crum Scholarship is now awarded annually to help similarly passionate individuals attend Balkan Camp.

[25] In 2012, the East European Folklife Center (EEFC) listserv hosted a discussion of early Camp history. On May 21st, Sandy Ward confirmed that the first Camp was held in 1974. "By 1st camp, I mean 1st week-long Balkan Camp," she writes. "It was clear at this time that there had already been a tradition of weekend gatherings of Balkan musicians at Sweet's Mill. For me, it was an eye-opener. I'd never seen a gaida, hadn't experienced live Balkan music (only records in folk dance groups), had never met such an open and free group of people." In a subsequent post, Mark clarified that this shift was facilitated by accordionist Nada Lewis. More information can be found in an interview with Miamon Miller in the Spring/Summer 2000 *Kef Times*. The history of Sweet's Mill is chronicled at www.musickfalls.org/history/html.

38   One Heart, Many Voices

None of us got paid anything because there were all of these other
expenses. But I got all of my friends to teach again—none of this
could have happened without people donating their time. Ethel
Raim was the first vocal teacher; somehow we had money to fly her
out from New York and to pay her some tiny amount. She ended up
being the first Balkan vocal teacher that a lot of people were exposed
to, and Bob Leibman was the first dance instructor, and members of
Pitu Guli were the first instrumentalists! It was more academic those
first few years because it was a class for credit—there were cultural
and musical lectures. The whole camp cost sixty dollars to attend.[26]

With Mark at the helm, the first Sweet's Mill Balkan music
and dance camp was a resounding success, establishing a model
reproduced to similar acclaim the next summer. For Mark,
however, the future was far from assured. "There were problems
from the beginning," he asserts. "First, we were hardly getting
paid, so we couldn't continue that way. And not everybody could
handle camping out! Some people said, 'I hear what you're doing
at Sweet's Mill, but I just can't be in a tent and bring my own
food.'" Fortunately, there was a ready alternative. In the spring
of 1975, a group of folk dance enthusiasts from the Humboldt
Folkdance Factory in Arcata had launched their own weekend retreats,[27] held at Camp Mattole on northern California's
ruggedly scenic Lost Coast. Interested in live accompaniment,
they hired Pitu Guli to perform for their evening dance parties.
Then, the following year, Camp Mattole was logged, forcing
the Humboldt folk dancers to relocate. "They found this place

---

[26] Ethel Raim presently serves as Artistic Director of New York's Center for
Traditional Music and Dance. Conducting research for the Smithsonian Institute in
the early 1970s, she traveled to the Balkans with Martin Koenig, and together they
released the two-LP set *Village Music of Bulgaria* on Nonesuch Records. Throughout
the 1960s, she performed with The Pennywhistlers, an ensemble that was instrumental in bringing Balkan and East European vocal music to folk music enthusiasts in
the United States. In 2012, she was awarded the prestigious Botkin Prize, given by
the American Folklore Society "to recognize lifetime achievement in public folklore"
(http://www.afsnet.org/news/110145/Gates-and-Raim-Awarded-2012-Benjamin-A-
Botkin-Prize.htm).
[27] In the Spring/Summer 2001 *Kef Times*, Kim Wollter attests that inspiration for the
Arcata camp also came from Sweet's Mill.

called the Mendocino Woodlands, and that summer we had a weekend there, at Camp Three," Mark narrates. Captivated by the Woodlands facility, he again saw room for improvement, this time with regard to programming. "It was a camp of mainly partying, with a few dance classes, but no musical instruction," he notes. With a rush of conviction, he turned to the Woodlands as a site for the realization of what had quietly become his dream. "In 1977, I looked into the Mendocino Woodlands campground and planned the Mendocino Balkan Music and Dance Workshops," he states.

Independent of an existing folk dance organization or workshop series, Mark's dream was manifest through the combined investment of participants from Sweet's Mill and Camp Mattole, who came together around the common factor of Pitu Guli. "The thought of doing everything for a camp like that—organizing the whole kitchen scene?" he begins:

> I had no clue about any of that! That's why the Arcata people can take as much credit as they like—it couldn't have happened without them. I was the music programming guy, but they did everything else. The first week at Mendocino cost about one hundred dollars, and it was held at Camp Two. There was a small dance hall where we ate and danced; we had to move the tables and chairs for dancing and then move them back again! It was dusty, and there were hardly any places for classes, but about one hundred and twenty people came. And it's been at Mendocino every year since.

The first Balkan Camp served a purpose beyond the integration of the Sweet's Mill and Arcata folk dance demographics. Treating the inaugural session as an opportunity to extend a hand across the United States, Mark invited the members of two East Coast ensembles to teach at Mendocino, paving the way for the *American* Balkan Scene members experience today. "Here we were—Pitu Guli—with our California fans, but we had started hearing about people on the East Coast," he explains:

For example, there was a band called Novo Selo in Philadelphia—their strength was Macedonian village music, while ours was Bulgarian. And then there was a women's singing group in New York, Ženska Pesna. Unlike AMAN and all of the other women's singing groups in the country, which were doing Kutev-style polyphonic arrangements, Ženska Pesna was doing monophonic and drone-based village songs. They were mainly all former students of Ethel Raim—Carol Freeman and Carol Silverman—and they were doing tons of research in the Balkans every summer. That was actually the vision of the first Mendocino Camp—to bring us all together. And that was the staff—Pitu Guli, Novo Selo, and Ženska Pesna. It was my dream, and it happened! It's amazing.

Also significant is a legacy pertaining to ideas about Balkan folk music. As founder and program director, Mark focused the Camp curriculum on the Bulgarian *bitov* repertoire and instrumentation. With Novo Selo and Ženska Pesna also oriented toward village traditions, his personal proclivity was bolstered by his choice of instructors, canonizing *bitov* as the unofficial first language of American Balkan musicians.[28] Here, the picture begins to sharpen. As Camp convened once, twice, and into perpetuity, new alliances formed, and old alliances strengthened. Individuals who enjoyed playing music together one summer opted to solidify their association, prompting a bloom of fledgling ensembles eager to partner with existing folk dance organizations. Indeed, what commenced in the late 1970s was less the birth of a new entity than a layering of musicians who were themselves veteran folk dancers atop an audience already attuned to Balkan sounds and styles, and it is precisely the magic of Camp that it facilitates a sense of national

---

[28] In a personal email dated August 8, 2012, Mark clarified that Macedonian *izvorno* music also played a formative role in the early days of the Scene. "It's true that I was much more involved in *bitov* than *izvorno*, especially in terms of the UCLA class, and class offerings at the camps," he writes. "Whenever Pitu Guli provided live music for folk dancers, though, we would always do a *bitov* set and an *izvorno* set. I always had a strong interest in the general concept of (pan-Balkan) village-style instrumental and vocal music and dance, rather than the socialist ensemble arrangements. Bulgaria, however, has been my focus." My research suggests that this applies to many other founding Scene members.

unity while functioning as a breeding ground for a diversity of regional circles.

It is tempting to wax rhapsodic when relating an origin story. Yet Mark makes it clear that his vision concerned Balkan Camp, and Balkan Camp alone. "I really had no long-range objective, to be perfectly honest," he avows:

It was always just, "Let's make sure Camp happens next summer." It was really too much for one person—I was really going nuts—so how could I have a vision of anything more? Actually, there *was* one thing. I had a vision of a building—an East European Folklife Center—where it wouldn't be just one week a year. We'd have teachers from the Balkans and ongoing classes and workshops and concerts. I visualized it being in the Bay Area because it seemed like the most interest was there. That was a vision that I always had, and if I'd had millions of dollars, I would have done it. But that's all!

Having reached the extent of Mark's ambition for the American Balkan Scene, I prepare to entrust its story to my remaining interviewees. Working within the Scene community, however, I have come to expect that individual narratives will overlap, articulating a rich and incisive commentary when juxtaposed. To provide as nuanced a portrait as possible, then, I have invited Mark to reflect on more recent trends, generating an historical framework for subsequent chapters.

First, we advance to the year 1982, which saw the more comprehensive fulfillment of Mark's original vision. Specifically, when it appeared that interest in the Balkan Music and Dance Workshops would continue to rise, he was advised to form a non-profit corporation, a step that required the appointment of a board of directors. "We *called* it the East European Folklife Center," he laughs:

It was Carol's idea to call it that, but it really was just a center in name. There was a board, but it wasn't very functional. Really, the main rationale for incorporating had been to get grants, and we only got one! I put so much time into getting that one grant—it was from the New York State Council for the Arts, and it was about five thousand dollars. And that was to hire local ethnic Balkan musicians and to reach out to local ethnic communities. But the whole thing was so much work, and gradually I handed it over to other people. I got people to help with Camp registration—first it was Miamon Miller, and then Bill Cope, and then Rachel MacFarlane. Pretty soon I was doing zero administrative work, though I continued to be involved with programming.[29]

Another development occurred in response to growing awareness of Mendocino Balkan Camp among Balkan folk enthusiasts nationwide. By the early 1980s, the number of attendees hailing from outside California was such that the formation of an additional, East Coast Camp was proposed:

One summer, David Bilides and Henry Goldberg said, "Hey, maybe you should have a camp on the East Coast!" So we started the East Coast Camp in 1983 with their help. It's been a lot more difficult; we've never had a single location like with Mendocino, and it's always been more expensive. That one grant ended up coming in handy though—we used it to get going on the East Coast.[30]

With the incorporation of the East European Folklife Center (EEFC) and the inception of the East Coast Balkan Music and Dance Workshops, the Scene flourished as membership increased. Then, quite suddenly it seemed, Camp enrollment suffered a sharp decline. Some blamed this on the diminishing vitality of the International Folk Dance Movement, a trend linked to the aging of participants. "There was a low point in the mid-'80s when we thought we would have to stop having Camp because we couldn't make ends meet—we had trouble getting even one hundred and twenty people in those days," Mark recalls:

[29] Carol Silverman is Mark Levy's musical as well as life partner.
[30] East coast Camp has been held in Ashokan and Iroquois Springs, New York, and Ramblewood, Maryland. A detailed history appears in the Fall/Winter 2000 – 2001 *Kef Times*.

It's incredible what's happening today, where you have to sign up early to get a spot. We used to have meetings, like, "How can we get more people to come?" And people would say, "Ah, but the folk dance scene is fading." And it's true—they're *still* having trouble attracting new people. For example, a few years ago, I was hired to teach at Folklore Camp a week before Balkan Camp—it's a mainstream international folk dance camp also held at the Woodlands campground. When I went there, I felt like I was back in the '60s, but the average age was about sixty or seventy, and there were hardly any young people at all.

Hoping to revitalize the Camp population, Mark revisited the tangle of affinity and purpose that had driven his work over the previous decade, scrutinizing the implications of a tendency to prioritize music. "At first, I had had an agenda of offering what nobody else was offering," he states:

There were plenty of opportunities to take folk dance classes, but I wanted to focus on the music. Ultimately, though, I think that's maybe one of the reasons that we had declining enrollment. It was finally like, "Well, we always hire just one dance teacher, a couple of singing teachers, and twenty instrumental teachers." So we increased the dance component and added more singing. And that helped a lot!

Revitalization was unexpectedly hastened by a shift in the relationship between the American Balkan Scene and the Balkans. Previously, the majority of American Balkan musicians had learned to play from other American enthusiasts, unable to benefit from interaction with musicians behind the Iron Curtain. Then, in 1989, the fall of communism across Eastern Europe opened an unprecedented opportunity for intensive intercultural exchange. With the EEFC, Mark acted immediately to organize an American tour for Georgi Doičev, a *gajda* player he had met in Bulgaria. Doičev brought a band, Bulgari,[31] and Bulgari taught at both Camps the following summer.[32] "It was totally amazing. And that was

---

[31] Christened by Carol Silverman, "Bulgari" translates to "Bulgarians."
[32] Doičev also served as leader of the UCLA Balkan Ensemble between 1992 and 1993.

it!" Mark exclaims. "Waves and waves of musicians came after that. The best singers came. And then Esma Redžepova?! Yuri Yunakov?! I mean, it was like people leaping out of album covers!"[33] The response was ambiguous. "You'll get different stories from different people, but it wasn't all joyful," Mark allows. "I hate speaking in these terms, like, 'It wasn't all wonderful having the Bulgarian musicians.' It *was* heaven, for some people. But it was challenging for others." Recent efforts to proportion time and energy aside, the arrival of native musicians propelled the focus of the Balkan Music and Dance Workshops still more firmly toward music, triggering fear that this would necessarily come at the expense of dance. Also controversial was the introduction of new musical genres and styles, as feedback from native musicians effectively put the Scene's devotion to the Bulgarian *bitov* tradition on trial. This was acutely personal for Mark, who was forced to confront the possibility that his aesthetic gravitation toward *bitov* music had become an ideological extension of his cherished commitment to music as a vehicle for popular unity. "Like I said, it was never a righteous stance," he asserts:

> It's just that somehow I'm more moved by the village way of playing music. When Yuri Yunakov came, he cranked up the sound system, and that alienated a lot of people. Ultimately, though, that was just his aesthetic. Wedding music performed on amplified instruments is a grassroots thing that *became* village music. But polyphonic choral arrangements? Villagers don't sit around the table doing that! I've always had this vision of Camp being what people actually do in villages, not the government-run ensembles. So it was an adjustment.

---

[33] Esma Redžepova is a Romani singer celebrated internationally as "Queen of the Gypsies." Born in 1943 in Skopje, she began touring with her future husband, the late Stevo Teodosievski, at the age of fourteen. She remains one of few Romani musicians hired to teach at Camp.
Renowned as a pioneer of Bulgarian wedding music, Yuri Yunakov was born in 1958 to a Turkish Romani family. He performs internationally with the Yuri Yunakov Ensemble and for the native Balkan community in his adopted home of New York. In recognition of his efforts to promote Romani music and culture in the United States, Yunakov was named a 2011 NEA National Heritage Fellow.

Ironically, lasting engagement with native Balkan musicians has since led Mark to the revelation that Bulgarian *bitov* music was itself perhaps the ultimate expression of government ideology—a reimagining of folk tradition engineered to project continuity between the urban western aspirations of an intended socialist future and the rural agrarian rhythms of an idealized past. "It turned out that this was total hypocrisy on my part—I just didn't know," he remarks:

> In the beginning, I just loved the *bitov* sound. But I was totally brainwashed by the Bulgarian party line! It's embarrassing, really. According to the Bulgarian government, "The only true folk instruments are *gajda, kaval, gŭdulka, tambura,* and *tapan,* and they play together." "*Bitov* music is the *source* of the polyphonic arrangements." "Clarinet and accordion are *classical* instruments." I guess I just swallowed it up! And then the aesthetic of even the *bitov* musicians—it turns out they're ensemble musicians, and they have that ensemble aesthetic; their training is based on the music being concert music, not music for dance.

In becoming aware of the inherent incongruity of his aesthetic-cum-ideological bias toward what he had embraced as the iconic Bulgarian village tradition, Mark perceived a parallel irony in the demographic of individuals affiliated with the Scene. As it turned out, a number of native Balkan musicians had been living and making music in the Los Angeles area prior to 1989, rendering their absence from Camp largely a consequence of his failure to court them.[34] "Again, you have to understand this in terms of my obsession with Bulgaria, and with Bulgarian *bitov* music," he explains:

---

[34] "Actually, the one ethnic we had from the beginning was this fellow Nestor Gergievski, who was a huge influence on my life and many others," Mark later explained. "He was a very decent drummer and *zurla* player, and a fantastic dancer. He was always there on Wednesday nights at The Intersection, and he was at all of our events. I used to play with him—just clarinet and *tapan*—at the Macedonian picnics in LA for the Macedonian community. So he was my link!"

For example, had I been a real *tamburica* person, I'm certain that we could have had *tamburica* players at Camp. Chris Yeseta from AMAN was a Croatian-American *tamburica* musician! But I was only peripherally into that. We also didn't have any Greeks, and there were Greek-American clarinet players all over the place. And Serbian-American accordion players. There were many "ethnics" that we could have made connections with, but I was totally obsessed with all things Bulgarian and to a lesser degree Macedonian. And I wasn't even interested in those instruments! You have to remember that in the early years, the only instruments taught at Camp were *gajda*, *kaval*, *gŭdulka*, *tambura*, and *tapan*. The idea of a clarinet class? That was too modern! And we never had amplification for the evening parties. I had this thing called the "ethnic police"—I used to carry around a whistle, and if there was anything that sounded too modern, I would blow it. Now if I did that, I would be blowing my whistle every two seconds![35]

Intimating the direction toward which the Balkan Music and Dance Workshops have since evolved, Mark adds that at one point he entertained the idea of writing a paper "paralleling the developments at Camp with developments in the Balkans." Intrigued, I ask him to elaborate. The following is his response:

Well, first we started on folk instruments without amplification and without using written notation. The music was very improvisatory, going from one set of phrases to the next. In the village in the old days, you wouldn't have singers with the instrumentalists—the whole alternation between singers and instrumentalists got started with amplification! So then we had amplification, clarinet and accordion, and wedding music. And today we have ensembles playing in clubs and people not coming through dance. Who would have known?

---

[35] A lack of amplification meant few performance opportunities for singers, a fact Mark sees as having made the nascent Scene heavily male dominated.

2

Dena Bjornlie

*We return now to the mid-twentieth century and the story of
Dena Bjornlie, who was introduced to Balkan music as a young
folk dancer in Los Angeles. An indirect beneficiary of Mark Levy's
Balkan Ensemble, Dena went on to perform with Medna Usta,
which recorded the album responsible for my first encounter with
the American Balkan Scene. An analysis of her experience with
Medna Usta and later ensembles alerts us to issues of authenticity
and identity as they arose in the context of intensified interaction
with the Balkans and are being revisited due to interface with the
American public at the onset of generational transition.*

*Predating my awareness of Balkan music, the Balkan Music
and Dance Workshops, or the American Balkan Scene, I knew of
Dena as a close friend of my mother's best friend from childhood.
An unanticipated benefit of this project has been the opportunity
to become personally acquainted with Dena, completing a circle of
friendship almost four decades in the making, with Balkan music
the most serendipitous of threads.*

Dena Bjornlie was born in 1955 in Los Angeles, California. She
delighted in her parent's eclectic record collection and sang in her
school choir before taking lessons on piano and recorder. Coming
of age at the height of the International Folk Dance Movement,
she traces her awareness of folk dancing to the eighth grade, when
a group of her friends began practicing Israeli folk dances during
recess. "My friends were Jewish, and they were just learning these
dances. They must have picked them up at temple," Dena states:

> They used to dance right there at school—it must have been either
> lunch or morning break. I just remember being on the edge of a
> parking lot, somewhere on the fringes of campus, and they started

teaching me these steps. I had always loved to dance; I took ballet from the age of six until nine, and I would put on a record and just dance around the living room. So when I got introduced to folk dancing, I really enjoyed it.

As described in Chapter 1, international folk dancing in Los Angeles revolved around a network of folk dance cafes,[1] where recreational and professional dancers mingled nearly every night of the week. Dena and her friends frequented these cafes throughout their teens, initially with parental assistance. "We didn't have our driver's licenses yet, so our parents actually drove us to another part of Los Angeles, very far from where we lived, and then they'd pick us up when we finished," she recalls. "Looking back, I can't believe they did that! And then later on we drove ourselves, staying at the cafes until all hours of the night."

At first, the young dancers patronized Hadarim,[2] a venue run by Israeli choreographers Shlomo and Dina Bachar, who structured their offerings in accordance with a trend toward regional specialization. "They had a different kind of dancing on each night of the week, and then on the weekends they had a mix of dances," Dena explains. "We'd go there—this big crowd of teenagers—and I'm sure the owners weren't pleased because we never bought any food or drink while we were there. We just paid the fifty-cent cover charge!" As they expanded their range to encompass a greater cross-section of the cafe circuit, Dena and her friends observed a parallel tendency to favor repertoire from the Balkans. "Eventually, we found out about all these other cafes," she recounts:

> One of the main ones was called The Intersection—I think it was the first one, and it closed maybe ten years ago. They did a lot of Balkan stuff, and there were different people who taught

---

[1] The last such venue, Cafe Danssa, closed in in 2007. Dena danced there for a short time, though she recalls that the repertoire was predominantly Israeli. Cafe Danssa was also the original site of Café AMAN, a monthly gathering hosted by former AMAN musicians and dancers.

[2] Officially known as Hadarim Folk Cafe.

each type of dance. Though of course none of the teachers were from the Balkans—they were all Americans! Later, we went to another cafe, Gypsy Camp, which was owned by a Romanian guy named Mihai David. By then, Balkan dancing was all that interested us, and we stopped pursuing anything else.

Balkan Fascination author Mirjana Laušević links the rise of a national Balkan folk dance contingent to the appearance of recordings that enabled dancers with a penchant for Balkan material to immerse themselves in its stylistic subtleties. In Los Angeles, the UCLA ethnomusicology program provided site as well as stimulus for a gathering of forces devoted to the study of Balkan music and dance. "The main place we danced was at UCLA, which had an International Student Center with a Friday night folk dance," Dena states:

And then there was this graduate student named Bob Leibman; he had done a lot of research in Macedonia, and I went to his dance classes all the time. He would show films, he played great recordings, and his classes had a ton of cultural information. In the cafes, there wasn't much information presented—just the dances. Though I think there *was* an assumption that you knew a fair amount because of the presence of the UCLA ethnomusicology program; because of that, there was more general knowledge.[3]

As Balkan enthusiasts in Los Angeles, Dena and her fellow young dancers looked up to the AMAN Folk Ensemble, acclaimed for elaborate arrangements of Balkan and Middle Eastern music and dance. Too young to audition for AMAN, they set their sights on Koroyar, an amateur Balkan folk troupe led by a man named Richard Unciano.[4] "It was a really quirky group, and I actually

[3] Dena clarified in a follow-up email that these films were shot by Leibman. This is confirmed in the Fall/Winter 2003 – 2004 *Kef Times.*
[4] According to Dick Oakes, Unciano grew up in Los Angeles, where he was exposed to the traditional music and dance of the Armenian immigrant community and later taught at Hadarim, The Intersection, and other prominent folk dance cafes. In 1964, Unciano embarked on the first of three research trips to the Balkans, where he learned from village and conservatory dancers alike. Koroyar (a combination of

have no idea how we hooked up with them," Dena laughs:

> Basically, AMAN was for college-aged people. And anyway, who
> knows if we were good enough because they had real auditions!
> Koroyar had people of all ages and ethnic backgrounds—there was
> a guy from Armenia and a guy from Japan. I must have been sixteen
> when I joined because I remember we drove ourselves to rehearsal.

The most significant feature distinguishing Koroyar from
AMAN was the nature of its repertoire. This became a point of
pride for Dena, whose attraction to the glittering artistry of the
latter ensemble soon gave way to affection for the more unassuming beauty of the dances she learned from Unciano. With this,
she absorbed the rhetoric he employed to describe the dances
he taught, so that their "village authenticity" came to constitute
a considerable measure of their appeal. "Richard Unciano had
gone to Bulgaria in the 1960s, and what was so good about his
group was that he absolutely refused to choreograph the dances
he had learned," she recalls:

> AMAN was beautiful to watch, but their repertoire was definitely
> choreographed to be entertaining—they did the basic dances, but
> they danced in a line facing the audience. Richard refused to do any
> of that. What we learned were these authentic Bulgarian, Turkish,
> Caucasian, and Greek village dances, which were often very simple,
> but wonderful. And you could see the difference! Dances that were
> choreographed had many different steps, whereas the dances that
> we did had just a few. In terms of performing, I wasn't immensely
> proud of the group; I think that it was very boring for the audience

---

the words *kolo*, *horo*, *oyun*, and *bar*) was notable for its inclusion of Pontic Greek
repertoire and for its attention to styling in music as well as in dance. "All the appro-
priate and typical embellishments, accidentals, accelerando changes, beat pattern
variations, internal phrasing, 'flavoring,' etc. in each melody were employed," Dick
Oakes reports. "Tunes were not simplified and were all played at the proper tempo,
whether fast or slow. So that all the music would sound exotic yet familiar, genuine
yet artistically accessible, provocative yet pleasing, the ensemble played authentic
folk instruments and standard orchestral instruments in several different kinds of
combinations" (http://www.phantomranch.net/folkdanc/perform/koroyar.htm).

to watch, and it was maybe even embarrassing at times. But we really loved the dances, and we learned so much. And there was a part of me that was proud that these were real village dances and that they were different from *other* real village dances that *other* people knew because they were from different villages! I always appreciated that.[5]

If Dena had begun to develop a taste for village authenticity in Balkan folk dance, her experience of Balkan music remained heavily mediated by the international folk dance model. Again, this was largely a practical matter, as it was difficult to find Americans who possessed Balkan folk instruments, not to mention who knew how to play them. Indeed, Dena reports, "One member of the group could play accordion, but even then we danced to recorded music, and most of our performances were to recorded music."[6] Recorded or live, Dena had been drawn to Balkan folk music since she first heard it at Hadarim and gradually accumulated a collection of albums popular with folk dance circles. Not content merely to listen, she began singing along:

> There were very few recordings of Balkan music available in those days, but the ones that we really loved were the Nonesuch Explorer Series records—*A Harvest, A Shepherd, A Bride* and *In the Shadow of the Mountain*, and then there was *Village Music of Yugoslavia*. The cool thing was that the recordings had the song lyrics printed in the liner notes. So we had the lyrics, and we learned to sing from the records. And then at some point

---

[5] Balkan village dances are traditionally performed in circular fashion or a line that twists and winds, perhaps around tables in a room. In general, notions of "performance" are secondary to group coherence and diversion.

[6] In addition to the influence of the international folk dance model, I initially interpreted Koroyar's use of recorded accompaniment as evidence of an ideological ethic reinforced by financial constraint. After reading my draft, Dena countered that the issue was more explicitly the lack of musicians. "There was more live music after I left," she wrote. "Richard always had the intent to have a band; it just took some years to develop. The year I lived in Florida he added gaida and clarinet. These instruments were pretty inexpensive to buy in the Balkans. Richard had a very nice gadulka and a few other instruments but no one to play them."

we learned how to pronounce the words—someone taught us basic Balkan pronunciation. We sang a lot in the car driving to folk dance rehearsals, and we sang a little bit in Koroyar.[7]

For Dena, as for folk dancers throughout California, exposure to Balkan village instruments intensified in the fall of 1971, when Los Angeles-based ensemble Pitu Guli embarked on a mission to provide live Bulgarian *bitov* music[8] for recreational folk dance events. The live music revolution took the folk dance world by storm. "We just worshipped Pitu Guli," Dena affirms. "They were playing all of these cool-looking instruments that many people had still only heard on the records, and certainly we danced to them whenever we could." Dena's gravitation toward Pitu Guli was strengthened by its evident rapport with Richard Unciano's passionate commitment to village music and dance. "It was very clear that the dances we did to Pitu Guli were *village* dances," she asserts.

Coupled with its pioneering live performances, Pitu Guli offered direct access to instruments and instruction through the UCLA Balkan Ensemble. Though she never enrolled, Dena credits then director Mark Levy with jumpstarting her career as a *gŭdulka* player. "You want to know how I started playing *gŭdulka*?" she asks. "It's all because of Mark." In the summer of 1972, Dena's family temporarily relocated to Florida, where she spent her senior year of high school. The move was challenging for Dena, who feared that her connection to the folk dance community would inevitably erode. "It was really hard for me socially because I was hooked into the folk dance scene in Los Angeles, and Los Angeles was the center of the world as far as I was concerned," she explains:

> It turned out there was a folk dance group an hour away in Orlando, and every once in a while, my mom would drive me to dance there.

[7] As noted in Chapter 1, the Nonesuch records were the work of Ethel Raim and Martin Koenig.

[8] As previously mentioned, Pitu Guli also played Macedonian *izvorno* music, though *bitov* was its primary focus.

It was a nice group, and I thought, "I can relate to these people!" But Orlando was far away, and in terms of where I was living, there was nothing—nothing at all.

A lull in her development as a folk dancer, Dena's year in Florida inaugurated a period of musical growth. Visiting Los Angeles for winter vacation, she met with a friend who was studying *gŭdulka* at UCLA and was inspired to do the same on her own. "While I was in Florida, my good friend took Mark Levy's Bulgarian music class at UCLA, and there were all these instruments!" she recounts:

> Some of them were his, and the others must have been part of the UCLA collection. My friend had a *gŭdulka* checked out to her, and she was learning to play either directly from Mark or from the guy who played *gŭdulka* in Pitu Guli, Stuart Brotman. When I returned to LA for Christmas and then again for the summer before beginning college, my friend showed me what she had learned. I really wanted to play. I can't remember the details, but either I borrowed my friend's *gŭdulka* or I got a hold of the one from our old folk dance group, Koroyar; there was this period of borrowing instruments wherever I could find them and learning how to scratch away.

Without formal instruction, Dena's experience of learning to play mirrored that of the earliest AMAN folk instrument enthusiasts. "I was basically winging it," she remarks:

> I listened to recordings, and I had sheet music, most of which came from Mark—he was the major source of sheet music at the time. I had been given the basic information about how to play the *gŭdulka*, which is that on the top string you play the first note with the end of the finger and the rest with the fingernail, while the other strings are just stopped with the ends of the fingers. If I hadn't had *that* information, forget it! I also had the basic concept of the tapping ornament that emphasizes the pulse of the music. But beyond that I just had to figure it out; I learned by playing around with the instrument. Ornamentation was the biggest struggle for me.

Despite steady progress, Dena felt inhibited by persistent dependence on borrowed instruments. Aid came from an unlikely source. Prior to leaving for Florida, she had developed an interest in old-time stringband music. Beginning with instrument acquisition, however, American old-time proved more accessible than Bulgarian *bitov*. "The difference was that I actually had a violin—my parents bought me a violin," she notes. In 1973, when Dena moved to Santa Cruz for college, these music-cultural worlds converged:

> In Santa Cruz, I met other people who were interested in old-time music. Through that crowd, I eventually met a fiddler who actually had a *gŭdulka* that he had had made for him in Los Angeles by a Bulgarian man—he had gone to Bulgaria and really loved the music and dance but ultimately did not pursue it. So he had this instrument and sold it to me, and that was the first *gŭdulka* that I had actually owned. Then I was *really* able to learn more.

The summer preceding her junior year, Dena took advantage of a UCSC incentive to attend the Sweet's Mill music and dance camps. "There was this camp called Sweet's Mill that I had been hearing about since high school, but I hadn't gone to it yet," she states:

> Sweet's Mill is a folk music camp that at the time had mostly American and Irish stuff. This one year, they added a Balkan music week that was set up as a UCSC extension class, and I went and got one or two units of credit from it. I took *gŭdulka* from Miamon Miller and a singing class from Ethel Raim, and there were dance parties every night. It was pretty amazing![9]

In Chapter 1, I identified Sweet's Mill as one of three streams of influence that came together to launch the first Mendocino Balkan Camp in 1977. As musicians who collaborated at Mendocino opted to continue their association, there was a proliferation of

---

[9] The first UCSC Sweet's Mill extension actually dates to 1974. Dena attended the second year.

American Balkan ensembles across the United States, whereby Camp became the nucleus of what members would term the American Balkan Scene. A testament to this process, Dena was able to join an existing ensemble before attending Camp. Her account paves the way for a discussion of issues Scene members faced as their music-cultural world underwent its first major transition.

In 1986, Dena accepted an invitation to play *gŭdulka* with Santa Cruz-based Medna Usta,[10] formed some months earlier by a group of women who had met at Mendocino. "I don't remember the specifics, but I lived about three blocks from where they rehearsed, and somehow we were acquainted with one another," she recalls:

> They said, "You should play with us!" and at first I thought, "No, I don't really play." And then I thought, "Well yes, I *do*, and yeah, I *could*." So I started going, and *yeah—I could*! It turned out we were all at a similar level, and it just fell together really easily. Conveniently, we had all of the instruments covered once I joined the group. Karen Guggenheim played *gajda*—she's actually someone who had gone to Bulgaria for a year to study *gajda* with Kostadin Varimezov. Anne Cleveland played *tambura* and sang. Ruth Hunter played accordion and *tambura*, and she sang too. Barbara Cordes played *tapan*, and she was the third singer in the trio. I wasn't singing with them then because they already had a trio, although I really wanted to because by then I had been singing for a long time.

Like its primary American model, Pitu Guli, Medna Usta drew much of its repertoire from Bulgarian *bitov* recordings, supplemented by material collected by Scene members who had traveled to the Balkans.[11] In Dena's words:

[10] During the eleven-year interim before Dena joined Medna Usta, she devoted herself to Sundanese *gamelan* music and dance. "Though I was very active musically in college and beyond (with various kinds of fiddle music, new music and early music, as well as gamelan), I was not playing gadulka with any regularity during that period," she explained in a personal email. "My involvement with Indonesian arts ... also explains why I was initially hesitant when asked to join Medna Usta."

[11] As with Pitu Guli, Medna Usta also performed some Macedonian music. "We

With Medna Usta, we transcribed songs off recordings. And by then Marcus Moskoff had published a book of *bitov* material, so we did some stuff from there. Some songs they were doing because they had learned them at Camp, which I had not started going to yet, but basically we just played what we liked. We chose songs that we thought were beautiful or fun, and we patched them together in medleys, putting two vocal pieces together or a vocal piece and an instrumental piece. I think we did some things that would strike Bulgarians as very odd, like, "Why would you mix songs from Pazardžik and Strandža?" I think that if you were Bulgarian, you wouldn't. But it was great for us, and people seemed to enjoy it.[12]

Born out of Balkan Camp in a bastion of Scene activity, Medna Usta was welcomed by an existing audience base. "Santa Cruz had a really strong folk dance community, so it was great to be in the middle of all that," Dena avows. Whereas Pitu Guli preserved its original focus on the California folk dance circuit, however, Medna Usta sought to reach a wider demographic. "At some point, we started to play regularly at this cafe in downtown Santa Cruz—CafeZinho,"[13] Dena narrates:

A lot of people who were into folk dancing would show up to dance in the courtyard, which had these fake cobblestones—I mean, it was really hard to dance! We did that for a number of years, and it was a wonderful thing because we got so much exposure. People would walk by and hear us who had never heard the music before, and it would either be, "Oh, that's too weird for me," or they'd be kind of curious. It got so we were used to playing for all kinds of people, and we got really good at answering questions. And we started getting other gigs too, outside of folk dancing gigs. Santa Cruz had a number of events throughout the year that featured live music; there were a lot of ethnic music groups in town, and we were one of the groups

---

didn't limit ourselves to bitov," Dena later wrote. "We used whatever recordings we could find. We then played them on the bitov instruments we had, sometimes substituting accordion for tambura."

[12] At that time, Marcus Moskoff was known as Marcus Holt.

[13] CafeZinho closed following the 1989 Loma Prieta earthquake.

that would often get asked to play. Then there was a modern dance troupe based here, Tandy Beal and Company. Tandy actually came to Balkan Camp for a few years—she got really excited about Balkan dance for a while, and we were included in some sort of grant she had to teach dance in the community. We were also hooked into the arts in the schools program, and we did a number of informative performances in conjunction with that—we gave demonstrations in traditional costumes and taught the kids some simple dances. And then we played at weddings but not for people who were from the Balkans. It was always something like, "My grandmother was Greek, and this reminds me of her," or else people's fantasy of what you see in movies of Jewish weddings. Like, "Oh—dancing! That's what I want at my wedding!" It always amazed me that people who had no connection to folk dancing were interested.[14]

An unexpected highlight of Medna Usta's performing career was a flirtation with the Northern California rock scene, perhaps the most extreme expression of the ensemble's openness to transcending established music-cultural boundaries. "Something that was really exciting was that we got to play in rock and roll venues a few times!" Dena exclaims:

There was this local rock band that got to be internationally famous—Camper Van Beethoven—and one of the guys in the band was friends with Anne Cleveland. We had played at The Catalyst, the biggest venue for rock groups in Santa Cruz; they had a dollar night where local bands could play, and that's where

[14] Dena later stressed that Medna Usta put considerable effort into securing outside gigs. In her words, "We had band photos taken at a professional studio and had a promo packet. We set up a number of concerts at the Kuumbwa Jazz Center in Santa Cruz. We also performed twice at the Freight and Salvage in Berkeley and several times for the In Toto concert series in Palo Alto. That said, it is true that a lot of gigs just came to us due to our exposure at our twice-a-month CafeZinho gig. Also, the fact that we were initially an "all girl" band and relatively young drew a lot of attention and interest. Even after Mark [Forry] joined us, we were thought of as an all-women band. The funny thing was we had not intended it to be all women—it just happened to turn out that way. But for many people in our audience it had significance."
The school arts program, officially known as Spectra (for SPECial Teacher Resources in the Arts), remains operative under the Cultural Council of Santa Cruz County.

Camper Van Beethoven heard us. They said, "We want you to open for us when we play here next month," and this time it was for a full audience. It was really fun. And then they asked us to open for their next show, which was at the Fillmore, so we played the Fillmore! That was one of our best gigs; we had our own dressing room stocked with drinks, and someone had drawn a sign with "Medna Usta" written in colorful '60s psychedelic lettering. The audience had no idea who we were, but they loved it, and they kept yelling, "Who are you? *Who are you*?" It was so much fun![15]

Dena made two albums with Medna Usa. "The first, *New Clothes and Ručenicas*, was literally made in a garage by this guy, David Larstein, who really admired our group," she explains. "He was part of the rock scene in Santa Cruz, and he said, 'Please let me record you guys!' It really has that garage sound—not at all professional—and we got a whole lot better later on." The second album, *All Dressed Up*,[16] was recorded in a studio at greater cost to the band. "It was totally worth it, though, because it was a good quality recording," Dena asserts. "By that time, Barbara and Karen had left the band, and we were playing with Mark Forry—he had gone to UCLA to get his PhD in ethnomusicology, and he played *kaval*." To promote the album, Dena submitted it to two leading folk music magazines, *Sing Out!*[17] and *Dirty Linen*, both of which published favorable reviews. "It was so interesting," she observes. "One review quoted this Bulgarian woman saying something like, 'I can't believe they're not Bulgarian!'—someone who didn't know who we were but had heard the recording." [18] At once an

[15] An additional rock appearance not listed here was at the DNA Lounge in San Francisco.
[16] The initial printing was 1000 copies.
[17] Interestingly, Ethel Raim was Music Editor of *Sing Out!* magazine between 1965 and 1975.
[18] The woman Dena mentions is Penka Kuneva, formerly affiliated with the Sofia Chamber Choir. The review reads as follows: "This is the most genuinely high-spirited and authentic Bulgarian music I've heard from the mouths of Americans. I played it for Penka Kuneva, past assistant conductor of the Sofia Chamber Choir in Bulgaria, and she said: 'I'm raving about this group. I would never guess they are not Bulgarians. And their music is so joyful, so rhythmic.' That joyfulness is also reflected in the group's name (*Medna Usta* means 'honey lips'), the recording's title, and its brief, lighthearted translations of the wry texts. Many Balkan ensembles focus

evaluation of Medna Usta's sound and an articulation of surprise at the novelty of an American ensemble performing Balkan music, this response was hardly one of a kind. As Medna Usta continued to broaden its range beyond the folk dance audience, confusion regarding members' ethnic and musical backgrounds seemed to abound. "Very often, people would ask me, 'are you of Bulgarian descent?'" Dena recalls. "They'd talk to me, and obviously I was American, but they'd ask if I was of Bulgarian descent because *why else* would I be playing this music?" Illuminating the specter of misrepresentation encountered by American Balkan musicians on the public stage, such confusion looks ahead to Chapters 3, 5, and 6, in which I examine the implications of Scene ensemble Brass Menažeri's engagement with the Bay Area hipster sphere. More immediately, it provides an introduction to questions of authenticity and identity brought to the fore by a major evolutionary process that intensified interaction between the Balkans and the American Balkan Scene: the post-1989 influx of native Balkan musicians into the United States.

First, a word on authenticity as it applies to ethnographic analysis. In general, I agree with contemporary ethnographers who caution against devoting excessive ink to what is authentic or inauthentic about a given cultural form, as this risks reducing culture to a dichotomy of right and wrong that may then be upheld as a proxy for some larger belief system. Treated theoretically, however, authenticity serves a valuable ethnographic function. Explicit or implied, labels of authenticity signify at the intersection between self and culture, separating what (we deem) we are from what (we deem) we are not. Whatever the intent with which they are assigned, such labels thus carry the deepest echoes of our views on social life, offering the researcher

---

exclusively on a cappella music, but this recording features hot dance numbers as well as unaccompanied songs which are the trademarks of the style. As Penka's approval indicates, the instrumentals (featuring strings, kaval and percussion) really cook. The vocal segments are really fresh, too, avoiding the more familiar covers of Koutev arrangements popularized by Ethel Raim and the Pennywhistlers as well as the homegrown English-language odes to the strength and sensitivity of women. Great songs, tight ensemble work, and a clear and convincing vocal style are high points of the recording" (*Sing Out!* 1993).

a vital indicator of wider trends in how individuals interact and identify.

Though it has only just been described, the concept of authenticity is central to the entirety of this book, bridging the gap between aesthetic and ideology in Mark Levy's narrative and informing conversations about identity and tradition in this and subsequent chapters. Having traced the consequences of Mark's pursuit of the Bulgarian *bitov* repertoire and instrumentation, I link changes in Dena's understanding of authentic *gŭdulka* technique to a shift in the structure of authority experienced by American Balkan musicians in the context of increased intercultural exchange.

Previously, Dena alluded to a struggle with *gŭdulka* ornamentation. "I had been given this limited knowledge about ornamentation, and I knew that it didn't sound quite like it did on the recordings," she explains. Unable to determine the precise adjustment required to bring her ornaments into agreement with those of her Bulgarian models, she proceeded despite a nagging impression that her technique was somehow flawed. Then, in early 1989, she had a lesson with Marcus Moskoff, who supplied her with the technique she had failed to unearth on her own. She tells the story as follows:

I had seen Marcus playing *gajda* in Los Angeles, but he had since taken up the *gŭdulka*, and he was considered to be the best American *gŭdulka* player. He taught at Balkan Camp for a number of years, but then he returned to Bulgaria to study with Mihail Marinov, one of the best *gŭdulka* players, and discovered that he needed to relearn his ornamentation. That lesson with him was one of the key moments in my playing. I knew that he had studied in Bulgaria, and I knew that the ornaments he was doing sounded like they did on the recordings—they had that characteristic barking sound. He was very good at articulating what was going on, and I could see what he did and put it together with what I heard. Though afterwards I couldn't play for months! I had to start all over—to reprogram my fingers and my brain.[19]

Recognizing the limitations of self-guided study, Dena welcomed firsthand instruction. Granted a new method of ornamentation firsthand, however, she evaluated it against the ornaments she heard on recordings of Bulgarian *gŭdulka* players, a circuitous process through which she bolstered her confidence in its overall accuracy. The stage was set for change when she attended her first Balkan Camp at a critical juncture in its role as the heart of the American Balkan Scene. Beginning in 1989, the fall of communism across Eastern Europe made it possible to bring native Balkan musicians to the United States. "Sometime around 1989, the EEFC hired Georgi Doičev, the *gajda* player, to teach," Dena recounts:

Our first Bulgarian! It was so exciting. And then the following year Doičev brought a band over—Bulgari—and there was a *gŭdulka* player, Aleksandur Georgiev, in that group. That was fantastic, and we took lessons from them at Camp. It was a big thing, the change of the culture at Camp. All of the instruments had been taught by Americans, and then with this influx of not just native musicians, but native musicians of the highest caliber … by the late '90s, it was very different than it used to be. To me, it used to feel more like a really big private party as opposed to an official workshop, and all of the American bands got to play in the dance hall, whereas now it's mainly the Balkan musicians—that's what I miss. In terms of the educational experience, though, I feel like I'm learning a lot more.[20]

[19] Mihail Marinov performed in Bulgaria with a group called Trakijska Troika.
[20] In a follow-up interview, Dena clarified that the hiring of native Balkan musicians slowed after Bulgari, accelerating again in the late 1990s around the time Esma Redžepova arrived.
There are two main performance venues at Mendocino Balkan Camp. The dance hall is a large open building with a polished wooden dance floor. Modeled after an intimate café ubiquitous throughout Southeastern Europe, the *kafana* is a small dark room with a drink counter and limited space for dancing. Prior to the late 1990s, American bands held court in the dance hall. With the exception of such storied groups as Édessa, Ziyiá, and Brass Menažeri, priority is now given to native performers.

The most immediate shift involved the experience of teaching and learning at Balkan Camp. For Dena, this was manifest in uncertainty over how to reconcile her revised ornamentation technique with that advocated by the *gŭdulka* player from Bulgari. "Under communism, there were these music conservatories that arose, and certain aspects of playing were standardized," she states:

> There were things the Bulgarian *gŭdulka* player showed me that were very difficult, and there really didn't seem to be a solid technical reason to do them. Mostly, they had to do with the motion of the fingers during ornamentation and with how you actually hold the instrument. By this time, I had been playing the *gŭdulka* for years with a hand position that felt very comfortable, and he had this position that had a certain *look*—his instrument was positioned higher on his torso, his hand was very straight, and he would lift his fingers up very high when he played the ornaments. I thought, "I don't know, it's really hard to do it that way," and in general when you play an instrument, you're told *not* to lift your fingers so high because it's inefficient! I had been willing to redo my ornamentation with Marcus because I was convinced that what he was doing in terms of the sound was right and that what I was doing was wrong, but I definitely wasn't convinced about the hand position.

This is an important distinction. Following her lesson with Moskoff, Dena adopted his technique because it produced ornaments like those she heard on recordings of native musicians. Paradoxically, then, she was immediately wary of the Bulgarian instructor's hand position, which she felt to privilege an institutional aesthetic at the expense of basic musicianship. Driven by an instinctive urge to defer to his native authority, however, she pushed aside her skepticism and "made an effort to try." The matter resurfaced in 1996, when Dena was asked to teach *gŭdulka* at Balkan Camp. After continued experimentation failed to persuade her that the position in question was anything other than "unnecessarily difficult," she had ceased all efforts to incorporate it into her own technique. Still, she admits, "I ended up teaching it because it seemed like I should—like it was the official way."

Clarity came in 1998, when the EEFC hired a different Bulgarian *gŭdulka* instructor, Nikolay Kolev,[21] who did not use the position Georgiev had taught. "He didn't hold his hand that way, and he's known as a darn good player," Dena remarks. Inquiring, she learned that the position was indeed an example of standardized conservatory technique and thus antithetical to the village ideal upon which the Scene was founded. "I asked Nikolay about it, and he said that when he started at the conservatory, he was already a teenager and had been playing competently for a long enough time that they didn't make him change his position," she relates:

> He felt the same way—that it didn't make sense to hold your hand like that. I feel bad because I made it excessively hard for my poor students at Camp, but it seemed right at the time. I felt that it was my job to teach that position because it seemed like the Bulgarian way. I've never gone back to it myself, though, and I wouldn't teach it again.

As we attempt to grasp what Dena's narrative implies about the impact of intensified intercultural interaction on the structure of authority experienced by aspiring American Balkan musicians, it is helpful to consider how that structure initially formed. Headed by Mirjana Laušević's teacher-ethnographers, the emergence of a national Balkan contingent was marked by heightened awareness of Balkan folk music. With respect to actual music-culture, however, a pervasive abstraction endured. This furnishes an explanation for the power of early music-cultural intermediaries such as Marcus Moskoff and Mark Levy, whose overseas training was understood to invest them with the ability to convey authentic information to their fellow enthusiasts back home. Whatever the correlation between their teachings and the reality on the ground, these esteemed individuals would serve as the voice of authenticity for the Scene population as long as the source of authenticity remained abroad. Then, with the fall of the Iron Curtain, the music-cultural worlds of the American Balkan

---

[21] Kolev relocated to New York in 1995 and maintains a close relationship with the Scene. Today, he performs with his wife and daughters as the Kolev Family Ensemble and with *bitov* band Kabile.

Scene and the Balkans commenced to collide. The consequences were most conspicuous at Camp, where American instructors were within a decade largely replaced by native Balkan instructors. Yet to suggest that the post-1989 transition amounted to a total restructuring would be a gross oversimplification. Rather, I see the fact that Dena did not unquestioningly adopt the hand position presented by the *gŭdulka* player from Bulgari as evidence that what she calls "the change of the culture at Camp" should be interpreted as a thorough review of the systems of ideology and authority that had fueled the birth of the Scene, awakening members to the inherent contingency of their vision.

A comparison between Dena's experience with Medna Usta and with later ensembles reveals a parallel shift in American Balkan musicians' approach to engagement with Balkan music and their concept of music-cultural identity. This begins with an expansion of the definition of Balkan folk music recognized by the Scene.

As established in Chapter 1, the Balkan Music and Dance Workshops coalesced from efforts to promote the dissemination and performance of Bulgarian *bitov* music in the United States. These efforts sparked an increase in the incidence of affiliated individuals traveling to the Balkans, where they were exposed to additional genres and styles. Among the first genres to cross the radar of the Scene was Bulgarian wedding music, characterized by rapid, virtuosic playing on amplified accordion, clarinet, saxophone, electric bass, and drum kit and often associated with the Roma.[22] Dena was introduced to wedding music as a member of Medna Usta. "We got a copy of a cassette," she recalls. "There was this man named Bruce Cochran who had gotten a copy in Bulgaria, and it was going around. I think I had been aware of it—of this other kind of Bulgarian music—but I didn't have a recording of it until then, and certainly with Medna Usta I didn't play it." After Medna Usta disbanded in 1992, she played with a

---

[22] For a socio-political analysis of wedding music, see "Bulgarian Wedding Music between Folk and *Chalga*: Politics, Markets, and Current Directions" by Carol Silverman.

succession of ensembles that looked beyond *bitov* to incorporate the repertoire, instrumentation, and aesthetic of other, wider Balkan traditions. In contrast to Mark Levy, who was one of many Scene musicians and dancers reluctant to accept that amplified accordion and clarinet had penetrated the vocabulary of village musicians, Dena celebrated the expansion of her musical horizons as a catalyst for creativity and growth. "Medna Usta basically broke up when Ruth moved to Boston, but Anne and I were still in town, and we wanted to play again," she narrates:

> We started playing with Lisa Ekström, who plays accordion and sings, and we hooked up with Mary Hofer, who plays clarinet. We also had a fabulous drummer, Peter Romeo—a Greek-American who grew up in the Greek community in Pennsylvania. His family was actually from a part of Greece that's now part of Turkey, so he had a lot of knowledge about Turkish language and culture. He played *dumbek*, Anne played *tambura* and sang, Mary played clarinet, I played *gŭdulka* and sang, Lisa played accordion and sang, and we had bass players occasionally. We played a lot of Romani material, and we were going for more of a contemporary sound. That group was called Voluta Vox; we played for a few years, and we made a recording, though we got a lot better later on. After that, I had a similar group, Top Dog Run, which faded out about a year ago. That was also Lisa Ekström, Mary Hofer, and myself, and then Tom Farris, who played drum, and Bill Lanphier on bass. Tom could play *tapan*, but he also played drum kit, so some of our music was very modern—kind of pop-ish. Folk with a pop accent! It wasn't strictly wedding music, and of course we couldn't approach the proficiency and speed of the Bulgarians, but we tried to capture some of the energy. Our repertoire was about half Bulgarian and half Romani; the Romani songs were Lisa's specialty in singing, and then I would sing the Bulgarian songs, and we'd back each other up.

In addition to what they imply about the diversification of material practiced by Scene musicians, differences in genre and style contribute to the rhetoric Dena employs to position Medna Usta, Voluta Vox, and Top Dog Run on a comparative temporal continuum. Referring to Medna Usta, she states, "We didn't play music that was contemporary in Bulgaria at the time." By the same equation, she offers that Voluta Vox "sought more of a contemporary sound," while pronouncing the music of Top Dog Run "very modern." Manifest most explicitly in Mark Levy's ambition to write a paper "paralleling the developments at Camp with the developments in the Balkans," historical comparison proves critical to understanding trends observed at the level of the Scene. The reason is clear. As a music-cultural ecosystem with an intercultural design, the historical trajectory of the Scene is by definition a function of its evolving relationship with the Balkans and thus a function of the music-cultural evolution of the Balkan region. Investigating what makes Voluta Vox and Top Dog Run more in line with contemporary Balkan practice is of value precisely because it compels us to contemplate both the respective processes shaping each music-cultural realm and the history of contact between them, calling attention to how this history is articulated in the work of Scene members.

As the preliminary focus of instruction at the Mendocino Balkan Music and Dance Workshops, the Bulgarian *bitov* tradition was canonized as the unofficial first language of the American Balkan Scene. Far from arising in a vacuum, however, early emphasis on *bitov* reflected the confluence of values and beliefs with currency among key music-cultural actors at the outset of exchange. When Mark Levy embarked on his initial journey to the Balkans, he had already gravitated toward village repertoire and instrumentation, which he cherished as a vibrant alternative to the more generic AMAN orchestra. Returning from Bulgaria, where the *bitov* ensemble was promoted as the village prototype for the radio orchestra, he enlisted Pitu Guli on a mission to bring live *bitov* music to the California folk dance circuit, triggering a chain reaction whereby his aesthetic-cum-ideological predilection was embedded in the consciousness of his fellow American Balkan musicians and dancers.

Meanwhile, the music-cultural climate in the Balkans continued to evolve, with significant recalibration following the collapse of the Soviet Union. When the first Bulgarian musicians arrived at Mendocino eager to teach and perform a variety of genres and styles on acoustic and amplified instruments alike, the Scene was forced to confront the reality that Balkan folk music was not circumscribed by ideals of village tradition. The effect was profound, deepening an incipient rift between *bitov* devotees and individuals willing to draw from a broader palette, while prompting musicians to reconsider their relationship to the music they performed. Illustration is available in Dena's account of playing with Medna Usta, Voluta Vox, and Top Dog Run. Like Pitu Guli, Medna Usta did not eschew creativity in all forms but took pleasure in compiling medleys from songs originating across Bulgaria. Still, I see a difference between the juxtaposition of regional idioms and the integration of repertoire and instrumentation from disparate traditions. Indeed, as the perpetual replication of an archetype of authenticity gave way to a more vital, organic approach, it could be said that firsthand intercultural interaction opened the door for American Balkan musicians to cultivate their own artistic identities in conversation with Balkan folk music.

The concept of identity brings a deeper story to light. Prior to 1989, Scene members united around collective pursuit of Balkan music and dance, extrapolating a music-cultural connection that was for most ungrounded in experience. Face to face with representatives of the Balkan region, these same individuals were made more viscerally aware of the artifice of their community—captured, as it were, in the floodlights of their own Americanness. At that moment, the question of how to play authentic Balkan folk music was subtly reframed, becoming the question of how to play Balkan folk music authentically as an American Balkan musician. In Dena's words:

My question is, "To what degree can Bulgarians recognize their own music in what I do?" In other words, how thick is my American accent? For me, it's very important to try to play my instrument as authentically as I can, which means really trying to get the ornaments. What's interesting to me about music from around the world is the differences, and the ornaments are one of the main things that make Bulgarian music different. That's why I don't like fusion music; I'm not saying it's wrong or anything, but something that absolutely does not interest me is taking a melody from one type of music and playing it in a totally different style. The ornaments give this music life, and on that level I really try to be as authentic as I can. As I've said, ornamentation is something I've had to work on over the years, and it's something I will definitely zero in on when I hear Americans playing—either, "They've got the ornaments," or, "They don't have the ornaments." Other Americans just hear a Bulgarian melody, and that's enough for them. For me, the ornamentation has to be there or it's just not pleasurable to listen to. Then again, I'm not trying to play *totally* the way Bulgarians play! The Bulgarians I come in contact with tend to be really highly trained conservatory musicians, they play incredibly fast, and they take old melodies and put interesting new twists on them. That's something I love to hear, but it's not necessarily something I could do or would even *want* to do myself. I'm happy approximating an old-time village sound. And I love having the freedom as an American to play pieces that Bulgarians would no longer play or might not group together. I look at that as something that makes my version of Bulgarian music different from Bulgarians' versions. And I think it *should* be different because I *am* an American![23]

For Dena, adhering to a specific model of tradition for the sake of authenticity is less important—less authentic, even—than giving voice to the junctures as well as the disjunctures that structure the relationship between music and musician. She refines this view in her treatment of vocal performance, weighing the significance of attempting to sound like 1) a Bulgarian singer, 2) an American Balkan singer, and 3) an American Balkan singer exploring her artistic identity through Balkan folk music. "I feel the same way about singing, in terms of getting the ornaments right, as I do about the *gŭdulka*, but with singing there are other considerations," she reflects:

[23] When speaking of music from distinct cultures, Dena employs the term "differences" with reference to qualities of instrumentation, intonation, vibrato, and timbre.

As Americans, we don't speak the same way—our vocal placement is different—and it's easy to get to this place where you sound like an imitation. The trick, then, is sounding reasonably Bulgarian without sounding like you're imitating. If you're singing on a recording, it's more acceptable, but if you're singing in person, the same singing can come across as sounding like imitation or affectation. It's interesting. When I first started singing, I was listening to the old field recordings; I've always loved the hard-voice village-y stuff, which I think many Americans don't like, and I was really trying to get that sound. But most of the Bulgarian singers that I've worked with are conservatory trained, and their voices are different from the older village style. So what *I* do vocally has definitely evolved, and then I've learned that *every* singer is different.[24]

At first glance, this discussion mirrors Dena's perspective on authenticity and identity in relation to her experience as a *gŭdulka* player. Upon further meditation, however, it becomes apparent that she attaches greater importance to demonstrating her inherent distance from the Balkans when performing as a vocalist. One explanation is the medium of sound production. Whereas the instrumentalist is responsible for enlivening a material object, in the case of the singer, music and breath issue simultaneously from a single source. This provides a rationale for Dena's fear of sounding like an "imitation" when singing, as any perceived posturing would implicate her body as well as her expression. Another explanation is text, which poses the challenges of pronunciation, translation, and meaning. Dena makes a point to translate the songs she learns and endeavors to grasp their context. Ultimately, however, she indicates that for her, lyrics are a gloss on music regardless of language. "In general, I like to know what the songs I'm singing are about, though I've definitely performed songs I don't understand," she suggests:

[24] Words westerners use to describe Bulgarian village singing include "strident," "brassy," and "nasal," though the latter is a bit of a misconception. Conservatory-trained singers cultivate a more classically oriented sound that preserves distinctive national elements. As is typical of music given a "world" designation, the exotic and the familiar are juxtaposed to broaden accessibility and appeal.

And then even if I *do* understand what the words mean, I don't always know what the tone is in Bulgarian. Sometimes I can't tell if something is funny or not or if it's happy or sad. I learned a song from Donka Koleva where a girl is making a present for a boy because she really likes him, and he says not to bother because he's got another girl somewhere else who he plans to marry. When I heard that, I said, "That's really sad," drawing on my own personal experiences of being rejected in life. And Donka said, "Actually, he's doing her a favor—there's no way she's going to get him!" It's just hard to know, culturally, and anyway maybe that's just Donka's personal feeling! But then, lyrics are not the most important thing for me even in my own language; the words are not the first thing that I listen to when I listen to a song. For me, if a song has good words but bad music, forget it! On the other hand, if a really beautiful melody has so-so lyrics, I'll still perform it. The music is most important, and the words are an overlay—that's where I start from in any kind of music.

Despite her professed ambivalence toward text, Dena admits to having modified lyrics that conflict with her basic values or potentially those of her audience, a nod to the frequency with which folk songs reference beliefs and practices that seem outdated, confusing, or even offensive when carried across music-cultural lines. More than a remedy for reconciling different backgrounds, she associates this with her aforementioned need to clarify that she in no way assumes the ability to perform Balkan music as anything other than an American Balkan musician. Embracing any confusion or discomfort she experiences in relation to a particular song as not only unavoidable but instructive, she deems mindful adaptation a sign of deference and respect. "There's this whole 'killing Turks' genre," she states:

It's such a significant part of the history and the repertoire, but I don't always feel comfortable singing about it—bragging about how many Turks you're going to kill. Especially because there are Turks in the folk dance community! With my bands, we've gone so far as to edit verses out of songs. There was one song comparing Christianity to Islam, and Christianity "smelled" like incense and fresh basil, while Islam "smelled" like burned silk. It was interesting, but one band member in particular didn't feel comfortable singing that verse in front of an audience. And verses get edited out by Bulgarians too, just like in American music. Verses get lost. You have all of these epics that told very long stories, and now only the first three verses are ever performed.

As with her approach to text, Dena accepts the ebb and flow of music through space and time, envisioning tradition as a living organism with the capacity to respond to a changing environment. With this, she reminds her fellow American Balkan musicians that their opinions and choices have little if any immediate bearing on the reality of music in the Balkans. "Once the music comes over here, it's really quite a different thing," she asserts:

Look at American blues—many white people play blues now, but it's not any less valid because it's being played by white people who might happen to be educated members of the middle class. It can still be good music! Certainly, I don't think in terms of us preserving something for Bulgaria or that Bulgaria will somehow rediscover their music through us. Bulgarians *could* rediscover it by Americans going over there and expressing interest in it—that can happen, and I think it happens all over the world. But it's not the same tradition! Once it's in another context, it's not the same tradition. And then of course whatever we do with the music here, it's not the same tradition in Bulgaria anymore either—many of the older styles are performed less frequently now. But that's just what happens. It remains to be seen what will happen over there. Hopefully, young people will rediscover it. And because there are a lot of Bulgarians living here now, that will be interesting to see as well. I'm really curious about their connection to Bulgarian music, and especially that of their children.

This chapter has heretofore examined issues of intercultural authenticity, identity, and tradition as they pertain to intensified interaction between the American Balkan Scene and the Balkans. To conclude, I have asked Dena for a survey of subsequent trends linked to the rise of a new generation of American Balkan musicians passionate about musical innovation and the pursuit of new audiences.

Previously, Dena extolled the breadth of exposure she enjoyed with Medna Usta, which supplemented regular folk dance performances with public events. Today, she plays almost entirely for folk dancers. "With Top Dog Run and with Verna Druzhina, the band I'm with now, it's really just the folk dance crowd,"[25] she explains:

> Really, I think this trend continues because we don't play anywhere that other people will hear us. Top Dog Run only played for folk dance groups; we played somebody's fortieth anniversary party, but they were both folk dancers too! We kept saying, "We've got to get out—we've just *got* to!" But it never happened. With Medna Usta, it often just came to us. And with Top Dog Run and Verna Druzhina, we haven't expanded our audience at all.

Audience expansion acquires new urgency in light of diminishing interest in folk dancing nationwide. Like Mark Levy, who attributes this contraction in part to a faltering youth demographic, Dena identifies age as central to her concerns. "Until recently, our audience was just people my age and older, and that was always frustrating because we wanted younger people to get involved," she states:

> With my new band, we kept saying, "We've got to get out so other people can hear us," and we found a good venue and started playing last January—a restaurant that had a really good space where you could move the tables around for dancing, and there was a little stage for us to perform. They were very accommodating, and for four months in a row, we had a once-a-month gig. We figured out after the first time that we needed to get a younger band to play on the same bill because that automatically drew a younger audience. Which was exactly what we wanted! But then

---

[25] Verna Druzhina disbanded in 2011. I have elected to preserve the present tense in pertinent quotations to maintain spoken integrity.

the restaurant closed. It was such a disappointment for us, and a number of people have told me they were disappointed when it closed because they were enjoying the music. So now we're looking for other places to play. Public places, because if we rent a place, we'll have the same scene—the same folk dance crowd. Which is great, and that's mainly who came to the restaurant anyway, but at the restaurant there were also always people in the back who would have never heard this music otherwise and who were interested.

Interaction between musicians and dancers is vital to the fabric of the Scene. Yet if there is some consensus that a downturn in folk dance activity renders this relationship less sustainable, efforts to attract a new audience are often resented by veteran folk dancers. And in this way it is important to consider age—or more specifically, generation—as it applies to the Scene population. When Mark invoked the decline of the International Folk Dance Movement, he did so not to illustrate the plight of American Balkan ensembles facing audience attrition but to help account for a crisis of enrollment that beset the Balkan Music and Dance Workshops in the mid-1980s. Stimulated by the arrival of native instructors, revitalization later drew strength from an influx of young American musicians distinguished by a lack of folk dance experience and acute sensitivity to the workings of the music-cultural mainstream. From the perspective of what is retrospectively framed as the first generation, then, the root of tension is a difference in *approach*, as constituents confront the possibility that these young music-cultural émigrés will shift the focus of the Scene while destabilizing its traditional boundaries.

Dena acknowledges that the process of generational transition will require continuous conversations and an openness to change. Ultimately, however, she welcomes this as a necessary trade-off for the health and longevity of the Scene:

I'm so thrilled that so many young people are interested, but I've noticed that most of them did not get into it through folk dancing—they came to it from a very different place. It's not wrong, it's just not my generation—it's not how we got into it. People come to it for different reasons, and you just accept it. And the main thing is that the Scene continues. That's most important.[26]

[26] Revisiting this in 2013, Dena expressed that she now feels greater nostalgia for the marriage of folk music and dance traditions that defined the early Scene.

3

Rachel MacFarlane

We turn now to the story of Rachel MacFarlane, who discovered Balkan music at the University of Kansas in the mid-1970s. Later, Rachel sang and played baritone horn with Brass Menažeri, a Bay Area band at the heart of my analysis of generational transition. Until late 2011, she presided as General Manager and Program Director of the EEFC, working to shepherd the Scene toward a future consonant with its founding design. Decades of intensive academic and independent research have garnered Rachel recognition as a scholar among her fellow Scene members, who respect her for her conviction that music should be engaged with mindfulness to context.

When I met Rachel at the 2007 Mendocino Balkan Music and Dance Workshops, I was already familiar with the scope of her influence, which is credited in a humbling array of publications and recordings released by American Balkan musicians and dancers. Embodying the front between the past and evolving present of the Scene, she is perhaps the ideal figure to carry us into the second half of this book.

Rachel MacFarlane was born in 1958 in Orange, California and became aware of Balkan folk music through her involvement with the International Folk Dance Movement. In contrast to the majority of what I henceforth term "first generation folk dancers-turned-musicians," her introduction to folk dancing was preceded by academic pursuit of East European languages and cultures. "When I was in junior high, I got interested in learning Russian. I don't know why—I just did," she states:

An astute teacher noticed, and she gave me a textbook, so I started learning it on my own. My father was in the military, so we moved every couple of years, and by the time I was in high school, I ended up at a school that offered Russian. I took two years of Russian, in the tenth and eleventh grades, and then we moved again my senior year.

In 1976, Rachel enrolled at the University of Kansas with a major in Slavic languages and literatures. Her first week on campus, she noticed a sign-up sheet for international folk dancing. "This was at the tail end of the really big folk dance craze," she recalls. "There I was, a seventeen-year-old freshman, and I wanted to find ways to meet people. So I went, and I got completely addicted to it. It was perfect!" Mirroring a national trend, the campus folk dance organization specialized in repertoire from the Balkans. This was also perfect for Rachel. "I found Balkan dances to be the most exciting, and I thought Balkan music was just so cool!" she exclaims. "I remember specifically hearing *zurnas* for the first time on a recording; it was very compelling to me." With growing interest in the Balkans, she shifted her studies from Russian to Serbo-Croatian, nurturing an impassioned belief in the interconnectedness of a given region's expressive forms:

> I was lucky because the Slavic department at school wasn't limited to Russian—there were Balkan languages as well. Pretty soon I got interested in the literature and culture, and I started trying to transcribe song words. That was great language practice—you can really learn a lot about a language by studying folk songs! My thread has always included language and culture studies; there has always been an academic component to whatever I do.

At the University of Kansas, Rachel enjoyed dancing to, listening to, and learning from Balkan folk songs. She made no attempt to play Balkan music herself. "It wasn't just me, though," she notes. "At that point, none of us were getting into actually playing the music—that hadn't really touched the Midwest. We listened to recordings and we danced to recordings, but the idea of live music was still pretty new." Change came in 1980, when she relocated to Seattle for graduate school and encountered a professional folk ensemble that featured live accompaniment.

"I completed four years at the University of Kansas, and then I decided to go to the University of Washington," she narrates:

> There was an ensemble there that I had seen on tour—it's called Radost, and it's still in existence today. Radost did big staged choreography—mostly Eastern European stuff—and by the time I moved to Seattle, they also had musicians who played. By then, there had been groups like AMAN that were exploring traditional instruments, and more dancers were becoming interested in performing Balkan music.[1]

Rachel auditioned for Radost shortly after her arrival in Seattle and served for three years as a dancer and a costume designer. Her initial musical activity was peripheral to the ensemble. "Somehow, I hooked up with some people who were connected with Radost and with other groups in the Seattle folk dance community, and we started playing music together," she explains:

> We did a lot of *tamburica* music, and we did some Serbian stuff. I sang, and they handed me a *tamburica* instrument—a *brač*—and said, "Here, play this." And a *frula*, which is a Serbian fipple flute. So we all learned to play some simple things together. Really, it was a whole new dimension for me, and pretty soon I got more interested in playing music than in going folk dancing!

Like many American Balkan folk dancers-turned-musicians, Rachel *approached* Balkan folk music with little prior musical experience. "I liked to sing, but I had never been in any groups except a glee club here and there," she states. Around 1982, she joined Ostali Muzikaši, an assemblage of Radost-affiliated musicians with which she toured Bulgaria and the former Yugoslavia. In addition to its influence on her understanding of Balkan music and music-culture, the tour exerted an indelible

---

[1] Founded in 1976, Radost performs Balkan and East European music across the Pacific Northwest. In recent years, the ensemble has prioritized Bulgarian material, embracing the opportunity to collaborate with members of the local Bulgarian immigrant community. Other collaborations include fusion projects with non-folk dance groups. The word *radost* means "joy" in languages of Slavic origin.

impact on her personal life, igniting a chain of events that cul-
minated with her entrance into Balkan Camp and the American
Balkan Scene. "To make a long story short, I ended up staying
in Macedonia and marrying a Macedonian man," she recounts:

> Eventually, I brought him back to the States, and we tried to set
> up our life in Seattle. He was a musician—he played *kaval* and
> *gajda* in the Northern Macedonian village style. One day, I got
> a call from a man named Mark Levy—I did not know Mark at
> this point—and he said, "We'd like to invite your husband to
> teach at the Balkan Music and Dance Workshops in Mendocino,
> California, this year." That was the first that I had heard of Camp.
> So he taught for a couple of years, and I went along as his spouse
> and interpreter. And that's how I got introduced to the Scene!

Even in a supporting role, Rachel made a strong impression
on Camp founder Mark Levy, so much so that, in 1988, after she
and her now former husband had parted ways, Mark asked her
to teach singing at Camp. "It seems so funny now," she remarks.
"The Camps have really evolved, and we've gotten a lot more
native talent to teach since then. But at that time the instructors
tended to be Americans, and I was happy to share whatever I
could." In consultation with then ethnomusicology graduate student Sonia Tamar Seeman, Rachel focused her class on *čalgija*,
an urban Macedonian genre combining *ut, kanun, tarabuka*,
and *dajre* with clarinet and violin. "Sonia was also involved
with Balkan Camp, and she was researching *čalgija* in Skopje,"[2]
she states. "We wanted to get some of this music out there, and
people were ready!" Rachel's statement alludes to the expanding definition of Balkan folk music recognized by the Scene:

> Camp had started out with Bulgarian village music—Bulgarian village
> instruments and Bulgarian village singing. That's what people were
> originally interested in. When my husband taught, he was teaching

---

[2] Currently a professor of ethnomusicology at the University of Texas at Austin,
Seeman recounts this experience in the Fall/Winter 2004 – 2005 *Kef Times*.

Macedonian folk instruments, and that was already a step in a new direction because Macedonia was a region that hadn't been explored as much yet. By the time I came to teach, there was an interest in urban music. This was around the time that wedding music and Greek urban music were also introduced, and it kept going from there.

Rachel maintained a steady presence at the Balkan Music and Dance Workshops over the next five summers, continuing to teach while taking a variety of classes. Then, in 1993, Mark Levy invited her to sit on the board of the EEFC, granting her a voice in Camp administration that augmented her position within the Scene.[3] From 1998 to 2011, Rachel presided as EEFC General Manager, overseen by a seven-member volunteer board that convenes from across the country to make decisions pertaining to membership, programming, and finance.[4] During her tenure, the EEFC adopted a consensus model as a more inclusive alternative to standard voting procedure, a move board members hoped would bring the organization into greater harmony with Scene ideology. "We've had some wonderful board members who are interested in working with the consensus model," she reflects. "It was an important step for us, and I'm proud of how well we've done with it."

Though the EEFC remains operative throughout the year, its primary function is to facilitate the Balkan Music and Dance Workshops, now held annually on both coasts. "We are first and foremost an educational organization," Rachel avows. "That said, our goal is not so much to do research ourselves but to present an opportunity for other people to educate the members of this community. We have a formula for our Camps so that we don't have to constantly reinvent them or even to innovate much at this point." To use Rachel's term, the Camp "formula" refers to efforts to hire instructors who will aid the EEFC in bringing its educational objectives to fruition. If this formula has encouraged

---

[3] Prior to the 1990s, most board members were drawn from the roster of Balkan Camp instructors. As the latter group broadened to encompass native Balkan musicians, the board shifted to favor the greater EEFC community, where long-term investment is more guaranteed.
[4] The workings of the EEFC board are detailed in the Fall/Winter 2002 – 2003 *Kef Times*. An analysis of recent developments can be found in this book's Conclusion.

continuity in Camp structure, however, these objectives have themselves evolved, shifting in tandem with two evolutionary processes this book has already explored: 1) intensified interaction between the American Balkan Scene and the Balkans and 2) rising interface between the Scene and its American music-cultural surroundings. I revisit the first process to gain insight into the changing educational fabric of the Balkan Music and Dance Workshops, laying the groundwork for a portrait of change at the level of the EEFC.

When Rachel began teaching at Mendocino Balkan Camp, the staff consisted almost entirely of American Balkan folk dancers-turned-musicians, many of whom had studied overseas. With the fall of the Iron Curtain in 1989, the EEFC seized the opportunity to hire musicians direct from the Balkans, leading to a contemporary ratio of approximately ⅔ American and ⅓ native Balkan instructors.[5] "We've been really lucky—we've found incredible people to teach," Rachel affirms. "Some of them have moved here, some happen to be in the country and we manage to get them, and some of them we sponsor. Some have been one-time instructors, and others come again and again, year after year."

The indisputable advantages aside, it is important to note that the intercultural hiring process introduced enduring administrative challenges. Most tangible are those involving the logistics of overseas exchange, a category that encompasses everything from aiding incoming instructors in obtaining visas and other necessary travel documents to making transportation arrangements and booking a corresponding North American tour. Also noteworthy is the challenge of establishing trust with candidates for each position, a task that requires sensitivity to individual responses to the Camp concept. "Before anything else, we have to ask, 'Will they get it? Are they going to be comfortable in this setting?'" Rachel explains:

---

[5] This ratio encompasses both dance and music instructors.

Sometimes we have to get someone who's been to Camp to talk to the person, especially if they're not American. There was one instructor in particular who took a couple of years of talking to before he was finally convinced to come. He had ideas about "those Americans," like, "Are they crazy or what?—what do I want to be around them for?" But he ended up being one of our most loyal teachers. He came, and he understood the community—he got it.

Logistical or conceptual, elements of these challenges carry over into the Camp environment, with implications for the educational experience of attendees. Illustration begins with the question of how to assess teaching ability when a prospective instructor resides overseas, made more complex by the specter of conflict stemming from the juxtaposition of disparate teaching and learning styles. In Rachel's words:

Some people are well-known teachers—they know how to teach, and they understand how Americans need to learn. Others don't, and sometimes it's difficult for us to find out before the first day of Camp. But sometimes even if people don't know how to teach or don't know how to teach Americans, you can still get a lot out of just watching and listening to them play. You hope people will accept that, but we get complaints about it all the time. There was one person I remember who was almost in tears, he was so frustrated. He's a good musician, but he had to write everything out; he started in classical music, and there was no way that he could just sit in class and learn the tunes by ear. There was another person who consistently wrote in her evaluations that she would have liked to have songs all charted out. And it never happened—it's just not going to happen. There's a *culture* of learning by ear at Camp, and there's a *culture* of observing and not having charts for everything. But it was very frustrating to her; she couldn't learn by someone singing at her.

The above quotation harbors an intriguing contradiction. If Rachel seems at first to link oral transmission and related tension to the arrival of native Balkan instructors, her reference to a "culture of learning by ear" indicates that this was by no means a novel approach. Confirmation is found in the narratives of Mark Levy and Dena Bjornlie, which furnish examples of veteran folk dancers who taught themselves to play Balkan music by following along with available recordings. To grasp the significance of this tension, then, it is first necessary to determine the root of the culture Rachel describes. Here, I invoke a prevailing assumption that oral transmission signifies as the traditional mode of teaching and learning among Balkan folk musicians. Borrowing from Chapter 2, I replace the word "traditional" with "authentic," positing that Americans who advocate for transmission without transcription do so in part because they see it as a way to tie their activity to their vision of authentic musical practice in the Balkans, conferring that authenticity on the music they produce while augmenting their authenticity as musicians. But what of those who require notation to learn? As might be expected, most deem authenticity a poor substitute for accessibility and its sovereignty an affront to the atmosphere of inclusivity that gave early folk dancers-turned-musicians the confidence to attempt to play Balkan folk music before *any* form of instruction was widely available. From this angle, conflict over oral versus written transmission can be interpreted as a balancing act between two ideological pillars that predate the Scene: 1) the ideology of authenticity and 2) the ideology of inclusivity.

This is not to suggest that the influx of native instructors is in any way irrelevant. Previous chapters offer evidence that efforts to reproduce authentic repertoire and technique gained urgency as the arrival of native Balkan instructors gave aspiring American Balkan musicians a sense of proximity to what they perceived as the source of that authenticity, prompting them to think critically about their relationship with Balkan music-culture, while bringing latent ideological fissures to light. Such is the interpretation embraced by Rachel, who argues that it is a willingness to learn from tension and debate that best captures the impact of the post-1989 transition at Camp. "We *have* had some culture clashes—there *have* been some difficult times. But I actually think that's educational too!" she proclaims:

Throughout all of this, one of my main complaints has been the romanticization of the Balkans. I remember when people started talking about our community as a "village," and they're thinking about some sort of romantic village in the Balkans. I really resist that. Often, I feel that people are saying, "Here we are—we're emulating the happy peasants!" Well, we're doing their dances, and we're singing their songs, but we're *not* going one step further. I think that we need to look at the Balkans with a clear eye and to accept the beauty that comes out of there, but we also have to know that Balkan cultures are just as complicated as American culture, and there are a lot of bad things that go on. Not to demonize anybody, but to accept the existence of prejudice. It's not just a bunch of happy peasants jumping around in colorful costumes! And we *have* to understand things in the context of history. People have an idea that peasants don't play with amplification, and that's been a major thing at the workshops, for sure. You see these musicians coming in from the Balkans—actual exemplars of this music—and *they're* amplified. For them, it's not even a question. But we've had people say, "This isn't right! This isn't the way it should be!" And it's like, "No. This is real life. It is what it is. The Balkans have evolved—it's not the turn of the century anymore. People in the Balkans are just as modern as anyone else, and we have to understand modernity as part of their culture.

Taking an historical view, Rachel attests that changes in the educational fabric of the Balkan Music and Dance Workshops have paved the way for a restructuring of the educational objectives of the EEFC. "In terms of Camp and the EEFC today, we try to cover as much educational ground as possible, including old stuff as well as new stuff," she begins:

Underlying everything, though, we try to maintain a sense of what is traditional. For me, the question is, "Is it played? *Has* it been played? Is it something that people have enjoyed as part of their own culture?" A lot of the Romani music that's taught at Camp is highly composed—it's not necessarily "of the people." But it's *real*. Another interesting example is the Bulgarian choral music. I definitely resisted having any of our Bulgarian teachers teach that stuff because, as I see it, this is music that was composed and performed in a rarified environment, sponsored by the Socialist government. It didn't come out of the villages, and it didn't even come out of the towns. But it's fun to sing, and people enjoy it! At the same time, part of me still feels that I don't ever want that stuff to dominate. There's enough of that already, and we need to be a repository of material that's more basic. What we can do is to provide people with the basic vocabulary; whatever they choose to do with it is their business, but they need to know the underlying vocabulary!

This is formally articulated in the EEFC Mission Statement, drafted in 1994. "The Mission Statement was very important for the EEFC," Rachel asserts. "We publish it in newsletters and online, and we've pretty much kept it as a guidepost throughout all of these years." Though not explicitly a response to the arrival of native Balkan musicians, the Mission Statement bears witness to the ensuing redefinition and growth. A version is included below:

The East European Folklife Center (EEFC) is a non-profit membership organization whose mission is to educate the general public about the folk music, folk dance, and folklore in the Balkans through promoting and sponsoring activities which honor and celebrate the richness of these cultures; and to foster understanding and respect of all peoples through shared experience of Balkan cultures.[6]

Having charted the post-1989 transition at the level of Balkan Camp and the EEFC, I treat this as a platform for investigating heightened interface between the American Balkan Scene and its music-cultural surroundings linked to impending generational transition.

---

[6] In 2011, this was altered to read: "The East European Folklife Center (EEFC) is a non-profit membership organization whose mission is to promote, celebrate, and educate the public about traditional and traditionally based music, dance, and cultures of the Balkans" (www.eefc.org). This revision was conducted as part of a wider restructuring detailed in the Conclusion.

By the mid-1990s, a decline in enrollment perpetuated by an aging population led many to fear for the survival of Camp and the Scene. The threat of extinction was eased by a wave of young American musicians credited with mobilizing a new generation. "There was actually a time when we were very worried about Camp because the population was falling off," Rachel recalls:

> People were getting into their forties, and there just didn't seem to be anybody new coming through. Campers brought their children, but there were no twenty- or thirty-year-olds—nothing in between. And then around 1997, the year that Esma Redžepova came, there was this influx of young people. Maybe Esma had broader appeal or somehow people knew about her, but they came to Camp and it just fed on itself.[7]

Asked to characterize these young music-cultural émigrés, Rachel echoes Dena Bjornlie in highlighting a discrepancy in *approach*. "What I've seen is a gradual movement from people coming into the Scene as folk dancers and *then* becoming musicians to people coming in *as musicians* who don't know a thing about the dance," she states. "They come in having heard world music or the Bulgarian Women's Choir[8] or something like that; you can hear so much more nowadays than you could twenty years ago." She follows this with a meditation on the role of the EEFC in negotiating demographic change:

> We're at an interesting crossroads, and I'm not sure what's going to happen. A lot of the originators of the Scene are getting older, and they're not going to be involved for that much longer. Our challenge is to ensure that something keeps happening, and that is of course entirely related to making sure that young people come to Balkan Camp. We need outreach, and we need to keep the younger generation involved in our decision-making process. At

---

[7] The Fall 2002 – 2003 *Kef Times* mentions the early filling of Mendocino Balkan Camp, expressing concern that this might eventually require denying admission to veteran attendees.

[8] Rachel uses the term "Bulgarian Women's Choir" to refer explicitly to Le Mystère des Voix Bulgares. Others apply it more generally to the Bulgarian choral phenomenon, which gained ground among western listeners in the early 1990s.

the same time, we need to be ready to keep up with the new form that all of this is necessarily going to take. We have to be open to things moving in a direction we might not all be happy with—it all depends on who is coming up through the ranks and what experience they bring. People come with different knowledge and different views of music and culture. We have to adapt to that— we have to *rejoice* in it, you know? It's a challenge, but keeping a wide age range involved will ensure the longevity of the Scene.

It would seem hardly remarkable to suspend Rachel's narrative here, as though in the interest of ceding the stage to an individual able to provide a second-generation perspective firsthand. This is the approach of Chapters 1 and 2, in which Mark Levy and Dena Bjornlie comment on but do not fully engage with the experience of second-generation musicians. Yet failure to include a more integrative perspective would be to turn a blind eye to one of the most definitive characteristics of the Scene today: its intergenerationality. Two factors make Rachel an ideal figure to bridge generational narratives. Most obvious is her former position as EEFC General Manager, which situated her at the administrative center of events and processes related to Balkan Camp and the Scene. Also significant is her involvement with Brass Menažeri, among the most prominent of a handful of intergenerational American Balkan ensembles and the subject of the next section.

Directed by former jazz and klezmer musician Peter Jaques, Brass Menažeri juxtaposes first generation folk dancers-turned-musicians with young musicians who came of age nearer to the American music-cultural main-stream.[9] Self-advertised as a "powerhouse brass band," Brass Menažeri is distinguished for taking primary inspiration

[9] Some readers will recognize that Brass Menažeri disbanded before this book was published. Such is the challenge of writing about living people within an evolving community: everything is subject to change. Here, I have elected to preserve the tense of my original discussion and interview quotations because I feel that they retain immediate significance. The circumstances surrounding Brass Menažeri's dissolution are noted in the Conclusion.

from a contemporary Balkan tradition. "A lot of the music Scene members play is becoming archival," Rachel explains:

> People in the Balkans are not playing that stuff anymore, and some people feel that we are somehow preserving this music by continuing to play it. But the music that Brass Menažeri performs is *living*—it's not music from fifty years ago that Balkan musicians no longer perform. It's living and developing, and it's still part of people's lives. We definitely perform older pieces, but we also listen to current recordings and perform stuff that just came out in Serbia, Greece, and Macedonia, with attention to newer ways of playing.

With respect to instrumentation, Brass Menažeri is modeled on a Balkan brass band. Far from imitating Balkan brass recordings, however, members draw from Balkan and non-Balkan traditions to craft a unique sonic profile further imagined through original composition.[10] At the same time, the ensemble has shown increasing commitment to the Balkan brass style, a shift Rachel portrays as directly proportional to Peter's investment in the Scene. "I remember when Brass Menažeri first started out," she reflects:

> Peter was originally a klezmer musician, so he was using a lot of klezmer ornamentation, and a lot of the stuff we were playing came out sounding like klezmer music. Until he realized, "Wait a minute, there's *way* more to this," and devoted himself to studying it and figuring it out. And it *shows*. It's incredible! He does a lot of his own arrangements; we've done a Persian piece and some Indian stuff, and right now we're working on an original composition by Peter that's in the style of south Serbian music. He's a really intuitive musician—one of those people that just picks things up. But I saw this shift in his music as he started going to Camp and being more exposed to these top musicians, American as well as Balkan. It was like he realized, "I can emulate their style *and* go forth."

---

[10] Echoed in Chapters 4 and 5, Rachel observes that Brass Menažeri mirrors the practice of contemporary Balkan brass bands, which juxtapose Balkan, Bollywood, and even mariachi sounds and styles.

Brass Menažeri's evolution aside, as a first-generation folk dancer-turned-musician who learned to play in part by emulating recordings of native Balkan musicians, Rachel continues to wrestle with the second generation's propensity to treat Balkan folk music as a vehicle for creative expression. "I've had a lot to learn," she allows:

I'm kind of a purist, and I want to play this music how it's supposed to sound. But I really do see the value in how young musicians like Peter can put themselves into the music and how I can contribute to that as well. They do their own arrangements, and every now and then a little jazzy lick will come out—something that's not pure Balkan, but it still works. Being in a band with some of these younger people has been an incredibly wonderful experience for me. I don't resist innovation as much as I used to—I used to get really upset over that kind of thing. But that's my own philosophy; I don't want to impose it on anyone else. And anyway, no matter what you do, no matter how traditionally you play, the music is *still* going to change. Even if you try to imitate a recording, even if you do a faithful cover of a song, it's *still* going to migrate as you play it—as you play it over, and over, and over again. You can't help that—it's part of the musical process! But how far you go with it is the thing. To me, as long as no one is trying to *deceive* anyone, it's fine.

This is a provocative statement, meriting further inquiry. What does Rachel mean by "deceive," and what does this tell us about her attitude toward musical innovation as an element of generational transition? The answer proceeds from her aforementioned conviction that music should be engaged with frank attention to context, centering on an analysis of her approach to text. In the previous chapter, Dena Bjornlie identified knowledge of text as integral to her role as an American Balkan musician, though she admits to having performed songs she has not translated or struggles to comprehend. Rachel is more stringent on this account, arguing that it is the responsibility of the vocalist to develop an informed emotional language for each song presented. Cognizant that her lifelong research renders her singularly adept in this regard, she is celebrated by the Scene for her willingness to proffer linguistic and cultural counsel. "People ask for translation and advice, and if they're really sincere about it, I'm happy to give the help," she states:

> The more people know, the better. Knowing what you're singing about adds an entire dimension to how you sing and to how you sing for an audience. With Brass Menažeri, there are often times where we have an audience that includes people who are from Balkan countries, and knowing the language means that I can enhance our ability to communicate with them. I'm *always* thinking about the text when I'm singing; I *always* take pains to know the meaning of the words coming out of my mouth. Even if I don't speak the language, I feel that I can convey the emotion of the songs because I know what they're about. And even if audience members don't understand the text or have no experience of the culture, the fact that you're giving a performance that is emotionally informed … people can read each other's emotions, and they can feel something of what is behind the song.

The desire to communicate is complicated by the fact that folk songs are often intensely emblematic of a specific place and time, demanding delicacy on the part of musicians wary of voicing sentiments they personally reject. Yet whereas Dena might alter or even excise a sensitive verse in the interest of performing an otherwise pleasing song, deeming this a sign of respect for the boundaries that distinguish her reality from that which the text evokes, Rachel encourages mindful immersion in the experience of dissonance and tension:

> I think in general it's easy for American singers to get very cavalier about singing Balkan songs. They form their mouths around the words, but they don't really know what they're saying. I mean, it's just fun to *sing*! But sometimes you really have to think about whether you should sing a certain song, because of the lyrics. There are, for example, songs that indicate old prejudices. I collaborated on some collections of Macedonian folk songs with a man named David

Bilides; we took recordings, and he transcribed the music while I translated the words. I remember one song in particular—many Americans had performed it already. It has to do with this girl who's talking about meeting up with a guy whose skin is dark, and she tries to scrub the blackness off of him. I was shocked! They called the guy an *arapče*, which means little Arab in Macedonian, though it could also just be used to mean somebody with swarthy skin. And I thought, "Should we put this in the book or not?" In the end we did, but we included some notes about it. I thought, "People need to know about this, and they need to decide for themselves if they want to sing it."[11]

From the foregoing discussion, it is possible to state with some certainty that Rachel would apply the term "deceive" to any approach that obfuscates the vital interconnectedness of music and music-culture, impeding performers from making informed decisions about how to honor that connection in their own practice. As for what this implies about her response to the innovative sensibility of the second generation Scene, I infer that she would likely object to practices that foreground creative expression without audible rootedness in tradition, divesting the music of obvious music-cultural identity to give it unfettered potential as art. This requires additional scrutiny given recent innovations in performance context and audience

[11] Both volumes of *Macedonian Folk Songs for Voice and Tambura* are available through an informative companion website, www.izvormusic.com.
Some songs are deemed inappropriate for particular contexts. In Rachel's words, "A recent example is that Brass Menažeri just played a wedding, and one of the new songs in our repertoire is this Bosnian song. I'm really the only one in the band who speaks with any fluency—any of the languages—and Peter said, 'Here's this song,' and I said, 'That's great, but give me a chance to translate the lyrics.' So I looked at them and they're devastating—it's about a woman in an open casket floating down a river. So I translated it as quickly as I could, and I sent it out. I'm not the one who's singing it—Briget is singing it. I said, 'Is this on the set list for this wedding? We can't, we *can't*.' I said, 'I *insist* that we cannot sing this at this wedding. I don't care if a soul does not understand what the words are. *I* do.' And I thought, 'It's inappropriate. Just because it's a nice tune doesn't mean that you should be singing about death and coffins at someone's wedding.' So I convinced them that we shouldn't do that piece. And we can do it elsewhere—it doesn't matter. We can go to a club and play it. I just think that it would have been bad luck for the bride and groom to be subjected to this song, even if they didn't know what it meant."

demographic also pioneered by young American music-cultural émigrés.

In 2004, Brass Menažeri made a foray into the Bay Area hipster sphere, where it continues to perform at nightclubs and bars for an audience that is generally without exposure to Balkan music or music-culture. Having played almost exclusively for folk dancers, Rachel credits second-generation Menažeri musicians with granting the ensemble access to the club circuit. "I think the only way we could have done this is because we have so many younger members in our group," she reflects:

> If we consisted only of late forty- and early fifty-year-olds, which is what part of our band is, we never would have gotten noticed in the club scene. A couple of people in our band have played in other groups, and they have been exposed to some of these venues. So now our whole group is connected!

Brass Menažeri has enjoyed surprising success with the hipster audience, satisfying one-time listeners while establishing a loyal audience base. For Rachel, however, it is important to note that club performances carry their own challenges, chief among them that of upholding a commitment to linguistic and music-cultural integrity in a setting hardly conducive to discourse on translation and meaning. Hoping to mitigate this challenge, Brass Menažeri's second-generation contingent broached the possibility of performing songs in translation, a proposition Rachel fervently opposed. "We recently started talking about performing lyrics in English—English translations of Balkan songs," she relates:

> They said, "Then people could understand them—maybe this could open up more understanding!" But I said, "*No*. No, no, *no*. I really draw the line here." These songs are *songs*, and if you take away the language and substitute English words, they're not at all the same anymore. I got the reason for it—it was about accessibility. They wanted people to understand the profundity of some of the lyrics,

and that's impossible if they don't know the words. And I said, "Well, not all music *has* words, and people still get something out of it then!"

Despite the inevitability of future quandaries, Rachel is enthusiastic about the idea of lasting engagement with the Bay Area hipster sphere, which she sees as affording Brass Menažeri a degree of freedom precluded by the expectations of the folk dance audience. "I love the club scene!" she exclaims:

Part of it is that there's so much enthusiasm. People get out there, and they love it—they get ecstatic. Brass music is loud and direct; the sound just kind of invades your body, and the rhythms are so compelling. And it's accessible! The instruments aren't weird, they're just familiar instruments doing things a different way. I think people just love it—even if they don't understand it, they love it. When we play folk dance gigs, often the dancers don't like what we do because we're too loud or we don't play something the way they know it. In the clubs, we can just get out there and *play*. And people dance! They don't care. It's usually too crowded to do anything but just jump around anyway, but you see these dancers get into a sweaty ecstasy. *That's* the appeal for us.

The vitality of Brass Menažeri's relationship with the club audience warrants further attention in light of fear that a sustained influx of musicians without folk dance experience will deal a decisive blow to the already tenuous balance between music and dance at the core of the Scene. Just as she credits second-generation Menažeri musicians with inspiring their first-generation peers to expand their musical and music-cultural horizons, however, Rachel believes the second generation to be developing in conversation with the first. "I remember when some of these young hipster types first came; they brought all this great musical skill, but at first they just jumped around and waved their arms on the dance floor," she recounts:

Then, as the years went on, you saw some of them saying, "I'm going to get in the dance line." So they started to learn more about the dance, and they started to actually *feel* the music, instead of it being a purely intellectual interest, like, "Oh— that was a funny rhythm." Feeling the rhythm in your body through your feet can only help your sense of meter or the way you approach a particular dance tune. It's made a huge difference for my own band members; it makes their music a lot better, especially when we play for folk dancers. We're not returning to the old folk dance days—it's not like that at all—but I've seen these particular young musicians become so much more broadened and enriched by taking the opportunity to get in the dance line.

With growing recognition of the need to foster comprehensive intergenerational dialogue, in 2008, the EEFC appointed a pair of youth liaisons to take the pulse of young Camp attendees. Though too early to report a conclusive outcome, expectations are high that this and future efforts will help members of the emergent generation to feel appreciated as inheritors of the Scene while enabling veteran musicians and dancers to shepherd its evolution. This is the vision behind the EEFC Vision Statement, drafted in the early 2000s[12]:

- We will remain connected to the authentic traditions of music and dance while also being attuned to ongoing and changing cultural trends.
- We will be open and welcoming to all people of all backgrounds.
- We will maintain the highest possible degree of scholarship and teaching.
- We will have the financial and structural resources to meet the evolving needs of our community.

The prospect of generational transition elicits considerable tension, particularly where matters of tradition and innovation are

[12] A revised version was devised between 2011 and 2012 in tandem with changes to the Mission Statement. It currently reads: "We envision a global community of passionate amateurs and professionals, sharing what we know and love about Balkan music, dance, and folklore. By inspiring and supporting research and study in these fields, we preserve both historical and living traditions for future generations" (www. eefc.org).

concerned. Yet this does little to discourage Rachel from celebrating evidence that the Scene will endure as a cohesive community bound by shared passion for Balkan music and dance. "We really try to incorporate everybody—that's what I love," she affirms:

This year, I saw it especially—at both workshops. There was such a wide generational range, and people were getting along with each other no matter how young or old they were. Everybody's learning from each other, standing next to each other in class, playing with each other, dancing with each other. Because ultimately we all love the music, you know? And that matters most.

4

Eva Salina Primack

In Chapter 2, Dena Bjornlie spoke of performing with Medna Usta in the courtyard of a Santa Cruz cafe. It is with a nod to these courtyard performances that I begin the story of Eva Salina Primack, a talented young vocalist who discovered Balkan folk music in the early 1990s. Coming of age in the world of Balkan Camp and the Scene, Eva benefitted from close interaction with native Balkan instructors and later identified with the influx of young American music-cultural émigrés that would herald the rise of the second generation. In an ongoing quest to identify and position herself within and beyond the boundaries of the Scene as traditionally defined, she upholds a commitment to personal expression as the most honest form of engagement with musical tradition, seeking to communicate freely, constructively, and with all the power of her voice.

I met Eva in the summer of 2007, when I attended her class at the Mendocino Balkan Music and Dance Workshops. Though all of my teachers were wonderful that year, I was particularly struck by Eva's ability to articulate the joys and the complexities of intercultural exchange. Eloquence and passion spin a glimmering thread that envelops us in her narrative.

Eva Salina Primack was born in Santa Cruz, California in 1984 to an extended family of craftspeople and artisans. "We've got architects, carpenters, painters, and basket makers," she states. "I was exposed to visual arts a lot as a very young child." An avid musician, Eva's uncle harbored a deep affection for American folk music, and his sing-alongs were a highlight of family gatherings. "We would go to my aunt and uncle's house for holidays or birthdays, and we would inevitably end up in their living room at the piano," she recalls. "Even though I was only two or three years old, I would sit in the middle of everything, on the piano bench next to my uncle."

At three-and-a-half, Eva accompanied her preschool teacher into the studio to sing in the chorus on his latest recording project. "My teacher dabbled in children's music, and he would invite a group of kids to record with him," she explains. "The thing is, I can't really remember starting to sing, but I can remember when I *sang*." As the recording session ended and the children filed out, Eva wandered back into the empty studio. Hearing her voice, the technicians rushed to restart their equipment. "Everything had been shut down, but I walked up to the mic and started singing 'You Are My Sunshine,'" she states. "They heard me, and they were like, 'Wait, wait—*wait!*' while they turned everything back on. Then they said, 'Okay, now do it again.'" The resultant thirty-second track was included on the recording.[1] "They ended up using it because I didn't have a little girl's voice when I was a little girl," she avows. "They captured something of me then that really is a pleasure to hear now."

When Eva was five, her grandfather began giving her tapes of Yiddish music, which she describes as "these old guys singing this Yiddish Sinatra kind of stuff that I never responded to very well." One song made a positive impression. "The song was 'Tum-balalaika'—a sweet Yiddish song—and I recognized it from a songbook my uncle had owned. When I was six, that was the Yiddish song I knew how to sing; I taught myself to sing it," she explains. Around the same time, a family friend gave Eva's parents a copy of a Yiddish album by NAMA,[2] an offshoot of the AMAN Folk Ensemble. Though Eva is half Jewish, as a child her attraction to this album stemmed from "a deep, unfiltered emotional connection" to the "warm" and "unpretentious" voice

---

[1] Copies of the album *Little Jimmy's Favorites* are available through CD Baby (www. cdbaby.com).

[2] Ironically, Eva later discovered that the B-side of her NAMA recording featured tracks by Nevenka, a women's vocal ensemble with which she would later perform in Los Angeles. Formed in 1976 "by women who shared a common interest in the complex harmonies and compelling rhythms typical in Balkan music," Nevenka seeks to emulate "the Eastern European tradition ... [of] women of all ages making music together" (www.nevenka.org).

of NAMA's singer, Pearl Rottenberg. This was combined with a powerful urge to add to that voice her own. "All of the words had been Xeroxed from the LP jacket in their English transliteration," she recounts:

> I figured out pretty quickly the five or six songs that were my favorites, and I learned to sing them—this phonetic way of learning. The thing about Yiddish music for me was that it was like a reflex. I remember it being completely effortless and natural for me when I was a kid; the words fit so well in my mouth.

Struck by their daughter's musical feat and linguistic dexterity, Eva's parents found themselves grappling with the question of how to nurture her evident gift. "My parents thought, 'What are we going to do for/with this child, who has this natural ability to sing the Other?'" she states. The answer was hidden in plain sight. In preparation for the birth of her brother, Eva's family had recently exchanged their one-bedroom apartment for a house three doors down the street. Across from their new home lived Susan Wagner, a member of the local Balkan and Jewish music and dance community. "It was this beautiful synchronicity that there had been this local movement in Balkan music," Eva notes. "Many people had been involved—Karen Guggenheim, Barbara Cordes, Dena Bjornlie, Jana Niernberger, Anne Cleveland, Mark Forry, and Ruth Hunter—and once a month, Susan hosted a gathering of musicians and dancers at her house."[3] Becoming acquainted with Wagner, Eva's family began to attend these gatherings, where Eva was often the lone child in a room full of adults. Rather than impede her inclusion, her youth propelled her unselfconsciously into the dancing fray. She was met with similar warmth:

> At some point, my family and I started going to the parties across the street. Soon, we had a little more knowledge, and we started

---

[3] Participants called these gatherings *večerinkas*, a Bulgarian word used to refer to evening soirees.

learning all the dances. My parents were shy in the beginning, but I was always right there in the dance line. And most people were there with me! When you see a kid who's six or seven and they're that focused, you just want to *grab* them—you know they're going to get so much out of it.

More than she relished the dance line, Eva loved to "get up and sing 'Tum-balalaika'" for the assembled guests. "Sometimes I would start it too high, sometimes I would sing it in the right place, but I would sing it for them," she recalls. Keen to encourage her interest, her parents contacted a local klezmer musician to inquire about lessons. He replied that he was unavailable to teach at the time. With the precision of hindsight, Eva regards his rebuff as providence in disguise. "Thankfully, he had his reasons because of what came next!" she exclaims.

After purchasing multiple flea market accordions, Eva's father had begun taking lessons from American Balkan vocalist and accordion player Ruth Hunter, whom he knew from Susan Wagner's house and from her appearances with her band, Medna Usta, in the courtyard of CafeZinho. Unable to find a Yiddish instructor for Eva, he asked whether Hunter would be willing to provide lessons in Balkan singing. "Ruth was skeptical at first, like, '*How* old is your daughter? *Seven?*'" Eva laughs. "But she agreed, and once a week, she walked up the hill with her accordion on her back to give me lessons." Ruth began by teaching Eva a Croatian New Year's song. "It was not a complicated song, but I loved it," she affirms. "It felt good—it felt really, really good—and we grew to like each other pretty quickly, Ruth and I."

Within a year, Eva's mother also commenced to study with Hunter, and Balkan music seemed destined to become a central force in the family's life. Recognizing this, Hunter directed them toward the Mendocino Balkan Music and Dance Workshops, where she felt Eva could receive guidance to cultivate her inherent potential. "Ruth said, 'Look, if you really like this music, there's a camp that happens in Mendocino every summer,'" Eva explains. "In 1992, we went to Balkan Camp, and we've been there every year since." For Eva, the progression from singing and dancing at Susan Wagner's monthly gatherings to taking classes at Balkan Camp "felt perfectly natural," and with her exuberance and poise, her presence did not go unnoticed. "It was crazy because there were all these grown-up people playing great music," she describes:

> Before we went there, I had started singing some Bulgarian songs with Karen Guggenheim, an American woman who played *gajda*, so I was already familiar with the different instruments. Karen was a great support figure for me. I have many, many aunties and surrogate mothers in this community—they had their eyes open for me when I was a little kid. But I was fearless when I went to Balkan Camp the first time. The funny thing is, I have very few memories of my childhood outside of Balkan music. Even though Mendocino is something that happens only once a year, that community had already begun to define me when I was eight years old.

Eva attended her first Balkan Camp at a fortuitous time, just as the influx of native Balkan instructors began to accelerate, taking shape as a long-term trend. "When I came into the Scene, it was right after the end of Communism in Bulgaria but right before the wave of immigrants started to come over," she notes. "Those were the years when the staff lineup really began to change, and when I was eleven, Petrana Kučeva and Tatiana Sarbinska were hired to teach singing at Camp." Previous chapters have examined the post-1989 transition, which afforded Scene musicians unprecedented access to repertoire and instruction while challenging accepted ideas of the relationship between the American Balkan Scene and the Balkans. Some individuals experienced this on a personal level, undergoing a parallel shift in their understanding of what it meant to be an American musician devoted to Balkan folk music. In Eva's case, almost no shift was required. Due to the serendipitous triad of youth, ability, and circumstance that characterized her entrance into the Scene, she was exposed to Balkan music in a series of direct doses that wound an intricate web between her budding music-cultural identity and music-cultural experience in the

Balkans. Above all, it is an aura of intercultural ambiguity that makes her story unique.

The first such dose came in 1995, when Bulgarian vocalist Tatiana Sarbinska[4] took Eva under her wing. "Tatiana kind of adopted me as her protégé, and when she would come to the West Coast, she would give me lessons," she states:

> I learned from Ruth, and then, while my voice was still very malleable, I started learning from Bulgarians. I've had the exact opposite experience of most people here, in that this was the first musical language that I spoke. It never felt like an Other to me because I had no knowledge of any other way to sing.

The second dose can be traced to 1996, when the women of Boston-based "global music ensemble" Libana[5] hired Sarbinska to take them to the International Folk Festival in Varna, Bulgaria, and Sarbinska invited Eva to accompany her on an extended six-week tour. Eva marks this "a turning point" in her relationship with music and culture. "I taught myself how to read Cyrillic before I went, and then we were there in the thick of it, in another world," she recounts:

> That summer, I went from this kind of topical understanding of Balkan culture through Balkan Camp, where the ethnomusicologists were my idols and everything was filtered through the redwoods, to really seeing the way that people lived in Bulgaria. By the end of the trip, I could have functional conversations with people in

[4] Before emigrating to the United States, Tatiana Sarbinska was a featured soloist with the Pirin Ensemble and taught at the Academy of Music, Dance, and Fine Arts in Plovdiv. Today, she serves as founder and director of three American Balkan ensembles: Divi Zheni and Zornitsa in Boston and Orfeia in Washington, DC.

[5] Libana was formed in 1979 by "a group of women sharing a passion for international music, dance, and women's issues." Members hold an abiding commitment to "dynamic cross-cultural understanding, profound healing, and widespread peacebuilding" through "the artistic expression of the global community" (www.libana.com).

Bulgarian. I could order breakfast for twelve people and deal with all of the financial transactions and all of that; there was this sort of vernacular cultural interaction that I became acquainted with. And I think that I learned an incredible amount about the music just by *being* in the country. Because this music does not exist without its immediate cultural context—without the comforts and discomforts, the smells and the tastes, the sounds of nature, the land, and the smoke of the diesel cars. It *all* informs the music.

In addition to what it taught her about life and music in the Balkans, Eva's experience in Bulgaria prompted her to confront her concept of self as an American Balkan musician. Over the course of her travels with Sarbinska and Libana, she was troubled by an inability to translate her natural social facility to the reality of interacting musically overseas. As part of the tour, Sarbinska arranged for her to give a solo performance during several of Libana's sets. Exhilarated by the opportunity to perform the music she loved in its native land, she infused each song with childlike reverence. Shortly thereafter, she learned that aspects of her conduct had been found to conflict with cultural norms:

I would dress up in traditional costume, and I would go and sing in front of however many people—these old unaccompanied songs. Here I was, fully immersed in the culture, but there was implicit cultural protocol that I did not comprehend. I think that I was perceived as being somewhat selfish because I didn't have these tools—these very *adult* tools—that were also completely *culturally* foreign to me. I was twelve years old.

Another source of discomfort for Eva was a discrepancy between her expectations for the tour and the manner in which it unfolded. "I have a great deal of respect for Tatiana. She was incredibly generous with me. But ultimately it felt like I was there as her protégé; I had a few songs she had taught me that I would sing for people when she asked me to," she explains:

I think it was nice for her to have me there, in terms of the trip not being what I had expected, which was an opportunity to *learn*, but rather an opportunity to be shown around. I wasn't taking lessons there, and really there wasn't much music at all. I recorded some older men that Tatiana arranged to sing for me, some Romani kids singing on the street, a group of old *babi* sitting at a long table and singing these songs with endless verses, and parts of a Romani wedding that one of Tatiana's friends took me to just outside of Blagoevgrad. But that was it! I have one tape from the tour. I felt like while I definitely got an unfiltered *cultural* education, it was not the unfiltered *musical* education that I had hoped for.

In pondering the dissonance that surrounded her initial journey to the Balkans, Eva developed a precocious awareness of the relationship between music, musician, and music-culture, a complex figuration that becomes infinitely more convoluted in situations of intercultural exchange. Yet she experienced this enlightened cultural confusion on her own, as a child, and in a foreign country, and it left her feeling isolated and bewildered. "When I came back from my trip to Bulgaria, I didn't really sing for a whole year," she states.

It was against the backdrop of the 1997 Mendocino Balkan Music and Dance Workshops that Eva felt prepared to resume musical activity. "Balkan Camp for me is like New Year's for so many others—it's my annual check-in with the community," she remarks. "You see where everyone's at, you hear what has transpired, and that's your cross-section of, 'How far have I come this year?'" With Camp as her guide, she designates that summer as a closing chapter of her childhood within the American Balkan Scene. Perpetuating the serendipity of her inaugural year, Eva's personal shift coincided with the arrival of the great Macedonian Romani singer Esma Redžepova, who brought her band, Ansambl Teodosievski, to teach and perform on both coasts that year. For Eva, the most immediate result was a new expressive palette, as Redžepova and Ansambl Teodosievski introduced her to a musical language with which she felt a deep emotional affinity. "As you know if you've seen Esma sing in recent years, it's this completely emotionally, physically, and musically unrestrained experience, and she brought something out of people that was in a way melodramatic, but also very positive," she begins:

> Being someone who has always loved extremes, I threw myself into her music. I was *infected* by Esma and by the intense little mass of cultural energy that she brought with her in the form of her band. I just watched that bustling excitement bounce off of everybody, whether it was the swooning women or the drinking and playing music until four-thirty in the morning. And of course I was there, at thirteen, in the middle of it all.

Identifying not only with Romani music but to some degree with Romani music-culture, Eva experienced a series of interactions with the Romani musicians at Camp that set her ambiguity into relief, intimating the potential consequences for her life within and beyond the Scene. She tells the story as follows:

> That year, Esma decided that I was a good candidate to marry her accordion player, who was in his twenties at the time. He was courting me on a pretty basic level, but I was freaked out. I was someone who was intellectually used to the world of adults, but in terms of coming into adolescence, this was completely foreign to me. It was flattering, of course—I was being included in their cultural conception of how these things happen. But it was totally not going to happen for me! The next year, Esma and her band returned to Camp, and I was a year older, and in my own mind I was so much more grown up. I felt bad because I had scared them so much the year before by my response, and I thought, "I'm going to hang out with them, and I'm going to be part of this singing and drinking beer around the table." I was totally still a kid, but very good at pretending to be an adult. One night, they took me outside, and they said—all in Macedonian—"He really likes you, and we know you really like him. So don't tell your mom, and don't tell your dad, but now you're together."

Her professed naïveté aside, Eva was acutely aware of the delicacy of this situation. As a young woman in the throes of adolescence, she was both intrigued and alarmed by the attention. Any curiosity she felt was undoubtedly amplified by the idea that her identity had acquired sufficient fluidity to be valued in another music-cultural context. With this, however, she was humbled by recognition that she at least temporarily occupied a position from which to confirm or repudiate prejudices commonly leveled against the Romani people. "I didn't want to play into any cultural stereotypes—I didn't want to contribute to any negative associations that people have of Romani culture," she asserts:

> I went to Šani Rifati, who was one of my "uncles" in the Scene during my adolescence, and I said, "I don't need to make a scene, but can you just talk to them?" I didn't want to cause a scandal. It didn't occur to them that this was not appropriate behavior, so I thought, "If we just tell them it's not appropriate, everything will be fine."[6]

It was also during her adolescence that Eva began to collaborate with American Balkan musicians beyond Balkan Camp. "At this point, my family knew a lot of people in the Scene, and we would drive up to Berkeley to see George Chittenden and Lise Liepman play with Édessa and also to see some Ziyiá gigs,"[7] she states:

> When I was about fourteen, Édessa invited me to sing with them, and when I was sixteen, I was on the first Édessa record, *Édessa and Friends*. My brother and I sing this song, "Karavana Čajka," which is one of these popularized folk-style songs that often pair Romani melodies with Bulgarian lyrics. And then after Camp one year Peter Jaques and I said, "We should really start a band," and that was the beginning of what is now called Brass Menažeri. I must

---

[6] Romani dance instructor Šani Rifati was born in Priština in present-day Kosovo. After moving to California in the early1990s, he co-founded Voice of Roma, an organization that works to promote the rights and culture of the Romani people in the United States and abroad. For more information, see www.voiceofroma.com.

[7] Called Édessa Power Block at the time, this venerable ensemble is beloved by Scene members of all ages and backgrounds. Eva later appeared with Édessa for occasional gigs, including the New Year's party I attended at Ashkenaz in Berkeley.

Despite membership overlap, Ziyiá is distinguished from Édessa by a more explicit adherence to Greek repertoire.

have been sixteen or seventeen. It was around then that my own
life began to seem inseparable from the world of Balkan music; it
stopped being something that I got to experience only on occasion.

In time, Eva's growing investment in the Scene combined
with her emergent awareness of her intercultural ambiguity to
outline the shape of her mature music-cultural identity. Her
attempts to manifest this identity were challenged by the tenor of
their reception, as she found it increasingly difficult to reconcile
her activities and ambitions with the expectations of her Scene
elders. Charted over the remainder of this chapter, the music-cultural, intellectual, and artistic journeys Eva has undertaken
since her early teens can be interpreted as components of an
ongoing quest to define her position and purpose as a musician.

In 1998, veteran American Balkan musicians Nada Lewis
and Karen Guggenheim invited Eva to attend her first Sweet's
Mill music and dance workshop, initiating a journey that would
carry her beyond the West Coast Balkan Scene into its music-cultural periphery. Though her path was not without precedent
among her fellow Scene members, it held a particular personal
gravity, enabling her to breach a new stage in her musical development while illuminating a key element of her future role:

> When I was about fourteen, I started going to Sweet's Mill, which
> is essentially a big private party/music camp in which anybody and
> everybody can teach. It's split into these different sections, which of
> course are bleeding together more and more every year—Middle
> Eastern music, flamenco music, old-time music, and Balkan music.
> And it's historically very spontaneous—you either show up to class
> or you don't, and nobody bats an eyelash. There were certainly always
> musicians there of a very high caliber, but people go to Sweet's Mill
> to *play*—to play for eight hours *straight* if they want. It's also totally
> productive, but in a very different way; there's a ton of learning,
> exploring, and collaborating but less structured than Mendocino.

Separation between Sweet's Mill and the Mendocino Balkan Music and Dance Workshops proved to be of great significance for Eva, opening a space in which she felt at ease to extemporize on her musicality and skill. With burgeoning autonomy, she taught her first students at the Mill that year. "I had a wonderful time at Sweet's Mill because I was free from many of the associations that defined my childhood," she affirms:

> I wasn't interacting with people who had known me since I was eight years old and who didn't realize that I wasn't eight anymore. And it wasn't their fault! That's the way it is when you exist with someone from the time that they're a kid. But I got to come into Sweet's Mill as this teenager, with a few years of experience and a lot of energy. I taught singing that year, and for the first time, I could really play around with what I had learned, without fear of criticism and without being held to any standard of cultural correctness or purity.

As with her first summer at Mendocino Balkan Camp, Eva made a strong impression on the Sweet's Mill population, attracting the attention of musicians and dancers who would subsequently ask her to contribute to their work. One such figure was choreographer Katarina Burda, who invited Eva to sing with Aywah![8] a traditional Middle Eastern dance and bellydance troupe she directed in the San Francisco Bay Area. Performing with Aywah! had two major consequences for Eva. First, it granted her visibility within the Bay Area ethnic dance sphere. This visibility in turn issued her a platform from which to present her nascent public identity to the community that had supported her since childhood. "I started singing with Aywah!, and my mom would drive me up to San Francisco for rehearsals," she recalls:

> We did a bunch of concerts with me singing Romani standards—songs I had learned from Carol Silverman at Balkan Camp but had

---

[8] Aywah! performed repertoire drawn from North African, Balkan, and Middle Eastern traditions. Recognized as a pioneering force in the Tribal Fusion dance scene, the ensemble produced such eminent dancers as Mira Betz, Rosa Rojas, Elizabeth Strong, and Zoe Jakes.

really wanted to be able to perform with a band, and I was confident that I was ready to do it. People from the Bay Area Balkan Scene came to these concerts, and then I got to share with that community something that I had not done in the context of Balkan Camp.

Energized by her recent music-cultural excursions, Eva traveled to New York in 1999 to attend Golden Festival, an annual celebration of Balkan music and dance founded by Zlatne Uste,[9] members of which she knew from Mendocino. "I bought my own ticket, flew by myself, and stayed with Michael Ginsburg and Belle Birchfield in their apartment for the week," she explains. "This was *me* saying, '*I'm going to Golden Festival*'; I would make proclamations like that, and my parents let me go!" While in New, York Eva took advantage of the opportunity to become acquainted with several native Balkan musical luminaries who had settled in the area. "I met Yuri Yunakov that weekend—Michael and Belle took me to the Bronx to visit him," she states:

That same visit, I met Merita Halili and Raif Hyseni at their home in Caldwell, New Jersey. Merita gave me a singing lesson—she taught me "Doli Goca n'penxhere," which is one of her most well-known songs. So I went to Golden Festival and soaked all of *that* in, and I've been there almost every year since.[10]

By attending Golden Festival, Eva facilitated her introduction to the East Coast Balkan Scene. To build on this connection, she enrolled in the East Coast Balkan Music and Dance Workshops that summer. Here, she encountered the beginnings of a trend that would have profound implications for her approach to music making. Accustomed to interacting with musicians at least twice

[9] Zlatne Uste is heralded as the champion of Balkan brass music among American listeners. The ensemble is also noted for multiple appearances at Serbia's Guča festival, an honor until recently reserved for native bands.
[10] Merita Halili and Raif Hyseni are among the foremost Albanian musicians worldwide. Born in Tiranë, Halili debuted at the age of seventeen and performed as a soloist with the State Ensemble for Folk Songs and Dances. Later, she helped Albanian Radio and Television develop a more elaborate, accompanied version of traditional vocal music. Hyseni is from the Republic of Kosova and was renowned in Prishtinë before relocating to Tiranë and then to the United States.

her age, Eva was thrilled to discover that East Coast Camp harbored a vibrant youth population dominated by the children of American and native Balkan instructors. "I re-met Jesse Kotansky, the son of Steve and Susy Kotansky, that year," she recounts:

> He's a great musician who lives in New York. Though we had met as children—Jesse, Casey Ferber, and I—meeting again as adolescents was an entirely different experience. I also got to hang out with Danko Yunakov, Yuri Yunakov's son, and Varol Saatcioğlu, a young Turkish man who was nineteen at the time—he's a great Thracian *gajda* player who studied with Georgi Doičev and Vassil Bebelekov. My whole world ripped open that year because it was like, "I'm at Balkan Camp, and I'm hanging out with this core group of kids *my age*?" It was the first time those two things had converged for me.

A similar process was quietly underway out West. As on the East Coast, veteran folk dancers and folk dancers-turned-musicians had begun to have children. Many spent summers at Mendocino Balkan Camp, where they were shepherded through the dance line and exposed to Balkan folk music, benefitting from heartfelt encouragement and immediate access to resources if they expressed a desire to play. The birth of children was followed by an increase in traffic between Mendocino and Sweet's Mill, as "younger people from Balkan Camp started going to Sweet's Mill, and younger people from Sweet's Mill started coming to Camp." Though it elicited minimal complaint from the Scene, Eva experienced this as a disquieting convergence between formerly distinct areas of her identity and background. "And then these two worlds which had existed very separately for me were suddenly growing closer and closer together," she describes:

> It was great in a lot of ways, but it was also hard. It had been nice for me to have those two very different scenes. I had just been starting to understand the distinction between how things worked in one setting and the other. There's something a lot less formal about Sweet's Mill in comparison with Mendocino. But it was good because I got to see more of my friends

everywhere that I went, and for a couple of years, Balkan Camp shifted to the more social and less studious side of things for me.

In the wake of the Sweet's Mill exchange, the Mendocino Balkan Music and Dance Workshops played host to an influx of young musicians from the outside American music-cultural landscape. As indicated in previous chapters, the direct catalyst of this influx is difficult to discern. Certainly it drew energy from rising awareness of Camp within neighboring arts communities, a trend linked to traffic with Sweet's Mill. Another probable stimulus was the post-1989 appointment of native Balkan instructors who may have enjoyed name recognition beyond the Scene. Whatever the draw, as accomplished artists without a basis in folk dancing, these dynamic émigrés exerted clear pressure on the Camp environment. In Eva's words:

All of a sudden, there were all these pseudo-hipster San Francisco kids dancing all crazy in the middle of the circle and not doing any of the line dances and taking these wild solos that were completely foreign-sounding to *me* but were informed by whatever musical backgrounds they had had. Peter Jaques, Dan Cantrell, Ryan Francesconi, Tobias Roberson—I got to see this new wave come in. And they were received with some disdain! Balkan Camp is a village, and people responded in the way a village responds to something new—they talk, and talk, and talk, and talk, and *talk*.[11]

Eva was both intimidated and delighted by these young émigrés, with whom she felt a startling kinship. Nurtured in the bosom of Camp and the Scene, she sensed that what they introduced was new and provocative. At the same time, she perceived an affinity between their ideas and her own, auguring the extension of the aura of ambiguity from her music-cultural to her generational identity. "I was in this funny position that I often find myself in, where I can see the older generation's perspective, but I don't feel obligated to agree with it," she reflects:

[11] Cantrell, Francesconi, and Roberson were members of The Toids, a now defunct Balkan-inspired band discussed in Chapter 5.

I can understand the resistance to change, but I can also breathe a sigh of relief every time I see a new young musician come into the Scene. It was perhaps easier for me, being young and knowing how quickly *I* was evolving musically, to see that in a few years these new young people would be vibrant, contributing members of the community. I recognized that they had something to offer, and I knew that talent catches up to experience. And indeed it was only a short time before they were doing something innovative and beautiful with the music.

Throughout her adolescence, Eva's devotion to music consumed the majority of her time and energy. "I had what was in some ways a split identity," she suggests. "There was this person I was supposed to be when I was at school, but it required a lot of effort. It was when I left school and returned to music that my life began, every day." As college approached, it seemed this rift might be bridged through the study of ethnomusicology. For Eva, there was little question. "After growing up around ethnomusicologists yet not really knowing what ethnomusicology consisted of, there was no doubt in my mind from the time I was eleven years old that I was going to be an ethnomusicologist," she states. Mentored since the age of twelve by Bulgarian *gajda* player Vassil Bebelekov, then leader of the UCLA Balkan Ensemble,[12] her choice of institution was equally clear, sealed by the presence of ethnomusicology professor Timothy Rice, who had published a book on his fieldwork with Bulgarian *gajda* player Kostadin Varimezov and vocalist Todora Varimezova. Though Eva had yet to meet Rice, she was aware of his book and applied to UCLA hoping to study under his direction. The following is a summary of her application process:

> I was going to graduate from high school at seventeen, UCLA was the only school I was applying to, and studying ethnomusicology at UCLA was the only thing that I wanted to do. I was *totally* nervous. I had expected that I would be auditioning for Tim Rice, and I had prepared a mix of songs to sing for him—a Yiddish song, a slow

[12] Bebelekov's tenure lasted from 2000 to 2001.

Bulgarian song, a Rhodope song, and a song from a Greek-Albanian minority group that I had learned from Christos Govetas. I thought, "There's some really esoteric and interesting stuff in here. I'm going to sing this for Tim Rice, and he's going to *know* something of me." Of course, I saw him in the hallway outside, and he was walking in the other direction. I said, "I thought I was going to be singing for *you*," and he looked at me and—totally deadpan—said, "I know who you are." And I was like, "What does that *mean*?" I went in to my audition, and there were two men sitting at a table, in this very sanitized environment that is the university institution. I was petrified. I wondered, "Are *these* guys going to think that this repertoire is interesting?" In the end I got in, but I was really, really nervous about UCLA.

In 2001, Eva moved to Los Angeles to pursue a degree in ethnomusicology. Though she experienced the anxiety inherent in venturing off to college, this was assuaged by the promise of a familiar face. "I was still really nervous, but I thought, '*Vassil* will be here; Vassil will be my *anchor*,'" she explains. Something entirely different was poised to unfold:

I was walking through the ethnomusicology building with my parents, and I saw the list of student ensembles, and I saw "Bulgarian Music and Dance: Varimezovi." It was like the bottom fell out—"*Vassil's not going to be here?*" What I didn't know was that one of the "Varimezovi" was *Tzvetanka*. It turned out that Tim Rice had been working on funding for a long time, and he wasn't certain until the last minute that their visas would come through.

It was soon apparent that Eva's relationship with Tzvetanka Varimezova would signify as one of the most influential and rewarding of her life. "I hadn't really had a formal teacher since Tatiana, and there was definitely some lingering trepidation from my experience in Bulgaria," she notes. "But then I met Tzvetanka, and I just *knew*—from the *beginning*." Through weekly vocal lessons and a blossoming rapport, Varimezova guided Eva toward greater intimacy in her relationship with Balkan music. "From that moment, I began to work intensively with Tzvetanka, and every time I went to see her, it was like I was swelling with love for the music when I left," she affirms:

> My soul was remembering, "Oh, right. I *love* Bulgarian music—*I love Bulgarian music!*" I had forgotten. I had been bogged down by the politics of the Scene and by my trip to Bulgaria—all of these extra-musical experiences that I had had. It brought it all home in the most resounding way. Tzvetanka is my greatest inspiration as a teacher and as someone who interprets folk culture and is not afraid to *own* her expression. And all of those things she instilled in me. I could have learned one song from her and sung it for five years. Some weeks, we wouldn't even sing—we would just talk. I would talk about my experience of this music, and she would tell me stories about her early years and the challenges that she had faced. She is the best teacher—in any subject—that I have ever had.

If Eva's relationship with Tzvetanka Varimezova enriched her relationship with Balkan music, her experience of academic ethnomusicology exposed a disconnect between her *approach* and the culture of her chosen field. As a student at UCLA, Eva found herself reading and writing about music more than she engaged in firsthand musical exchange. What opportunities there were felt constrained by a pervasive abstraction. "My experience with Tzvetanka did so much to counteract my experience of ethnomusicology," she avows:

> Growing up with such constant access to the culture, it felt like the most artificial thing I could do—to create distance, to create this wall, to develop a whole different way of speaking about musical experience. I thought, "Wait, can't we just *live* it? Isn't *that* an option? That seems to be working really well for me!" I couldn't find the incentive to change the way that I thought about music and culture because, as I said before, *music does not exist without its immediate cultural context.* How can we sit in a room with no windows and look at a piece of paper and talk about culture and music? *How?* All of the theory—is there value in it? I don't know. I don't know! I have a degree in ethnomusicology. Has it brought me closer to

the music? I don't know! Did I perform outside of the Bulgarian choir when I was at UCLA? Not really! My love for music—which is the whole reason that I do it anyway—was not as deeply nurtured by the program as I had hoped. It felt like, "How am I giving back to this culture that has given me so much by writing papers and making generalizations and putting my *name* on them?" And something that makes me sad, to this really deep level, is that I found people working in the field to be *divided* by their common interests, rather than brought closer together by them. There's this false sense of ownership—this proprietary approach—which to me feels completely contrary to the nature of oral dissemination and transmission of culture. And what this illuminates is that my relationship with the native-born musicians and my relationship with the American musicians/academics are often diametrically opposed. I've never really questioned what the native-born musicians thought of me. They've consistently been the most clearly supportive and warm and generous, acknowledging a mutual understanding and respect for the culture. If I make a misstep, they let me know. And it has not always been so clear for me with the Americans.[13]

In 2004, at the end of her third year, Eva withdrew from UCLA. That summer, she became aware of a deeper disorientation. "After dropping out of school, I came to Balkan Camp, and I didn't take any classes—I just *couldn't*," she states. "I came and I sang, and I felt that people within the Scene were questioning how serious I was." Compounding her disenchantment with academic ethnomusicology, the sense that she could no longer rely on first-generation support plunged Eva into a period of profound uncertainty. "Having a difficult year at Balkan Camp, it felt like, 'Well, what do I do now? What is my role in this community?'" she recalls:

But then, making the transition in the Balkan Scene from childhood to adulthood was not an easy thing in general for me! When you're thirteen, you're still a kid, and there's this novelty—this

[13] Superdevoiche Bulgarian Choir performs music drawn from the Bulgarian choral repertoire. Varimezova successfully lobbied to include this music in the Balkan Camp curriculum.

spectacle—attached to you that dissipates pretty quickly. And then it was hard to work out what was being projected onto me and what *I* actually wanted to do with my music. Which is a totally normal thing for an adolescent, but I was working it out within this complicated community. Tatiana had wanted me to go to music high school; she wanted me to go to music high school in Bulgaria and then join the Pirin Ensemble. Somebody else wanted me to join The Tamburitzans. Other people encouraged me to try jazz. There were times when I did not feel supported—when I felt that my drive was perceived as a negative thing. And being opinionated and observant ... I was deferential to a point. But with the stubbornness of adolescence, if I didn't admire somebody as a musician, I was not going to be deferential to them. I felt like, "What do you have to say to me? You should support me in continuing the work you started, even if it means that I grow beyond this community." That was the crux of it all. I am thankful for those who came before me, but I needed them to trust that I would do something of integrity with what they had given me.[14]

Becoming involved with the American Balkan Scene as a child, Eva was treated to enthusiastic reception by first-generation folk dancers and folk dancers-turned-musicians, who welcomed her as a whisper of hope for the long-term vitality of their community. In gaining independence and proficiency, however, she perceived a growing unease surrounding the intensity of her ambition and began to fear that her music-cultural identity would be incompatible with the framework of the Scene. To understand why this came to a head following her departure from UCLA, I draw a connection between her experience of academic ethnomusicology and earlier, more visceral tensions. This connection hinges on the capacity of her intercultural ambiguity and associated musical fluency to destabilize the pillars of authenticity and

---

[14] Founded in 1937, The Tamburitzans is "a song and dance company" modeled after Croatian *tamburica* orchestras (http://www.duq.edu/life-at-duquesne/tamburitzans). Members are students at Duquesne University, who benefit from access to an extensive collection of folk costumes and other resources. Beloved Scene dance instructor Dick Crum served for a time as artistic director (Laušević 2007, 198). For more information, see Kolar, Walter W. *Duquesne University Tamburitzans: The First Fifty Years Remembered*. Pittsburgh: Tamburitza Press, 1986.

inclusivity that have long structured Scene ideology and activity.

Notions of authenticity embraced by the Scene are synthesized in a three-tiered model. Originating as an expression of Mark Levy's devotion to the Bulgarian *bitov* tradition, the first tier informs prevailing ideas about authentic musical genre and instrumentation. At the core of ongoing debate over oral transmission and amplification is the authenticity of practice and performance, here designated the second tier. Requiring a cognitive leap between musical activity and broader music-cultural experience, the final tier serves as a guiding principle for American Balkan musicians who uphold the fulfillment of previous tiers as a means to augment personal and collective authenticity, a way of thinking exemplified by what Rachel MacFarlane portrays as a common propensity for Scene members to identify with a romanticized image of the Balkans. As for what this implies about tension in Eva's relationship with the Scene, I argue that a significant proportion of first-generation musicians and dancers may have interpreted her ambiguity as evidence of an ability to attain a degree of authenticity they had not achieved yet toward which they still fundamentally aspired. Further insight proceeds from a review of how the ideology of authenticity has evolved, as it is hardly difficult to imagine that a smaller subset of the Scene population objected to the very idea of intercultural ambiguity, deeming it a matter of decency for Eva to demonstrate that she *approached* Balkan music unequivocally as an American Balkan musician.

What, then, of Eva's musical fluency, as the language in which her ambiguity is most directly expressed? Owing to the improbability of attaining such fluency in an adopted musical tradition, it would again be easy to dismiss any relevant strain as the product of envy and frustration. A deeper explanation evokes the legacy of the International Folk Dance Movement. With the exception of professional exhibition troupes such as AMAN and Radost, early folk dance organizations placed group participation over individual prowess, generating an atmosphere of inclusivity that emboldened the first American Balkan musicians to attempt to play Balkan music. Under the leadership of Mark Levy, who celebrated the folk dance world as a respite from institutionalized competition, inclusivity was later canonized as a tenet of the Scene. Without insinuating that Scene founders were in any way deficient in ability or achievement, this view furnishes what is perhaps the most basic explanation for tension in Eva's relationship with her first-generation peers, many of whom may continue to feel challenged by an outstanding young vocalist whose very presence could be construed as threatening to induce a culture of talent with the potential to restructure their community.

For Eva, these tensions sharply converged in the field of academic ethnomusicology. Driven by pursuit of a sort of intellectual authenticity that hinges on the dichotomy of researcher and subject, the majority of ethnomusicologists operate in a manner that purports to underscore native authority. At the same time, contemporary participant-observation methodology emphasizes the importance of firsthand musical activity, idealizing musical fluency as the manifestation of a more comprehensive music-cultural intimacy. This was initially a source of comfort for Eva, who applied to UCLA eager to embark on a journey she believed would sanction the intimacy that had complicated her role within the Scene. In the space between her response to Tzvetanka Varimezova and her studies, however, she noted a familiar irony: to satisfy the role of ethnomusicologist as prescribed by the academy, she would be urged to minimize both her intercultural ambiguity and the unfettered musicality on which it fed. No longer motivated to comply, she returned to Mendocino, where her renewed intensity and candor accentuated the politics of her youth, triggering a process whereby disillusionment with the academic sphere precipitated a larger crisis of faith in her position and purpose as a musician. Yet if her immediate response was one of alarm, it is here that an analysis of her mature music-cultural identity begins.

Back in Santa Cruz and feeling detached, Eva auditioned for Kitka, a women's vocal ensemble that specializes in the music of Eastern Europe and related traditions. Though Eva speaks of Kitka with earnest respect, she left the ensemble in 2006. "I have always been more attracted to the *zurna* and *davul* end of things—to the gritty, dirty, *crunchier* parts of culture," she states. "But I had amazing experiences performing and touring with them." Singing with Kitka had two major benefits for Eva. First, it offered her the structure she needed to solidify her ensemble technique. "I'm a musician who relies on the ability to improvise every time—that's just my personality," she asserts:

> It's the way that I clean, it's the way that I cook, and it's evident in my musicality, I think. But being in Kitka—singing with the same group of women and wearing the same costume and performing the same repertoire night after night—I learned how to be an ensemble singer. I learned how to execute things the same way every time. I learned how to be consistent. And just by virtue of singing so much, my voice became stronger.

In addition to its impact on her voice, membership in Kitka granted Eva the opportunity to participate in *The Rusalka Cycle*, a musical theater production directed by Ukrainian composer Mariana Sadovska and a focus of Chapter 6. Sadovska proved to be a key mentor to Eva, encouraging her to employ her singular fluency in articulating the inherent multidimensionality of identity and experience. "Mariana said something to me that just shook me, which was that, 'It's not always about how beautiful your voice is,'" she relates:

> Singing is in reality a varied aesthetic experience; there are so many voices that one person possesses, and there's no one-size-fits-all in terms of vocal quality. I left that conversation with a commitment not to finding the *one* voice that was me but to discovering the many, many voices that I could encompass.

Central to the formulation of *The Rusalka Cycle* was a research trip to Ukraine, after which Eva remained abroad for two months. In the course of her now solitary peregrinations, she began to reevaluate her priorities and ambitions.

One Heart, Many Voices

"I went directly from Kiev to Istanbul, which was a place that I had wanted to go for so long, musically as well as physically. And that I was kind of afraid of!" she exclaims:

> It's an interesting situation because just like how within the Balkan Scene there are not very many people that sing Albanian music, there are also not that many people who sing Turkish music. And being part of the Scene, there were times when I felt like I was not supposed to sing Turkish music. So I went to Turkey, and it was a huge affirmation for me. I met Selma and Rehâ Sağbaş, who are renowned Turkish musicians. I had become friends with their son when he was living in the United States, and in Istanbul, he introduced me to his community of young musicians and artists. And then I met Laurent Clouet, a great French clarinet player living in Bulgaria and Turkey, and I ended up going to a Romani wedding in Bulgaria with him a couple of weeks later. Meeting him and playing with him and then two days later running into this guy that I had met in New York at a concert—there was just phenomenal stuff like that happening. Doors—*cultural* doors, and doors of friendship—were being opened. I didn't take any singing lessons while I was there, but I met *people*—met *incredible people*.[15]

Leaving Turkey, Eva traveled to Greece, where she visited Ruth Hunter and her husband, Christos Govetas, at Govetas' childhood home. "It was their tenth anniversary party, so there was lots of music, and dancing, and dancing, and *dancing*. It was like *zurna* heaven!" she laughs. At some point during the festivities, Eva telephoned her father in Santa Cruz, seeking his perspective on her recent experiences. Their conversation centered on a reimagining of ethnomusicology and its role in her life:

---

[15] A major exception is Brenna MacCrimmon, a Canadian vocalist who has devoted herself to Turkish music since her teens. MacCrimmon is celebrated in Turkey, where she often performs with local musicians. Her collaboration with Turkish psychedelic band Baba Zula was explored in the 2005 documentary *Crossing the Bridge: The Sound of Istanbul*. MacCrimmon occasionally teaches at Camp and served on the EEFC board from 2008 – 2011. Her recordings include *Karşilama* (with legendary Turkish Roman clarinetist Selim Sessler), *Ayde Mori* (with Turkish musicians Muammer Ketencoğlu, Sumru Ağiryürüüyen, and Sevdet Erek), and *Kulak Misafiri*.

I had decided that after my trip to Europe, I was going back to finish school, but I was dreading it. I was dreading being in that kind of mentality again. And my dad said, "Look. Make your *own* ethnomusicology. Remember who the role models are for you." Many of the best ethnomusicologists I know lack academic credentials, but the significance of their work is unquestionable. It was just like, "Wow." *Major* shift in who I looked up to—the people who had lived through a good portion of their lives around this music, who were so well respected by musicians and dancers and citizens of the Balkans—and saying, "That's what I want to be. *That's what I want to be.*" Because anytime someone comes up to you with tears in their eyes and says, "My grandfather sang that song to me"—*that's* how my work is measured. I don't ever need to be published. I don't need that. I don't need a title. I don't want anyone to ever call me an authority or an expert, ever. *Because the culture is the authority.*

As Eva's idea of ethnomusicological inquiry shifted from academic research toward an integrative music-cultural immersion that seemed to confound academic epistemology, her response to Sadovska grew similarly more profound, so that she began to see music not only as a vehicle for the expression of varied personal temperaments but as a language through which the space *between* established music-cultural boundaries might be purposefully inhabited. Mingling with support she had received from Tzvetanka Varimezova and Ruth Hunter, this empowered Eva to embrace her intercultural ambiguity as fertile ground from which to give voice to the full complexity of intercultural experience. "When I was a teenager, I couldn't tell if I was more afraid of being really mediocre or really powerful. Because both are terrifying," she avows:

I wanted to be humble, but I had to realize that I can dream to be a singer, and that's what I'm going to do. And that's okay, *unapologetically so*. Because any criticism that I apply to anyone else, I apply equally to myself, if not more. Tzvetanka said something to me when I was in LA that has really stayed with me—she said, "Today, I'm going to teach you this song my way. Next week, I want you to come back and sing it *your* way." Getting that kind of trust from someone like her really propelled me deeper and deeper. And Ruth talks about me when she teaches at Balkan Camp—she says, "Eva, when she was eight years old, would *cry* if she couldn't get an ornament right the first time." Ruth saw that part of me, and she said to me, "You have to believe that there is something intrinsic in you that gives you purpose within this culture." And I do. I believe that now. I'm not here to replicate something—there's no point in doing that. "Izlel e Delju Hajdutin" was sung absolutely exquisitely by Valya Balkanska in 1967 on the recording made by Ethel Raim and Martin Koenig. I don't need to try to do that! There are these demigods of Bulgarian singing—these exquisite singers—and I can leave them be. I don't need to try to sound like any one of them. But there's that crucial step of saying, "*I think I know enough to make it my own now.*"[16]

Eva's resolution to draw strength from the ambiguity of her music-cultural identity has not eliminated all tension in her relationship with the American Balkan Scene. Still, there is evidence to indicate that a threshold of acceptance has been breached. In 2006, the EEFC hired her to teach an introductory Balkan singing class at the Mendocino Balkan Music and Dance Workshops. "Being invited to teach at Balkan Camp was a really important validation for me," she affirms:

It was like, "Wow. I am being asked to contribute what skills I possess." I just breathed this sigh of relief. It was like I was being given permission to be myself, and I was so grateful for that opportunity. The first year was rocky, emotionally working out this new place. And my recordings weren't all together, and I didn't have translations for my songs, and I didn't have great speakers to play the music on. But I learned a lot, and the next year was better, one reason being

---

[16] Other sources indicate that Balkanska recorded "Izlel e Delju Hajdutin" in 1968. The recording by Raim and Koenig to which Eva alludes was made internationally famous in 1977, when it was included on the Golden Records sent aboard both Voyager spacecraft.

that I had gone back and finished school. I have a degree in ethnomusicology now. And that in itself changed the way people saw me.

Her second year teaching, Eva drew method as well as material from her singular background, working to translate her experience into something of value for her fellow American Balkan musicians. In her words:

Piecing together my repertoire to teach the second summer, I thought, "There's something in these songs that people can latch onto, so that I can know that the music is inside of them." And I realized *that's* what I need to do—I need to give. I don't need to show, I need to *give*. So I put everything together, and it ended up working out. Balkan Camp that year was really good for me because I felt like, "I know if I'm responsible, I can come to Camp and fill all the needs—my needs and that which is asked of me." I can be a good teacher, and I can be an available teacher. And I just want to *infect* people with love for the music—that's the most productive thing. Because what I realized is that most people, especially with singing, are painfully aware of the inadequacies that they perceive in themselves. I don't need to remind people of that. I need to say, "Yes, but given whatever limitations you are experiencing, you can *still* sing, and you can *still* feel good." I want people to experience the joy of the music; that's the only thing that's important, and it's the highest thing that I can accomplish. And it will do more to bring people into the Scene in the end.

Having commenced to carve out a new role in the context of Camp and the Scene, Eva turned her attention progressively outward, tracing a path reminiscent of the one she had traversed in her early teens. In July 2007, she relocated to Brooklyn, New York, a move she had contemplated for some time. Her decision was spurred in part by a need to distance herself from the community of her childhood, in hope of gaining freedom to probe the boundaries of her expression. Another incentive was a desire to live in greater proximity to various Balkan immigrant communities, chiefly the Bronx Roma. "One of my closest friends grew up in the Macedonian Romani community in the Bronx—her father was one of the first Roma from Prilep to come over," Eva explains:

> Together, we've shared a lot of life experience, and we've found a reciprocity that encompasses many things, including exchange and discussion of Romani music, dance, language, history, and culture. Beyond sharing songs, she helps me to understand their lyrics and context, and she's introduced me to members of her community, who I now count among my friends. And all of this functions independently of the Balkan Scene.

In the months succeeding her first social gatherings, Eva's relationship with the Romani community significantly deepened, as her respectful and unassuming presence granted her a broader welcome. Building on the foundation of trust fostered in her relationship with Tzvetanka Varimezova and Mariana Sadovska, this budding acceptance reinvigorated Eva's faith in her ability to walk between music-cultural worlds, even as it informs her awareness of the enormity of her responsibility as a musician capable of such fluid exchange. "I'm beginning to see how things might move in the opposite direction—from me back to the culture," she recounts:

> Last month, Seido Salifoski called me for a gig—it was at Hungarian House in New York, and it was with his band, Romski Boji. Seido called me beforehand to talk about what we would play, and he was like, "Well, what are *you* going to sing?" So I'm wracking my brain, and I panicked. He said, "Don't stress out, this is just to see if we like the way you sound with the band." But I was so nervous as I was going there. *Because this was my audition.* But making a connection with members of that musical community, and then them asking, "Would you want to sing with us?" It's like, "*Are you joking?*" That's the final judge for me. And a big part of moving to New York is being able to play music where there are as many immigrants and children of immigrants in the audience as there are Americans. I want to make a music that speaks to a broader demographic, where

the essence is not compromised—where you're not capitalizing on stereotype or theater to communicate something. I want to perform in a context in which Roma will come, and they'll know that I know how to sing it the way it is or has been sung, but that—with that knowledge—I am making it into something of my own.[17]

This final provision is crucial. If Eva welcomes participation in the Romani music scene as both personal validation and an opportunity to promote understanding, she has equally come to see that an immigrant context is not the place for unfettered expressive freedom. "There are all these different realities going on for me at the same time right now," she reflects:

It's a big honor to be asked to contribute to the musical culture of a community. That's like things coming full circle, which is amazing, but in coming full circle, they don't necessarily move forward. It's kind of groundbreaking because I'm an American, but in terms of my own *artistic* identity, I desire further innovation.

I find three reasons for this distinction. First are the wishes of the immigrant audience, which tend toward familiar songs performed a familiar way. Next is Eva's embrace of the fact that her position within the Romani community demands the discretion expected of an honored guest. The third reason captures the complexity of this role. Asked to sing by Romani musicians who value her musical proficiency, the very idea of her wider ambiguity inevitably precedes her onstage, where it prefigures her performance as it does any she gives within the Scene. For Eva, then, true freedom of expression is predicated on the ability to make music unconstrained by labels, assumptions, and the expectations

---

[17] Born in Prilep, Macedonia, Seido Salifoski bridges a background in Balkan and Middle Eastern percussion with a jazz sensibility rooted in his studies at the Berklee College of Music. As a member of Paradox Trio, he "spearheaded the downtown New York Balkan Jazz movement" (http://www.seidoism.com/bio.html), which some see as a precursor to more contemporary "Gypsy punk" bands (http://www.allmusic.com/artist/paradox-trio-mn0000893034). Today, he performs with a diversity of musical projects and has taught at both Balkan Music and Dance Workshops.

they create. "The more that I grow as a musician, the more I make an identity for myself that is inseparable from music; the more natural this becomes, the more strongly I feel that I make music *for music's sake*," she states.

The most immediate incentive behind Eva's decision to move to New York was an invitation to work with Slavic Soul Party!, a Brooklyn-based ensemble that credits itself with having forged "an acoustic mash-up of Balkan and Romani (Gypsy) sounds with North American music, weaving the gospel, funk, dub, jazz, and Latin influences of New York's neighborhoods seamlessly into a Balkan brass setting."[18] Founded in 1999 by jazz vibraphonist and longtime American Balkan musician Matt Moran,[19] Slavic Soul Party! operates within and beyond the traditional boundaries of the Scene, performing at Golden Festival yet primarily at home in bars and jazz festivals popular with urban hipsters. Alerting us to issues that will receive further discussion in Chapters 5 and 6, Eva summarizes the challenges of marketing such an ensemble as she encountered them while preparing for a 2008 West Coast tour:

> It was the band's first time on the West Coast, and it was like, "Which audiences do we market to?" Trying to produce a show in San Francisco, it was like, "Do we go to Marin so that we can get folk dancers from Santa Rosa who wouldn't otherwise come to our show? Or do we go to the city, where there's a thriving hipster community? Or do we go to Burning Man?" I was talking to Peter Jaques the other night, and I said, "We can go to *all* of them. Because we can *play* for all of them." With the right knowledge, you can tailor a performance—you can be a single band that can do many different types of shows. The demographic should be varied, you know? Slavic Soul Party! has played in bars where people were taking off their shirts—where everybody was completely drunk

[18] See www.slavicsoulparty.com.
[19] As Moran explained in a personal email, Slavic Soul Party! was originally a quintet. The band's current nine-piece instrumentation dates to 2004.

before we even showed up to play. And also in concert halls. You see your audience, and you try to give them what they need.[20]

It was in advance of this tour that Eva began to experiment with a form of innovation that would implicate the very fabric of her relationship with Balkan music. In October 2007, Moran approached her with a request that she write new Balkan-inspired vocal music for Slavic Soul Party! to arrange and perform. Hesitant to compose lyrics in a Balkan language yet reluctant to pair Balkan melodies with English lyrics, she was initially paralyzed. Recognizing a rare opportunity for artistic freedom, however, she soon reconsidered. With the tour imminent, she reached a compromise between Moran's desire to augment the ensemble's creative oeuvre and her commitment to music-cultural integrity, a commitment she believed him to share. This involved the composition of original musical settings for existing Balkan texts. "It started when we were planning the tour; we were talking about adding repertoire," she begins:

I suggested a few tunes, and we put out some charts for them, as they're pre-established songs. But then the challenge came up. It was like, "We don't want to be a cover band, but where will our repertoire come from?" And that of course was put on me, as the singer—"Well, what are *you* going to sing?" For the tour, but there's also a longer-range goal of wanting to do something that is entirely original. And that brought up the question of lyrics because I said, "I don't want to write lyrics in English." I'm not quite ready to use this music—this *culture*—as a platform for some separate part of my identity. That would make it almost *too* personal, when I feel like music is already personal enough for me. And I just don't feel like the language sounds right with the music—it's some kind of disharmony, like they're dissonant with each other. So I thought, "Okay, well here's what I can do. I can look at all of these Romani songs that are floating around—even the more contemporary ones— and I can find some poetry!" Find some poetry and put it to new

[20] Burning man is a storied countercultural gathering in Nevada's Black Rock Desert. Brass Menažeri attended in 2008.

melodies. So rather than try to apply my own emotional knowledge of language through English, why don't I just get inside the original language, and then it will be as if I'm still speaking—I'm still *saying* something. And not everyone will understand, but that's okay.

Two months after her conversation with Moran, Eva was introduced to a song that inspired her to act on this vision. She described the experience to me just prior to the tour:

I'd been kind of stalling on this, like "What do I use? Where do I start?" Well, start where you are! So I was teaching a lesson in Brooklyn to a wonderful woman who has been involved in the Scene for a really long time. The first lesson I had with her, *I* taught her a song, and then I said, "Next time, why don't *you* bring a song that you love." She brought this song, which is a recording from the Hungarian Rom group Kalyi Jag, and she said, "I want to work on *this*." I knew the song on a skeletal level, and we sang through it a couple of times. So I'm watching her go through this process, and at the same time the song is *incredible*. It's called "Sar Čirikli"—"Like Birds"—and I haven't been this excited about a song for a very, very long time. Completely separate from the melody, which is one of my favorite melodies, is this super heavy-hitting text. By the end of the lesson, I had figured out a chord progression, and it's continuing to mutate, but I *couldn't* stop *singing it*. Of course, the sound is completely different from the recording, but it's analogous with the tradition. And at the same time, it's mine. And it's the first time I've ever, ever felt that. It's like, hearing something in one form and having something you can't suppress inside of you that says, "I'm going to bring it into *this* form and sing it with who knows *what* kind of band or maybe just sing it with my accordion, and I'm going to *say* something—*just say something*." So that's been this huge, huge thing because it's that first taste of, "Oh, there are *lots* of ways to do this!"[21]

As became clear when I heard Slavic Soul Party! perform "Sar Čirikli" in Eugene, Oregon, Eva's creative efforts bore fruit

---

[21] Kalyi Jag translates to Black Fire. "Sar Čirikli" appears on the Hungaroton album *Gypsy Folk Songs from Hungary*.

for Slavic Soul Party! as it embarked on its first West Coast tour. More relevant here is the long-term effect on her philosophy of engagement with Balkan musical tradition. Mentored by first-generation folk dancers and folk dancers-turned-musicians, Eva was exposed to Balkan music in the context of a community founded on adherence to an archetype of native authenticity. Simultaneously affirming and destabilizing this model, early and in-depth interaction with native Balkan musicians enabled her to develop a provocative ambiguity she later embraced as a source of communicative potential. Yet it was ultimately through affiliation with the second-generation Scene that Eva came into her own as a singer. Working with young American musicians accustomed to asserting themselves individually as artists, she experienced what it felt like to embody tradition by giving it creative rebirth in a language of personal resonance, empowering her to approach Balkan music—and with it, her voice—with new integrity and conviction.

Since 2008, Eva has played with an assortment of bands that have heightened her commitment to personal expression while refining her ability to communicate with a diverse audience. "In New York, I'm discovering that I can have multiple venues for expression, and there's value in all of them," she observes. One example is Which Way East, founded by Jesse Kotansky, with whom Eva shared her adolescence within the Scene. Conceived to explore the connections between Balkan traditional music and the contemporary music scene of New York City, Which Way East strove to be equally comfortable in concert and club environments. In Eva's words:

> That band has a great accordion player, a really great bass player, and a percussionist who has played with people like Lauryn Hill—he's very versatile and has a really nice groove. But none of them came through the Scene! We played a show at the Knitting Factory a couple weeks ago, and it was great. I sang "Tutti Frutti," which is a Romanian song from the movie *Gadjo Dilo*. The original has a dense filled-in texture, like it would have a *cimbalom*,

and then the singer just really soars above it. But when we were in rehearsal, I said to the drummer, "How about on the chorus we switch grooves? Like *entirely*." So we're doing the dense vampy stuff, and then it switches to super funk—like not really Balkan, but just this down and dirty groove. And all of a sudden it's hip-hop.[22]

Eva took a different approach with Kadife, an ensemble she formed in 2007 with musicians more directly enmeshed in the Scene. Distinguished by a focus on Albanian repertoire, Kadife channeled the first-generation ideal of adherence to traditional practice. "I started this southern Albanian band, and the individuals involved are wonderful people,"[23] she states:

There's Kazuki Kozuru-Salifoska, who's a drummer and very into Balkan music. And then Jesse Kotansky, and Demetri Tashie, who plays *laouto*. It was really funny—I had sent them some musical samples, knowing in my own mind what the music would sound like with the instrumentation we were going to use, but on the source recordings the production is just incredibly cheesy. And not everyone liked the songs I sent, but by the end of the rehearsal, they loved them! And in that way we're doing the opposite thing, where we're saying, "Okay, so *without* the Casio, what does this song sound like?" It's like we're going more traditional than the source recording—like beginning to imagine what the song would sound like if you scaled it back. So on the one hand, I'm trying to take the old and bring it forward, and at the same time I want to move the other way. Sometimes you can do that in the course of one song, with one band. And sometimes you need multiple contexts.

---

[22] Which Way East disbanded in 2011, well after the major interview conversations on which this book is based. As in previous chapters, I have chosen to preserve the original tense of all pertinent quotations to maintain spoken integrity and to acknowledge the continuous nature of change.
Shot in Romania with local Roma, *Gadjo Dilo* (1997) is the work of French Romani director Tony Gatliff. Music plays a prominent role throughout the film, both as an integral aspect of Romani life and as a narrative focus.

[23] Here again, I have elected to preserve the grammatical tense of my original interviews.

Eva Salina Primack   129

A groundbreaking project for Eva was Ash (Æ),[24] a duo she cofounded in 2007 with young vocalist Aurelia Shrenker, who pairs a passion for folk songs from Caucasus Georgia with lifelong interest in American Appalachian music. Beloved for heartfelt interpretations of Balkan, Georgian, and Appalachian material, Ash represented foreign territory for Eva in the area of repertoire and vocal technique. Manifest in the juxtaposition and interpolation of songs from disparate traditions, however, more innovative was the duo's desire to cultivate a language of expression that gave voice to their individual backgrounds while transcending music-cultural classification. "Singing with Aurelia has been so great for me because I get to sing in different languages and in different parts of my voice,"[25] Eva affirms:

A lot of the Georgian music has really beautiful poetry, and we did some overlaying of Appalachian music with Georgian, and Appalachian with Balkan. We want to *tell* more, to tell without speaking—to tell more stories. So what we decided to do was take this Appalachian song—Aurelia sings that once, and then I sing over it this old Rhodope song. We just kind of hold it until we cross at the right junctures, and hold those intervals. Or I sing the Appalachian song, and Aurelia sings a slow Georgian song over it. It's just so exciting. It's like, "Here we are! Both of these things happening at the same time!" We do different stylistic things, like I'll hold a note while she does a certain cascading ornament, and then we're back. And then we're apart. And then we're two traditions, and then it's one tradition again. I'm just *loving* doing that! And going through cultures that my identity is not already so set in—singing Appalachian, singing Georgian, and playing around within those—I'm able to extrapolate a lot, and to bring it back in. And that's just exhilarating.[26]

---

[24] Æ is an Anglo Saxon rune that Eva and Aurelia interpret as representing "something of a dual nature—not singular, not plural, but exactly two." Over time, however, the challenge of communicating with bookers, promoters, and audience members prompted them to exchange Æ ("Ash") for Ash (Æ).

[25] Ash disbanded in 2011. See footnotes 22 and 23.

[26] Innovative practices such as those explored by Slavic Soul Party! and Ash (Æ) have been received with enthusiasm in the hipster sphere. Interestingly, a similar approach can be found in the Balkan immigrant community, where young musicians integrate

Ultimately, investment in a diversity of musical projects that facilitate mindful experimentation has allowed Eva to begin to shift her attention from the politics of her position within the Scene to the shape of her artistic ambitions. With this, she approaches the realization of her goal to create a space in which she can sing without awareness of her identity prefiguring how her performance is received. "More and more, I have a thing where when people say, 'I want to introduce you to somebody,' I'm always like, 'I don't *want* you to introduce me to them.' I don't want to come before my music," she proclaims:

> I want someone to hear me sing and form their own opinion, and then it's on them to come talk to me. It's like, "You want to work with me on a *musical* level—that has to be there first. And *then* we take it to the personal." Somebody had been talking about wanting to introduce me to this DJ, but I have reservations about engaging with the so-called "Gypster" spinoff scene, owing mainly to their perpetration of romantic and negative stereotypes of the Roma, which I find to be equally damaging. A lot of the copy that people write about those events is like, "A lethal dose of gypsy firewater." If someone ever writes that about me, I won't use it on *my* press release! I try to hold the culture up as a mirror, and there are so many layers of prejudice in the sensationalist approach, particularly when you have an audience that isn't aware or doesn't care to be educated. But you can still be a model by demonstrating your respect. I can't convince anyone to listen to my music. But establishing a presence, cultivating relationships with multiple communities, and performing in a wide variety of contexts—*that's* the way to make meaningful connections. And people connect not because of any stereotypical or theatrical elements but just because it's good music. And that speaks volumes beyond any press sheet that anybody can write for you.

In light of Eva's artistic evolution, tensions that arose in response to her singular capacity to destabilize the pillars of authenticity and inclusivity at the core of Scene activity and

the music of their heritage with American genres and styles.

perception have modulated into concerns over how she might even unintentionally apply her talent to advance innovations that accelerate generational transition and the projected restructuring of the Scene. Without denying the legitimacy of these concerns, Eva asserts that she is motivated to innovate not for the sake of provocation but by an insuppressible desire to honor on all levels the music that has gifted her such passion and purpose, endeavoring to accomplish something she is uniquely positioned to accomplish at this time. "Whether or not it's been apparent to other people, my commitment to the music has never faltered," she avows:

> The music, and the culture itself … I would do more than I can presently conceive to work for it—to defend it. The culture is the way it is. We can't live in denial of any part of it. So what kind of positive change do I want to work towards affecting within it? And how can I communicate that more widely? I'm talking about evolution with compromise but not with sacrifice.

5

Peter Jaques

We return now to the late 1990s, when an influx of young American musicians drew a clear distinction between the initial and emergent generations of the American Balkan Scene. One of the "groovy San Francisco kids" whose arrival at Camp was noted by Eva Salina Primack was clarinetist and trumpet player Peter Jaques, who discovered Balkan music as a klezmer musician within the hipster sphere. As director of intergenerational ensemble Brass Menažeri, Peter endeavored to tap the living energy of Balkan brass music while honoring the legacy of the Scene by fostering innovation that retains audible rootedness in traditional practice. His comparison of performing for folk dancers versus hipsters offers a window into the politics of tradition, innovation, and represen-tation at the intersection of intercultural and intergenerational exchange.

I became acquainted with Peter at the 2007 Mendocino Balkan Music and Dance Workshops, where I was struck by his ability to radiate both infectious whimsy and devotional gravity as he played. Vision and verve similarly converged in our formal conversations, through which I came to admire Peter for his artistry, insight, and activist spirit.

Peter Jaques was born in Memphis, Tennessee in 1972. He began Suzuki piano lessons at the age of three, nurturing a keen aural facility. "Suzuki is taught mostly by ear, and I was good enough at playing by ear that I was able to fake out my teacher for years, so that I never learned to read music properly," he states. Peter's interest in music blossomed during his early adolescence, initially without exclusive focus. "I was a teenage boy, so it was the law that I had to play electric guitar for a couple of years," he laughs. "I did rock stuff, and then I switched to bass for a while.

Then I wanted something more portable, so I found my sister's old clarinet in the closet at home, and I stole it!" Smitten with the clarinet, he taught himself to play by imitating jazz recordings. "I would pick apart Coltrane tunes and Miles Davis—'50s and '60s jazz," he recalls. "But I didn't learn enough to be able to solo convincingly. Really, it was just noodling around."

As a student in computer science at Oberlin College, Peter found little time for musical activity. After graduation in 1995, he relocated to San Francisco, where he befriended an accordion player who introduced him to a new sonic landscape. Free from academia and freshly inspired, he devoted himself to music with new intensity and direction. "My friend and I started getting together to play all the time," he explains:

> She was into tangos and French music but also klezmer music, which I found that I loved. We were playing together every day, and after a while, it became apparent that we were mostly doing klezmer. More people became involved, and then suddenly we had a klezmer band, The Gonifs. That lasted about four years, though it still resurfaces on occasion.

In 1997, Peter enrolled in a Middle Eastern ensemble at the San Francisco Community Music Center,[1] through which he was exposed to Greek and Turkish music. "Both have a lot in common with klezmer, including some common repertoire, but the theory is more developed," he notes. "Turkish music especially has full-on classical theory, and that gave me a way of studying it more. But I didn't really play Greek and Turkish music; I was just using Greek and Turkish styles within the klezmer repertoire." The following summer, he underwent a shift in approach, prompted by an encounter with Balkan folk music and the American Balkan Scene:

---

[1] According to its website, the San Francisco Community Music Center is "the Bay Area's oldest community arts organization and San Francisco's largest provider of high quality, affordable music education" (www.sfcmc.org). The Turkish and Middle Eastern ensemble is led by Shirley Wong-Frentzel, who also offers instruction in harpsichord, recorder, and Chinese folk instruments.

One of the people I was playing with in San Francisco at the time was Matthew Fass, who was an integral part of this sort of alternative arts scene in the Bay Area. He was doing this show at CELLspace in the Mission, and he asked if I wanted to participate. We were taking a break during rehearsal, and I heard this accordion in the corner playing in 7/8. I had actually just written a tune in 7/8, which I thought I had invented, so I was both thrilled and outraged! I went over to Matthew and asked what he was playing, and he said, "Oh, this is a traditional Macedonian tune. I learned it at Balkan Camp last year, and if you really like it, you should come to Camp!" It just so happened to be a week before Camp in 1998, and it just so happened to be one of the last few years that you could call a week before and get a spot. It all worked out perfectly, and there I was. My first day, I'm taking clarinet with Christos Govetas, and my first night, Esma's band was playing. It was pretty much the best introduction I could have had!

Peter entered the Balkan Music and Dance Workshops familiar with elements of the Balkan musical language. "Playing Balkan music seemed easier than it was, at first," he remarks. "The scales were fairly familiar through klezmer and Turkish music, and they used some of the same keys." As he began to delve more deeply, however, he encountered formidable challenges. "The rhythms were the hardest part," he states:

> I had written that tune in 7/8, and I'd played a Turkish tune in 9/8, but the more complex meters like *leventikos* and some of the Bulgarian meters like *kopanica* and then getting into some of the southern Macedonian and northern Greek music where they actually *stretch* the rhythm—that was the stuff that blew my mind for a long time.

Beyond the fundamentals of meter and mode, Peter struggled to grasp the subtleties of style, confronting the residue of his *approach*. "Klezmer was my native language on the clarinet, so pretty much everything that I played came out sounding like klezmer," he laughs. "It was like speaking with an accent, and it took a long time before people stopped saying, 'Oh, you play klezmer music!' when I would play Balkan." Asked to pinpoint his accent, he highlights ornamentation. "The ornaments that are used are similar, but they're very subtly different, like the ramp that each note dives off of is shaped differently," he explains. "You almost can't express the difference—it's an intuitive thing. You just start to know when something is starting to sound like it's supposed to."

If I have hitherto characterized Peter's musical education as intuitive and self-directed, it is important to clarify that he learned to play Balkan clarinet with formal support, a testament to the timing of his entrance into the Scene. In contrast to first-generation musician Dena Bjornlie, who had to wait several years to address her stylistic and technical concerns, Peter benefitted from immediate access to skilled American and native Balkan instructors, who helped him to translate his klezmer accent into something stylistically more Balkan. "Michael Ginsburg has been an incredible mentor and inspiration to me," he affirms:

> He came to Balkan music through dance; he had already played trumpet as a kid, but he returned to it to play this stuff. His attitude is so supportive, maybe because of his background. There's not any sense of, "You have to have played this stuff for your entire life to be able to get it." I've always felt encouraged and supported by him, and then Christos Govetas and George Chittenden have also been very encouraging.

Timing was equally instrumental to Peter's relationship with Balkan folk music. Prior to the mid-1980s, he would have been guided to reproduce the repertoire, style, and performance practice associated with Bulgarian village tradition.[2] Nearly a decade after the arrival of the first native Balkan musicians, he instead embraced the opportunity to sample a variety of traditions and elected to focus on Balkan brass. "As far as who introduced brass band music, it might go back to Stewart Mennin," he suggests:

---

[2] Had Peter entered the Balkan Music and Dance Workshops at an earlier date, he would also have been encouraged to exchange his clarinet for a Balkan folk instrument.

He's a clarinet player, and he plays sax too. I think he started the brass band ensemble before Michael Ginsburg took over—I have a few photocopied charts of brass band tunes from the '80s that have his name on them. Obviously, Michael has been very influential as well. He started Zlatne Uste, which is a well-established brass band that plays very traditional versions of a lot of this stuff in New York, and they've actually been invited to play in the concerts at Guča a couple of times. He's been teaching brass band at Balkan Camp for years—at least as long as I've been going.[3]

Peter was drawn to Balkan brass music by its scope and exuberance. "When I heard Michael's class, I was really excited, and I thought, 'This music retains all of the elements that I really loved about all those other musics!'" he exclaims. "It's got the ecstatic and wild energy that klezmer music can have, but it also has the spiritual depth that I find in the subtler aspects of Turkish music. It's also just really fun, and you get this big group of people together to play." After participating in the Camp band in 2000, he was inspired to form his own brass ensemble. "I had such a great time that I wanted to keep playing," he states. "When I came home from Camp, I called up a bunch of folks from class who lived in the Bay Area, and I said, 'Hey, do you want to do something with this?'" The majority returned Peter's interest, and they met to play through their common repertoire. As one meeting gave way to many, a core group began to cohere, adopting the name Brass Curtain. This was soon exchanged for Brass Menagerie, attributed to a resident of the Mission District commune in which Peter was living at the time; when *Menagerie* became *Menažeri*, Brass Menažeri was born. "We had all the instruments we needed at the very beginning, except for mid-brass," Peter recalls. "It was me, Michele Simon playing *tapan*, Jeff Garaventa playing tuba, Mary Hofer playing saxophone, Greg Jenkins playing clarinet, and Eva

---

[3] Stewart Mennin established the Mendocino brass band in 1982 and extended it to both Camps the following summer.
Held annually since 1961, the Dragačevo Trumpet Festival draws several hundred thousand visitors to the Serbian town of Guča. International artists have been allowed to perform since the mid-1980s, and to compete since 2010.

Primack and Rachel MacFarlane singing."[4]

Headed by a recent American music-cultural émigré, Brass Menaženi was at its inception fundamentally intergenerational, juxtaposing first-generation folk dancers-turned-musicians with young musicians who had grown up at Mendocino. To fill in the missing mid-brass instruments, Peter contacted Rick Elmore, with whom he had collaborated in the klezmer sphere. "Rick's a trombonist and a tuba player who used to play with the Klezmorim[5]—he agreed to play with us, and he recommended Larry Leight, who also plays trombone,"[6] he explains. "Rick ended up leaving, but Larry has stayed with us, and he *was* our mid-brass section for a long time." Then, in 2002, Rachel MacFarlane took up baritone horn, redefining herself as the newest Menaženi mid-brass musician. "Rachel really threw herself into it, partly because she was bored sitting around at the gigs," Peter opines. "She enjoys singing, but only about a fifth of our songs are vocal songs." Next, Peter worked to strengthen the ensemble's uppermost range, a process he set in motion by embarking on an intensive study of the trumpet. Though individual musicians continue to be added and subtracted, this framework has since endured.[7]

Brass Menaženi lost little time taking its music to the stage. "We wanted to perform right away because this music is dance music, and if you're putting out that much energy, you want somebody to do something with it by dancing!" Peter proclaims.

---

[4] Rachel disputes this, maintaining that she joined Brass Menaženi later that year.

[5] Founded in Berkeley in 1975, The Klezmorim is widely regarded as launching the klezmer revival and originally incorporated East European folk instruments. Scene members who contributed to this ensemble include Nada Lewis, Stuart Brotman, and Miamon Miller. For more information on the revival itself, see Slobin, Mark. *Fiddler on the Move: Exploring the Klezmer World.* New York: Oxford University Press, 2000; Bohlman, Philip V. *Jewish Music and Modernity.* New York: Oxford University Press, 2008; Strom, Yael. *Book of Klezmer: The History, the Music, the Folklore.* Chicago: Chicago Review Press, 2011; and Freedman, Jonathan. *Klezmer America: Jewishness, Ethnicity, Modernity* New York: Columbia University Press, 2009.

[6] In a follow-up conversation, Peter specified that Leight was originally a jazz musician.

[7] Readers will recall from Chapter 3 that Brass Menaženi is no longer active. See footnote 9 on page 86.

In its quest to perform, the ensemble was aided by proximity to the folk dance audience, with which it felt an inherent affinity through its first-generation contingent. Yet interest in playing for folk dancers was—and remains—impossible to consign to a single generational demographic. Introduced to Balkan clarinet at the Balkan Music and Dance Workshops and mentored by first-generation folk dancers-turned-musicians, Peter experiences Balkan music as enmeshed with the Scene and thus with its traditional audience. Here, we see the concept of *approach* reconfigured as a sense of lineage, extending the desire to pursue folk dance performance to musicians with no basis in folk dance activity.

In October 2000, Brass Menažeri appeared in a Balkan showcase at Berkeley's Ashkenaz Music and Dance Community Center. Marveling at the size and solidarity of the crowd, Peter was struck by the vitality of the local Scene population. With this, he was humbled by acute recognition that he had much to learn. "Being in the Bay Area, I'm in one of the places where the American Balkan Scene is the strongest," he reflects:

I was impressed, like, "Wow—there are all these people who know all of these dances and go dancing every other Tuesday at Ashkenaz, and they have all known each other for at least twenty-five years!" It was really exciting, but it was also a little bit intimidating. I was this new guy trying to learn to play all this stuff, and here were all of these people who had been dancing and playing the music together for so long.

As Brass Menažeri sought to establish a connection with the folk dance audience, Peter's revelation was shared by his outside recruits, who shouldered the task of attempting to satisfy a roomful of dancers with needs and expectations they could not fully comprehend. The response was largely supportive. "We felt it immediately our first year at Camp," Peter asserts:

Even with a band that's only been around for six months and musicians who have only been playing this kind of music for eight months, people come, and they listen and dance, and you get to perform and learn what people like and don't like. Like,

"Oh—*that's* how fast a *kopanica* should be for people to actually dance it!" There are definitely people who will try to dance to anything, but then there are the times when even *they* say, "This is not working—your *maškoto* is not speeding up enough," or, "Your *kolo* is too slow!" If folks are dancing and they *stop* dancing, you know they're saying, "That's not working for us." You get those messages a lot, and you start to be able to read the dancers.

In their efforts to become attuned to the demands of playing for folk dancers, Peter and his fellow Menažeri youth benefitted from close partnership with their first-generation peers, who provide them with access to knowledge and resources predating the birth of the Scene. "It's a learning experience," Peter allows:

It's been really helpful to have more experienced people in the band. I often rely on Michele Simon to read the dancers for me because she's been doing this so much longer. She stands right behind me on stage, and she can check in with what the dancers want; she can start speeding up the music or tell me to speed it up. In general, the folks who have been doing it for such a long time have made it easier for the newer folks because they've got all of the source recordings, and they can do all of the dances, and they can teach them to us. Twenty years ago, if you wanted to learn a new Bulgarian folk dance, you had to go to Bulgaria! Then again, that's great because you see the context of the music. That means that a lot of the older folks have an insight into the music that the younger folks do not because we learned it at Balkan Camp instead of in Bulgaria or Serbia.

Intergenerationality is also a factor in Brass Menažeri's approach to the Balkan brass tradition. "I find that a lot of the older players are focused on playing very traditionally, while a lot of the younger players are very interested in doing something new," Peter observes. "But then, we walk that line fairly well in our band. What usually happens is that there's a lot of skepticism at first, but after we learn to play it, everyone likes it." To honor a spectrum of positions and preferences, the ensemble has assembled a repertoire that encompasses traditional and innovative arrangements of music learned from veteran American and native Balkan musicians, culled from historical and contemporary recordings of Serbian and Macedonian brass bands, and derived from assorted non-Balkan traditions, supplementing this with members' original compositions.[8] For Peter, however, it is critical to stress that members maintain a deep devotion to the Balkan brass style. "Our instrumentation is fairly close to what a lot of the Serbian bands use, but I still arrange pretty much everything," he begins:

> We want our own sound—our own take on things. Sometimes I write new instrumental parts for a tune or totally change its groove, but for other things it's just like resetting a trumpet part for the baritone horn. We've done some Bollywood tunes, some Greek *rebetika* tunes, and we had this Cuban song in our repertoire for a while. Yet all of this we try to do in a way that sounds like a Balkan brass band. *So what does that mean?*

Prompted to address the query he has just posed, Peter grapples with the question of how to define the stylistic essence of a given tradition. "I was going to say that just by playing it in a brass band makes it brass band music, but there's definitely something else that we're trying to stay true to," he states:

> On the one hand, I think that all of the instruments lend themselves to a certain sound, and most of us play primarily Balkan brass music, so that has become our accent. But there are idiomatic things as well, like the baritones doing the upbeat vamp patterns, the tuba doing the more agile arpeggios, the parallel third harmonies in the lead instruments, and the ornamentation that colors all of the melody lines.

Of greater significance is the question of *why* Brass Menažeri endeavors to perform traditional, non-traditional, and even non-Balkan material "in a way that sounds like a Balkan brass

---

[8] Peter later clarified that Brass Menažeri's original compositions were written by himself, Erik Oberthaler (who joined in 2003), and Darren Johnston (who followed in late 2007).

band." An obvious explanation is aesthetic, both as it informs personal taste and as a property of the music itself. In Peter's words:

> I love the sound of the Balkan brass band, and that's what I want to work for. And there's actually a tradition in the Balkans of arranging Indian film tunes. Like that song, "Ramo Ramo," one of the big hits of Balkan music—it's a Bollywood tune! I don't even know what the original version was anymore because it's become such a part of the Balkan tradition. There are definitely other tunes, because the Bollywood movies are very popular among the Roma in the Balkans; the Romani language is a Sanskritic language, and people can understand a fair bit of what's happening in a Hindi film. I like the aesthetic of what happens when those tunes are put on these instruments, and I try to work for that as well.

A more abstract explanation proceeds from the concept of lineage. Here, I invoke Peter's comment that, "a lot of the older folks have an insight into the music that the younger folks do not because we learned it at Balkan Camp instead of in Bulgaria or Serbia," reading in this the pervasive concern that, accustomed to treating music as material for the realization of an independent artistic vision, young American music-cultural émigrés will innovate for innovation's sake, disrupting the Scene's historical focus on continuity with Balkan folk tradition while failing to foster a personal relationship with the Balkan region. Somewhat ironically, then, it was in the course of his own first overseas venture that Peter began to dissociate innovation from art, envisioning it more broadly as an agent of identity and position between music-cultural and generational worlds.

In 2006, Peter was invited to accompany Slavic Soul Party! to Surdulica, Serbia, where the ensemble planned to attend Vlasinsko Leto, a regional brass festival. He described this experience to me in late 2007:

142   One Heart, Many Voices

Last year, Slavic Soul Party! went to Surdulica, where they had
arranged to study with Demiran Ćerimović and his band, Vranjski
Biseri. Matt Moran asked if I wanted to come along, and I got to
study trumpet for a couple of days with Demiran Ćerimović! I spoke
almost no Serbian, and he didn't speak any English, so without any
language, he would show me something and then I'd try to play it.
If I played it pretty well, he'd nod at me, and if I didn't, he'd play
it again so that I'd hear it the right way. It was just incredible![9]

That summer and again the following summer, when he
was privileged to witness Vranjski Biseri win best band at the
preeminent Guča festival, Peter sought opportunities to observe
and interact with musicians and audience members,[10] acquiring a
sense for the contemporary vitality of the Serbian brass tradition.
"Being in Serbia, the role of the music was made clearer to me,"
he affirms:

> They consider it part of their national identity, and the festivals are
> patriotic events in positive and negative ways. But most people are
> just like, "We're Serbian, we love being Serbian, and we love our
> music!" And it goes beyond the stage. Basically, what I saw was
> a bunch of people at restaurants, eating and drinking with their
> friends, and then the brass bands would come by. Diners would give
> a band some money and start requesting songs, and the band would
> then surround the table and play directly *at* them. Guča is normally a
> town of about 2,000 people, but it swells to several hundred thousand
> for the festival. There are not normally many restaurants in town, so
> people put up these open-air tents to serve food to the guests. In one
> of the restaurants, I actually counted seven bands all playing at once!
> And they're not playing the same piece because they're playing for
> seven different tables and each table is asking for a different song.[11]

[9] Demiran Ćerimović and Vranjski Biseri head a new generation of Serbian brass
musicians.
[10] Parallel to Peter's description, Rachel chronicles her experience at Guča with Zlatne
Uste in the Fall 2003 – 2004 *Kef Times*.
[11] Peter described the political tensions he encountered at Guča in our initial
interview. "Serbia was not too long ago bombed to oblivion by the United States, so
the fact that people are proud of who they are is important, and the brass music is

As a factor in the energy surrounding the Surdulica and Guča festivals, Peter perceived the potential for growth in the number of young musicians and in the enthusiasm with which they were received. "At Guča, we saw a band where everybody involved was under twenty," he recalls:

> The clarinet player was about nine, and he was fantastic. And the lead trumpet player actually was a girl, who was probably about fifteen or sixteen. You almost never see female musicians at these festivals, so having this sixteen-year-old girl leading this band was pretty fantastic. They had a huge crowd around them all the time—everyone loved them.

If Peter's experience in Surdulica and Guča led him to believe that interest in brass music spanned multiple generations, it simultaneously exposed a parallel with generational differences he encountered as a member of Brass Menažeri. "Demiran and a lot of his band are very young," he states:

> They're doing some very innovative stuff, like a lot of the younger bands over there, so it's not just the Americans that are having this divide. And I'm not even sure that it's a divide! It's just the way of music. You have the new folks doing something new and the folks that have been around for a long time saying, "That just doesn't sound right to me."

an expression of that," he began. "But it also takes on the ugly side of being an ultra-nationalistic rallying point to the degree where there are people selling t-shirts of well-known Serbian war criminals or the old Serbian king, who has become a symbol for the far right—for Serbian nationalism. That side of it is rough, but it's also part of the reason that the music is so popular in Serbia. As for how we were received, even with really nice folks that I've met, one of the first things that they'll say to me is, 'Your country bombed our country.' Which makes me think, 'Okay, they're not even really accusing *me* of being part of that—it's just the first thing that comes into their mind when they think of America.' But honestly, I've never gotten a comment like that from any of the Romani folks I've met. I can't really guess why, except that maybe Milošević was worth getting rid of in their eyes. I think he was worth getting rid of in a lot of people's eyes—he *wasn't* popular—but the United States bombing them also wasn't popular. Now that a few American bands have gone over there, people are getting used to the idea that folks outside of their country play and love this music. You still get questions like, 'Why are you into this? What does this mean for you?' But people are very generous."

Contemplating his trip to Serbia, Peter developed an appreciation for intergenerational tension as a response to musical innovation, itself an organic and even inevitable result of the persistence of a body of repertoire and practice over time. With this, he began to formulate an approach to tradition that accommodates this tension by articulating the disjunctures as well as the junctures between a group of musicians and the music they perform. Here, tradition and innovation lose meaning as properties of individual sounds, styles, and practices; rather, these signify as traditional or innovative based on how and in what context they are employed, so that each performance may be interpreted as a record of larger patterns of interaction and change. At the same time, it is by combining and recombining these sounds, styles, and practices in an informed and mindful manner that an ensemble crafts a purposeful identity and role. In Peter's words:

> I don't actually think you can go too far in personalizing music because ultimately you're the one playing it. Who determines what's the right way to play anything? I don't really believe so much in ownership of this stuff. I think music lives in the public domain. That's why Balkan brass band music is so rich—it's influenced by so many cultures, places, and times. That ability to take everything that you hear and make it your own is fundamental to any kind of music, really, and definitely to this kind of music.[12]

To bridge this with our earlier goal, for Peter efforts to perform a diverse repertoire "in a way that sounds like a Balkan brass band" serve as an attempt to give voice to the experience of engaging an already eclectic tradition as an intergenerational American Balkan ensemble operating within the intergenerational and intercultural framework of the American Balkan Scene. In adopting this approach, he sees Brass Menažeri as acknowledging the legacy and ideals of the first generation while pursuing patterns of innovation that more closely reflect

---

[12] Peter views Serbian brass music as integrating elements of Austrian, Hungarian, Greek, Turkish, Croatian, Bosnian, and even Italian, Spanish, and Mexican music.

the reality of its second-generation contingent, even as it mirrors a similar process among native brass musicians in the Balkans and beyond. All question of artistic capital aside, he argues that Brass Menažeri is invested in honoring the Balkan brass tradition by promoting its inherent capacity to resonate with integrity across music-cultural and generational lines.

In probing Brass Menažeri's relationship with Balkan brass music, I have neglected a practical incentive: the needs of the folk dance audience. "There's definitely an element of our audience wanting to hear something specific; folk dancers like music that's close to what they're familiar with so they can dance to it," Peter explains. Referring to a now defunct fusion ensemble at the periphery of the Scene, he offers illustration of what happens when musical innovation trumps *danceability* in folk dance terms:

> I remember when The Toids came to Balkan Camp in 1999—they did a *kafana* set, and the place was packed. People were completely floored by their music. They'd never heard anything like it! But they couldn't dance to it at all. Since then, The Toids have tried to accommodate people who really want to be able to love their music in every way—including being able to folk dance to it—without compromising their artistic vision. It's been challenging for them, and that goes for a lot of the bands that are doing stuff that's less traditional, including when *we* do stuff that's less traditional. We did a Persian tune that I arranged, and it was a convincing arrangement, but it was also something that folk dancers might appreciate but not know what to do with.[13]

Danceability is highly contingent on context. For musicians who play for Balkan folk dancers, the most basic component is

---

[13] Prior to disbanding in 2008, Toids members Dan Cantrell, Ryan Francesconi, Tobias Roberson, and Lila Sklar, were known for layering Balkan sounds and styles atop a dynamic, often meandering rhythmic structure, "maintaining a sensibility with roots in new music, jazz, songwriting, and improvisation" (www.myspace.com/toids). Note that I preserve the tense of my interview conversations.

meter. Balkan folk dances are built and defined on a set of metric patterns, and dancers determine which dance to perform based on the meter of the music they hear. With the exception of genres never intended for dance, however, Balkan folk music is similarly structured, so that more often an issue than meter itself is *danceability* within a given pattern.[14] This is on one hand a matter of tempo, as some dances require execution at a particular speed for optimal accuracy and expressive character. Also significant is what I term "flow," which applies to dances that incorporate changes in tempo, as musicians must take care to accelerate and decelerate without compromising metric integrity. Attention must finally be paid to stretched and/or truncated beats, as these are identified with dances of certain regions[15] and decidedly cherished as such.

A more abstract component of *danceability* is audience familiarity with the music performed. Regardless of whether they participate in musical activity, the majority of American Balkan folk dancers bear at least rudimentary awareness of Balkan folk music and may exhibit skepticism toward performances that deviate from those heard on standard folk dance recordings. If meter, tempo, and flow are critical here, instrumentation and arrangement are also key, so that some dancers may feel disinclined to dance to a given ensemble simply because of its innovative aesthetic. Inverting the question of audience familiarity, we encounter the idea that to give a performance that truly inspires folk dancing, musicians must be folk dancers themselves. Evident in the sentiments of Mark Levy, Dena Bjornlie, and Rachel MacFarlane, this idea suggests that folk dance accompaniment satisfies at a level far deeper than the accurate or even expressive execution of a metric succession of notes, benefitting in addition from firsthand experience of its physical manifestation. Redirecting our focus from music to music-cultural actors, the question of folk dance experience aligns *danceability* with *approach*, situating it within wider discourse on generational

---

[14] The exception is of course when fusion music is performed for folk dancers, as was evident with The Toids.

[15] Regions associated with such rhythmic complexities include southern Macedonia and northern Greece.

transition and what it means to invest in the Scene. In brief, if The Toids modified repertoire and delivery for occasional folk dance performances, Peter has urged his fellow Menaženi émigrés to learn to dance, encouraging them to cultivate an intuitive sensitivity to folk dance tradition that permeates their oeuvre and in the process reiterates an abiding commitment to the Scene.

While there are certainly individuals who remain wary of musical innovation, Brass Menaženi has earned the respect of many veteran Scene members. In December 2007, I traveled to Berkeley to attend the annual Ashkenaz Balkan New Year's Eve party, where Brass Menaženi shared the bill with renowned first-generation ensemble Édessa. Ashkenaz was filled to sweaty capacity with enthusiastic folk dancers that night, and Brass Menaženi was heartily cheered, a scenario allegedly repeated every December thereafter. Since 2008, Brass Menaženi has figured prominently at Mendocino Balkan Camp, and the EEFC listserv attests to regular performances for Bay Area folk dance events.[16] With this, however, Menaženi musicians have courted a new body of dancers, bringing their music to nightclubs and bars frequented by the hipster demographic.

The catalyst for Brass Menaženi's entrance into the hipster sphere was a chance encounter on familiar ground. "This guy named Sol Crawford heard us play at the San Francisco Kolo Festival in 2005,"[17] Peter explains. "He said, 'I love you guys, and I want you to play in my bar.' So we did!" Crawford turned out to be proprietor of Amnesia, a trendy Mission District venue where the ensemble has continued to perform. Though not something members were actively seeking, this connection opened Brass Menaženi to a dynamic new audience. "It's this whole other really interesting scene," Peter remarks:

[16] In later years, Brass Menaženi focused on contexts beyond the Scene, though Scene members were often present. Menaženi vocalist and percussionist Briget Boyle sees this less as a conscious dissociation than a reflection of audience energy and interest.
[17] Kolo Festival is a Bay Area celebration of Balkan music and dance held annually since 1951.

There are a lot of people out all the time, so we get a lot of walk-in traffic from the street. And Sol is known for having a lot of really eclectic folk music from a lot of different places, so people come by there on purpose to check out what he's got going on. We started playing there every once in a while, and all of a sudden, we had this whole slew of people who had never heard anything like our music or who *had* heard it but from a more mainstream group like Balkan Beat Box, which has moved very far from the tradition. And many people were impressed to hear something more traditional.

As the majority of patrons lack exposure to Balkan folk music, venues like Amnesia have created a space in which Brass Menažeri feels greater freedom to experiment musically. "Even stuff as complex as The Toids play, if you put it in a club like Amnesia, those folks don't tend to trip over it," Peter reflects. "It doesn't have to be at all like folk dance music, and it doesn't even necessarily need to have predictable rhythms; you can throw in funny transitions, and people will just jump around and have a great time." That said, club performances carry their own specifications with regard to *danceability*, requiring a re-concep-tualization of its relationship to meter. "We got so excited about the club scene that we stopped working on repertoire we couldn't perform in it!" Peter exclaims:

> We do a lot more *čočeks* now—*čočeks* and *kolos*. Things that are metrically simple and really easy for *anyone* to dance to. And we do a lot of tunes in the same meter so that we can medley them. If folks are really rocking out to something, but we're getting tired of playing the same tune, we can shift into another tune in the same meter—that way we can sort of seamlessly sculpt the energy, and nobody will lose interest. We've become more nimble that way, but at the same time, we've moved away from some of the more complex rhythms that folk dancers really like. Some work really well—*leventikos* actually works really well, even though it's one of the most complex rhythms we play. For some reason, people get that one—they can always dance to it. They can also usually do 7/8s, like *ručenicas*, but we don't do the stretchy *kopanicas* anymore—we

don't do the *maškoto* stretchy 7/8s. We sometimes do them for effect, like if we've just thrown down some really high-energy music, we'll throw in something that's a little less intuitive for folks to just listen to. But mostly we just try to rock the house the whole time, and that means a lot of *čočeks*, a few *ručenicas*, *kolos*, and *leventikos*.[18]

Distinguishing a broad range of metric patterns, each linked to a specific dance, folk dancers favor a set list that allows them to savor that breadth in order and in content. Accustomed to a succession of songs in western common time, club dancers improvise steps that draw on yet are not determined by meter. Here, the *danceability* of a song refers to the ease of intuiting a physical response, and priority is given to metric consistency as a means to build energy from one song to the next. Inasmuch as a pattern prized by the folk audience might prove prohibitive to club dancers, however, meter is still a concern. Where the club scene affords Brass Menažeri greatest artistic freedom is in the area of aesthetic. Presented with Balkan brass music, the average club attendee is hard-pressed to differentiate between traditional and innovative sounds, permitting Menažeri musicians to incorporate elements from Bollywood or jazz without fear of comment or judgment. Yet even were the club audience able to pinpoint a departure from tradition, it is unlikely that judgment would ensue, as the ability to forge a distinctive aesthetic is valued in the hipster sphere. As Peter alludes, this encourages the ensemble to retain a traditional sound as the basis of its unique appeal, a precept that is not restrictive only because it harmonizes with members' ideals.

Having investigated the impact of club performances on Brass Menažeri's approach to the Balkan brass tradition, it is important to consider the experience of the hipster audience. Namely, what do audience members learn about Balkan music

---

[18] What is significant here is not the medleys themselves but rather that club dancers are more apt to accept—and may even prefer—a succession of songs in one meter. Ironically, this evokes the lengthy *kolos* beloved by early folk dance circles. EEFC listserv subscribers have repeatedly inquired why dancers who previously appreciated medleys now demand greater variety. For pertinent threads, see postings from November 2009 and December 2011.

150 One Heart, Many Voices

and music-culture by hearing Brass Menažeri perform at a hipster club? This chapter concludes with a discussion of representation.

As another way to view the liberties and restrictions it extends, the club scene warrants scrutiny in light of rising interest in Romani (or "Gypsy") music among hipsters nationwide. Leading this trend are New York-based ensembles Balkan Beat Box and Gogol Bordello, which enjoy a passionate following that edges on the mainstream.[19] Founded independently of the American Balkan Scene, these ensembles exist in tacit relationship with Brass Menažeri and other Scene ensembles by expanding the audience for Balkan music in the United States. "I think the energy around us is in some way part of the scene around Balkan Beat Box and Gogol Bordello in New York—all of these folks who are remixing Balkan music and repackaging it for dance hall and rave crowds," Peter states:

It's kind of a hot thing right now, and people respond more to the energy and to the ecstatic side of things than to it being traditional or related to folk dance. It's amazing—people can just go to a random club now and hear this stuff. Balkan Beat Box and Gogol Bordello are also very popular among world DJs, and I think that the folks that like what they're doing might also like what Brass Menažeri does. A

---

[19] Balkan Beat Box emerged in 2005 from New York City's musical underground. Members are Israeli ex-patriots who advertise a "Mediterranean-inflected, globalized electronica sound" (https://www.facebook.com/balkanbeatbox/info). Gogol Bordello was formed in 1999 by New York-based frontman Eugene Hütz, a native Ukrainian who claims Romani ancestry. Both bands are notorious for provocative live shows, as indicated by the latter's mission statement, here reproduced from www.gogolbordello.com: "Gogol Bordello's task is to provoke audience out of post-modern aesthetic swamp onto a neo-optimistic communal movement toward new sources of authentic energy. With acts of music, theater, chaos, and sorcery Gogol Bordello confronts the jaded and irony-deseased.... From where we stand it is clear that the world's cultures contain material for endless art-possibilities and new mind-stretching combinations, raw joy and survival energy. We chose to work with Gypsy, cabaret, and punk traditions. It's what we know and feel. And many more are possible that can make the beloved statement of post-modernism 'everything is been done' sound as an intellectual error." For an in-depth discussion, see Carol Silverman's book, *Romani Routes: Cultural Politics and Balkan Music in Diaspora*.

friend of mine, David Satori, is actually playing around with remixing some of our tracks from *Brazen*, which in a broad sense is similar to what Balkan Beat Box does, but then again, what Balkan Beat Box is doing is not necessarily what I would want to do. They've carved a new path, and it's interesting to perceive these new audiences.[20]

Implicit in the previous quotation is the notion that association with Balkan Beat Box and Gogol Bordello is not entirely positive. Even as he commends these ensembles for making inroads into the hipster sphere, Peter contends that their music does not signify entirely as advertised. "I recently went to see Balkan Beat Box, which is in many ways similar to Gogol Bordello," he recounts:

I had a great time rocking out at the show, but I left saying, "That was a lot of fun, but what was Balkan about it?" Except for the fact that they used a sample from the Bulgarian Women's Choir, I'm not exactly sure what the word "Balkan" in their name refers to. Is it a marketing thing, because folks are into Balkan music right now? The saxophone solos were in Balkan style, but really it was more of a punk/hip-hop show. Something about commercialization and the production aesthetic … it doesn't retain what I see as the essence of this music. I think that if you didn't know the name of the band, you wouldn't know they have much to do with the Balkans.[21]

Advertised, respectively, as "Balkan Hip-Hop" and "Gypsy Punk," Balkan Beat Box and Gogol Bordello integrate Balkan, non-Balkan, and Balkan-inspired original sounds and styles in whatever manner seems best calibrated to realize their respective artistic visions. In contrast, Brass Menažeri devotes abundant care to preserving audible rootedness in the Balkan brass tradition. From the perspective of club patrons, however, these ensembles are easily conflated. "Sometimes people will

---

[20] Peter updated this statement in a personal email sent October 23, 2012: "David Satori/Beats Antique did remix 'Nesatovo' and 'Borino' from *Brazen*, as well as 'Phirava Daje' from our 2nd album."

[21] Here Peter refers specifically to Le Mystère des Voix Bulgares.

approach me after a show, and they'll say we sound like Balkan Beat Box or, even farther afield, Beirut,"[22] Peter relates. "It's frustrating, but it seems somehow inevitable." Not simply a question of marketing strategy nor of deliberate investment in the music-cultural mainstream, this inevitability proceeds from the basic reality that the public will more readily embrace the exotic when exotic elements are repackaged in familiar terms.

The implications of this representational imbalance highlight the artifice of a purely musical realm. Because Balkan Beat Box and Gogol Bordello are performing ensembles, reaching listeners through live appearances in addition to audio recordings,[23] it is necessary to assess how their conduct informs perceptions of the Roma in hipster culture. Behavior carries particular authority in the club setting, which does not lend itself to discourse on music-cultural context and wherein audience members do not typically approach a performance with the expectation of overt education. Peter portrays these ensembles as often trading in brash, theatrical antics that reinforce the inveterate image of the Roma as shiftless, immoderate, and immoral.[24] Against this, he

[22] Beirut is fronted by Zach Condon, an American musician who fell in love with Balkan folk music while vacationing in Europe. As reported by *Time Magazine*, the six-member band "has garnered a loyal following among indie rock fans, despite the fact that its music—global folk that relies not on guitar but on ukulele and brass—falls outside the mainstream even by the generous standards of indie music" (http://www.time.com/time/arts/article/0,8599,2091257,00.html). Since its emergence in 2006, Beirut's primary soundscape has shifted from Balkan to French chanson, Mexican funeral music, and most recently American pop.

[23] Audio later featured on movie soundtracks demands special scrutiny, as the music, musicians, and associated music-cultural context are then implicitly linked to the message and character of the film.

[24] This approach was prominently displayed in *The Pied Piper of Hützovina*, a film that shadows Gogol Bordello's Eugene Hütz on a trip to Ukraine. As in his live shows, Hütz conducts himself with abandon, seeming to perpetuate troubling stereotypes historically leveled against the Romani people. That same year, Hütz and a fellow Gogol Bordello musician joined Madonna onstage at Live Earth for what Billboard described as "a crazed hoedown version of 'La Isla Bonita'" (http://www.billboard.com/articles/news/1051072/live-earth-london-wraps-with-madonna-spectacular) juxtaposed with a Romani song. In the words of one Scene member who saw video footage, "She basically puts them out front in her show, and they do their 'Gypsy punk' show" (http://archive.iecc.com/article/eefc/20070711001), which in this case included suggestive gyrations and utterances. It is therefore interesting to note that Madonna has repeatedly called attention to the plight of the Romani people, often to the chagrin of European fans.

positions Brass Menažeri as unwilling to sacrifice music-cultural integrity for the convenience of a popular script. Yet here again we confront the unavoidable reality that Balkan Beat Box and Gogol Bordello maintain a solid advantage in terms of public visibility and clout. Amidst the swirling lights and gyrating bodies of the hipster club, stereotypes about what it means to be "Gypsy" are superimposed on Menažeri musicians, who find themselves complicit in a language of representation fundamentally dissonant with their values and vision. Peter characterizes the behavioral expectations he feels precede Brass Menažeri onto the club stage:

> There's this thing where folks are like, "Oh, you play 'Gypsy' music! I love 'Gypsy' music, and I'm a 'Gypsy' too!" Meaning whatever their romanticized notions of being a "Gypsy" are. I think that's what a lot of people were responding to at the Balkan Beat Box show that I attended. It was good music, and it was fun to dance to, but the front man is this crazy maniacal character, and he's flailing around the stage in a way that would be unremarkable for punk but with this drunken vibe that's definitely like what people's stereotype of "Gypsy" is. And I'm not claiming that they *created* that stereotype, but they definitely played into it, and as I understand it, no one in that group is Balkan or Rom or anything. It's funny that they're playing along those lines and promoting that—it's a whole side of this that I want to try to figure out. I want to find a way to let these people know that, "No, you're *not* a 'Gypsy,'" because there are all these people who actually *are* ethnically Rom, and they're living in refugee camps or they're living in cities, but they're discriminated against. It's kind of like if you were to go around saying that you're black or you're Jewish, and you're not. It's like, "Actually people get a lot of shit for these things, and you don't have to deal with that, so it's not quite the same thing for you to just be able to claim it."

When an ensemble leaves its home environment to explore a new music-cultural realm, it relinquishes a degree of control over the message it conveys. This loss of control is intensified for Brass Menažeri, which operates at the intersection of intergenerational and intercultural exchange. Performing for an audience of folk dancers, Brass Menažeri grapples with questions of tradition and innovation as they pertain to its position within the American Balkan Scene. Taking the stage at a hipster club, the ensemble stands in for a Balkan brass band, and it is this image to which members must most immediately attend.

Cognizant of the barriers to direct communication intrinsic to the club setting, Peter exhorts his fellow Menažeri musicians to fortify the integrity of their expression, hopeful that they might contribute to a shift in discourse surrounding the Roma. In the meantime, he encourages more tangible activism, deeming this the responsibility of *any* Scene ensemble with a public voice. In his words:

> I've definitely wondered if there are ways that we exploit all of this, but honestly, I feel so respectful of the tradition and fairly aware of the situation of the folks where the tradition comes from, and I do at least small things to help. Brass Menažeri plays benefits for the Voice of Roma foundation and for the Bread and Cheese Circus, which does circus workshops with refugee kids in Kosovo. That sort of activism has become very important for us, and it is something we will continue to pursue.

6

Briget Boyle

*In this final chapter, I trace the story of Briget Boyle, who com-
bined an early affection for singing with a sense of alienation from
commercial culture. Identifying with Balkan music at the College of
Santa Fe, Briget attended the Mendocino Balkan Music and Dance
Workshops and determined to invest in the Scene. As a member of
Kitka, she participated in The Rusalka Cycle, a vocal theater project
that inspires a meditation on the nature of a music-cultural world
engendered through intercultural exchange. A portrait of Briget's
experience performing with Brass Menažeri redirects our attention
to how that world is changing as innovations pioneered by young
American music-cultural émigrés prompt the Scene to revisit its
historical design.*

*I met Briget in 2007 at Mendocino Balkan Camp, where I
became intrigued by her experience as a relative newcomer negotiating integration into the Scene. In subsequent years, she has gained
recognition as a leading voice of the emergent generation, working
to increase public awareness of Balkan music and music-culture
while remaining attuned to the internal dynamics of generational
transition.*

Briget Boyle was born in 1982 in Sherman Oaks, a suburb
of Los Angeles. Music played a prominent role in her family life.
"My mother is an American country singer-songwriter, and my
father is a recording engineer for film and television," she states.
"We did not listen to music as a family that often, but there was
always music around." This was equally true of her experience
outside the home. "I spent a lot of time in the Hollywood studios,
and I was often surrounded by professional studio musicians,"
she explains. "My mother often worked as a studio singer, and
nearly all of her acquaintances were professionals."

Nurtured by the musical saturation of her environment, Briget began singing at a young age. Her training was informal and self-directed. "I studied voice briefly, but I learned the most about singing through listening to singers—pop, rock, and Broadway singers, singers in Disney movies, and my mother," she affirms. In the eighth grade, she founded an all-girl rock band called Zaccara, which performed Beatles covers and original compositions. As an adolescent, her interests broadened to encompass classic and early 1990s rock, R&B, rap, and pop—"basically anything I could get my hands on!" she exclaims. Following a flirtation with musical theater, however, she turned her attention to folk music. "In my late teens and college years, I became obsessed with folk singer-songwriters, and I started writing songs myself," she states. Briget was drawn to folk music for reasons beyond its aesthetic, driven by a desire to seek refuge from what she had begun to perceive as the institutionalized self-interest of commercial music-culture. This disaffection generated tension between her ambition and values. "I wanted to learn all that there is to know about music, but for a long time I thought that being a professional musician was not in line with making great music," she notes. "I know now that this is simply not true."

In 2000, Briget enrolled at the College of Santa Fe[1] with a major in music performance and composition. Her decision to begin formal study was fueled by recognition that she had "reached a plateau" in her songwriting practice. "I was really struggling with music at this point," she reflects. "I needed more tools, and I needed to find my voice." Heralding the start of a lifelong journey, her voice, as it were, found her. The first day of freshman orientation, Briget heard an announcement advertising a campus Middle Eastern and Balkan ensemble. "I had no knowledge of Balkan music or even of the Balkans as a region, so I thought, 'Why not try it?,'" she recalls. "I'd never heard of it, and I knew I should try new things." Directed by veteran Scene percussionist Polly Tapia Ferber,[2] the ensemble focused on instrumental music,

---

[1] The College of Santa Fe is now called Santa Fe College of Art and Design.
[2] Ferber is distinguished as the first female instrumental instructor at Balkan Camp. She shares her experience in an interview featured in the Spring/Summer 2003 *Kef Times*.

though students were also exposed to singing. "We didn't have a vocal coach, but Polly got a voice teacher from the college to help us with the harmonies," Briget explains. "We did some nice Kutev arrangements—mostly songs that Kitka had sung, because Polly knew Shira[3] and was able to get the music for us." She shares the memory of being "instantly swept away" by Balkan music:

> The first song I learned was "Što mi e milo," and the harmonies were like nothing that I had ever heard. The music spoke to me on a really intimate level, and I felt like I was *of* it in some way—it felt like what I had been seeking all along. I was also taking percussion lessons with Polly, and I was blown away by the subtleties of the rhythms. I could tell that the music was deeper than I could comprehend, which made me want to pursue it.

This was easier said than done. Introduced to Balkan music in a college ensemble, Briget struggled to find additional resources between terms. As one of only two students who "really got into Balkan music," her frustration was compounded by a hunger to connect with other musicians who shared her drive. "The first couple of years, it was just this thing that I was obsessed with!" she exclaims:

> I didn't understand it at all, and I thought I was the only person alive who was into it. It was scary, really. I remember watching the movie *Time of the Gypsies*, and by the end of it, I was just bawling. I didn't understand why, but I thought, "I need to do this, I need to be a part of this, and I need to find people who are as interested in it as I am."[4]

Relief came with an inexplicable charge. "In 2003, Polly said, 'Go to Balkan Camp—you'll be really happy,'" Briget relates. "I

---

[3] A member of Kitka since 1988, Shira Cion currently serves as Executive Director.
[4] *Time of the Gypsies* is a 1988 film by Serbian director Emir Kusturica. Shot in Serbian and the Romani language, it is a coming-of-age tale in which a young man with supernatural abilities becomes a hardened criminal. The soundtrack was created by Goran Bregović, who tours internationally with his Weddings and Funerals Orchestra. *Time of the Gypsies* has since given rise to a musical production, the *Time of the Gypsies Punk Opera*.

had no idea what she was talking about, but I *did*. And I *was*." It was at the Mendocino Balkan Music and Dance Workshops that Briget first experienced a manifestation of her ideal: a community bound by devotion to a rich tradition without commercial incentive. "That first year, I was like a kid in a candy store," she begins:

> I took five classes, and I never missed one. *And* I was dancing all night. It was just … the person that I was, was gone. I became a new person, and I had this completely new love. Going to Balkan Camp was like coming home, and all of the sudden I had this purpose.

As Briget would soon discover, however, Camp was a mere point of entry, accentuating the absence of a similar community in her everyday life. To borrow a phrase from *Balkan Fascination* author Mirjana Laušević, "as the sun [rose] after the final night of camp revelry," and "the magical spot [became], once again, a simple campground,"[5] Briget felt the bitterness of isolation return, now sharpened by nostalgia. "It was this week in the woods, and then I had to go back to my normal life," she mourns. "I had this purpose, but I didn't know what I was going to do with it."

Shortly before Balkan Camp, Briget had withdrawn from the College of Santa Fe and relocated to Austin, Texas, where she now attempted to form her own Balkan vocal ensemble. Undaunted by a tepid response, she resolved to practice on her own, sustained by hope that some as yet unfathomable opportunity would arise. Again, this transpired with the aid of Polly Ferber, who wrote to inform her that Kitka was holding auditions. "I contacted Kitka, and one thing led to another," Briget recounts:

> Right before my audition, I listened to my tapes from Michele Simon and Tzvetanka Varimezova's classes at Camp, and I just tried to have faith in myself that I could do this. I went into my audition, and I had no idea what was going to happen—I just sang and hoped that I was right for them. And it turned out that I was!

---

[5] Laušević 2007, 42.

Established in 1979 by members of the Westwind International Folk Ensemble,[6] Kitka maintains a fraught alliance with the American Balkan Scene, as many first-generation folk dancers and folk dancers-turned-musicians who respect the ensemble for its vocal prowess are reluctant to embrace it as a fitting expression of their ideals. The preponderance of dissonance stems from a discrepancy in musical orientation, as a preliminary focus on Bulgarian choral arrangements placed the ensemble in default opposition to Scene founders' quest to engage Balkan music in what they considered its iconic village form. Also significant is a staged delivery reminiscent of the Bulgarian choral phenomenon, as this diminishes Kitka's appeal for Scene members who restrict their patronage of American Balkan ensembles to those that cater to folk dancing. Notably, however, the decision to perform staged choral arrangements simultaneously opened the ensemble to a more eclectic audience, which today includes fans of women's and world vocal music who would not otherwise encounter the Scene.

For Briget, being accepted into Kitka felt like being adopted into a family, albeit one with a touring schedule and "a bit of a hierarchy for quality control." Beyond vocal finesse, she associates the latter with a commitment to music-cultural and representational integrity that evolved in tandem with a parallel consciousness at the level of the Scene. "Because we have a certain level of recognition, where we're seen as the experts in the field in America, it generates a lot of responsibility to be culturally, stylistically, and linguistically correct,"[7] she states. "But at the same time, we're not trying to sound like the Bulgarian Women's Choir.[8] We combine tradition with our own take on it. We sing

[6] Westwind International Folk Ensemble is rooted in late 1950s Los Angeles. In contrast to the majority of its counterparts, Westwind began as a gathering of singers, only later adding dancers and instrumentalists. A 1966 split into northern and southern contingents ultimately reestablished the group in the Bay Area. Westwind's repertoire derives from across Eastern Europe and the Americas, and many Scene musicians and dancers are past or present members.

[7] By the time this book went to press, Briget had left Kitka, a development noted in the Conclusion.

[8] As in Chapter 3, the term "Bulgarian Women's Choir" here refers less to a specific ensemble than to the Bulgarian choral phenomenon sparked by the international

160   One Heart, Many Voices

with *our* voices, and we want that to be reflected in the energy of the music." Over the past decade, this philosophy has fueled the development of a series of innovative theatrical productions that push the Scene's boundaries in new and provocative directions.[9] Of greatest relevance here is *The Rusalka Cycle: Songs Between the Worlds*, in which Eva Salina Primack also took part. The following section frames Briget's account of formulating and performing *The Rusalka Cycle* with observations I recorded in 2008, when I traveled to San Francisco for a preview of its second run.

Created by Kitka in collaboration with Ukrainian composer Mariana Sadovska and stage director Ellen Sebastian Chang, *The Rusalka Cycle* is a "vocal theater project" inspired by the *rusalki*, held throughout Eastern Europe to represent the "shapeshifting spirits" of "women who have died unjust or untimely deaths" and whose power to cause "crop failure, birth defects, and other calamities"[10] is annually appeased through the songs and rituals of Rusalka Week.[11] As a participant in this musical drama, however, Briget suggests that it derives much of its narrative and emotional force from the further integration of life and legend, serving as a meditation on the ensemble's experience of intercultural exchange. To understand how *The Rusalka Cycle* came to portray this particular plait of tales, we return to the spring of 2005, when Sadovska led Kitka and Chang on a three-week expedition to her native Ukraine.[12]

marketing of Le Mystère des Voix Bulgares in the early 1990s.

[9] Kitka's expansion into musical theater commenced in 2000, when it "received major grants from the National Endowment for the Arts and the Rockefeller Foundation's MAP fund to launch the *New Folksongs* Commissioning Project, which engages some of the most exciting voices in contemporary music to write new works that utilize Kitka's wide-ranging sound palette" (www.kitka.org/about/index.html).

[10] See www.rockpaperscissors.biz/index.cfm/fuseaction/current.press_release/project_id/339.cfm.

[11] Rusalka Week is observed in early June, during which time the *rusalki* are believed to be at their most dangerous, having left the rivers and streams to lure unsuspecting humans to their deaths. In so doing, however, they carry needed moisture to crops and must therefore be not only appeased but blessed.

[12] Kitka details its aspirations for this project in an official fundraising appeal. See

The expedition commenced in the city of Lviv, where Kitka met with theater professionals who encouraged members to cultivate a more embodied approach to singing, challenging them to reconsider their role as interpreters of folk culture. "In Lviv, we worked at the Les Kurbas Theater, where Mariana had studied," Briget begins:

We did movement workshops with the people who ran the theater and with a woman named Joanna Wichowska, who Mariana had worked with at Gardzienice, a movement- and music-oriented theater company in Poland. These people are extremely devoted—it's really serious and very physical and very musical. Joanna takes folk dances and twists them around, inserting some very dramatic movements into the basic rhythmic dance patterns. It was interesting; it's hard when you're really into folk dancing and you're particular about how it's done, and then you have to blow it all open and add all these weird arm movements!

From Lviv, Sadovska conducted Kitka and Chang to the village of Svarytsevychi, where they spent the Trinity holiday in the company of local women.[13] Immersed in rural Ukrainian life, *Rusalka Cycle* participants came to see these women as the primary keepers of traditional ritual and song. "It wasn't so much about *learning* from the women," Briget reflects:

It was more about observing them and listening to them sing songs we had already learned from Mariana—songs she had gathered during Rusalka Week the year before. Since we already knew how to sing them, it was mostly about getting an idea of their context and being part of the rituals. And then just being in the village and *seeing* these women ... their hands were rough and dirty, and they worked all day. They cooked, and they sang while they cooked, and they sang while they worked, and they

www.kitka.org/calendar/ukrainefundraisingappeal.html.
[13] Svarytsevychi is by Kitka's account "the last village in Ukraine" to practice the ancient Trinity ritual of parading "through the village singing songs to chase away evil spirits and invite health and fertility into each home" (Ibid.).

sang while they were doing the dishes. That was the biggest thing for me—seeing how much the music could be part of daily life.

If time in Svarytsevychi enabled Kitka to situate its intended material within the fabric of village experience, knowledge of this connection heightened members' awareness of their own inherent remove. Intimacy and deference weave a delicate balance that colors Briget's description of the Trinity rituals and proves critical to *The Rusalka Cycle* as a production. "The morning after we arrived, we went to the cemetery and were witness to a ritual in which people lamented at the gravestones of their loved ones," she recounts:

I have some really interesting videos of the grandmothers telling stories of their loved ones who had died, and they were making jokes! One of the things that was really funny was that somebody would be lamenting, and then she'd stop, talk to her friends, eat a piece of candy, and then go back to lamenting. I had never seen or heard of anything like that! Some people had been dead for a long time, and people were more casual there, but there were also some recent deaths like these two boys who had died in a fire. Their mother was there with their whole family, and they were all lamenting—wailing, really. In American culture, people barely cry, and there it was as if the louder and more passionately you lamented, the more respect you showed to the deceased. It was so intense. It was hard to witness because when you're not part of something like that, you feel like a voyeur. We kept our distance from the more recent losses.

Kitka's next destination was the capital, Kiev, where *Rusalka Cycle* participants consulted with a group of Ukrainian ethnomusicologists to strengthen their understanding of village music-culture. Though wary of a purely intellectual approach, this helped Briget to appreciate academic analysis as a complement to firsthand interaction:

Working with the ethnomusicologists was very different than working with the village folk. The ethnomusicologists taught us village songs that they had gathered, as well as different stylistic vocal techniques from different regions in Ukraine; we learned about the music from a more scholarly point of view. It was an interesting juxtaposition of learning styles. When you learn from the women directly, they're not like, "Well, this song is from the Poltava region." They just sing, and you take from it what you will. With the ethnomusicologists, it was a lot more technical. I think that when you look at this music from a scholarly perspective, something gets lost—you're not doing it from that very organic place. I felt like I was reading a textbook when I was learning from them. It was also very valuable, just a different perspective.

Leaving Kiev, Sadovska led Kitka to the village of Havronschyna, where *The Rusalka Cycle* acquired a potent ecological dimension. Confronting the enduring effects of the 1986 Chernobyl nuclear crisis,[14] members were struck by a parallel between the *rusalki* as "nature spirits" invested in the renewal of the "ecological balance" and the devastation wrought by "one of the greatest environmental disasters" of all time.[15] Sensitivity to the environmental ecology of the *rusalka* as symbol and subject in turn exposed a wider social ecology rooted in the power of traditional practice to spin a web of familiarity binding individuals to one another and to an altered or remembered homeland in times of crisis and change. "Many of the villagers had been moved to Havronschyna from a village near Chernobyl, and their traditions had been displaced," Briget explains:

It had been particularly hard to keep the traditions alive because the village that they had moved to was very Christian, and the rituals that they had practiced were Pagan. There had been a lot of conflict for about fifteen years, but I think the original villagers had gotten tired of all the trouble, and finally allowed the refugees to practice what they wanted.

[14] On April 26, 1986, an explosion within the Chernobyl Nuclear Power Plant released radiation across much of Europe. Contamination levels exceeding those deemed safe by health officials continue to be found throughout the affected area.
[15] See www.rockpaperscissors.biz/index.cfm/fuseaction/current.press_release/keyword_search/rusalka/project_id/339.cfm.

Illuminating the intricate web of nature, society, and culture, it was through the story of the Havronschyna villagers that the women of Kitka became receptive to the human core of the Rusalka Week rituals, infusing their work with what they felt was the universality of an archetype. To grasp the full ecological meaning embedded within the production, however, we must account for the fact that Kitka's attention to the *rusalki* stood in stark contrast to the value afforded the *rusalka* lore in modern-day Ukraine. It is important to remember that individuals maintain a relationship with tradition only as long as they wish to remain enmeshed in the lifestyle it evokes. In Havronschyna, as in Svarytsevychi, Briget was quick to observe a clear generational divide. "It was scary—the younger people are leaving the villages for city life because they need to make money, and the older women are the only ones still practicing these traditions," she states:

> These women are very old, and it made me really hope that these traditions can stay alive somehow. In that way I was really proud to be there because at least we were bearing witness. I don't believe that I, as an American, can preserve them in any real way, but the fact that I have them in my body—the fact that we took these songs and rituals and made a piece of art out of them—that's preserving them in *some* way, and that felt good.

Ultimately, Briget sees Kitka as having left Ukraine pregnant with the task of giving creative rebirth to what members now perceived as an endangered body of ritual and song with broad contemporary application. Yet if the prospect of extinction added a sense of urgency to their artistic endeavor, its underlying integrity was opened to doubt by the aforementioned discrepancy in respective attitudes towards traditional lore. Acknowledging this discrepancy and choosing to proceed, *Rusalka Cycle* participants placed themselves in a position from which it might have been conceivable to assert the role of music-cultural savior. Firm in her view that Kitka made no such claim, Briget offers the following anecdote to demonstrate that she and her fellow singers exerted great care lest they even *appear* to presume authority in their interactions with village women:

> In the second village, we recognized a song that the women were singing, and we were all feeling like, "Should we sing with them? Or should we just let them do their thing and watch?" And after about ten minutes of them singing by themselves, they were turning around and waving us into the line, asking us to join them. That was really fantastic!

Briget's interpretation of Kitka's experience with the Havronschyna villagers stands as one of potentially several. Amplifying the contingency of her account, we can only speculate as to members' response had they detected a different reaction to their activity in Ukraine. For now, I credit her reading as an approximation of that embraced by Kitka, Sadovska, and Chang and thus as a sort of music-cultural contract anchoring *The Rusalka Cycle* in the eyes of its principal actors, who returned to California confident that their vision had been affirmed. To initiate the process of crafting an artistic production, Sadovksa asked the women of Kitka to submit recordings of folk songs with which they felt a strong emotional connection, combining select elements with instrumentals, extended vocal effects, and other expressive devices to create a cohesive nine-movement song cycle. Significantly, she did not limit Kitka to songs with explicit reference to *rusalki* nor did she require that they originate in Ukraine. "There ended up being a Bulgarian song, a Bosnian song, a Serbian song—even an American folk song, Briget notes:

> Rusalka Week begins with Trinity Sunday, so the songs at the beginning of the show relate to springtime and to waking up the spirits. The second piece is a Russian drowning song, which was relevant in the sense that *rusalki* are often thought to be women who have drowned. Ultimately, Mariana took the energy of the songs and built them in a theatrical way, making an arc that described the experience of a woman passing from the world of the living into the spiritual world.

Next, Sadovska probed each singer's relationship with the material in the context of Kitka's recent travels. Though somewhat outside the story that participants had expected to portray, personal experience became integral to the fabric of the production.[16] In Briget's words:

Mariana would sing something to us and we would sing it back, and we incorporated movement, going deeper and deeper into the theatrical experience of the music. Through that process, she found things in each singer that she worked into the piece. It was very powerful, and it really took all of us on a journey through these traditions. The piece ended up being a chronicle of our trip to Ukraine, which also had a lot to do with the stage direction. Our stage director was fascinated by our individual experiences, and we spent a lot of rehearsal time talking about the women that we saw and other things that we experienced. We ended up including some of that in monologues between songs. The whole process was just so amazing. It was so transformative as a performer to explore these songs theatrically and really express our own beings through them.

Keeping the intricacy of its formulation in mind, *The Rusalka Cycle* was intended for a diverse audience whose knowledge of its concept and context would certainly vary. Citing the results of a survey conducted in conjunction with the inaugural run, Briget reports an impassioned yet ambivalent reception. Those who praised the production described it as "haunting" and "human," words that reappear in reviews featured on the Kitka website. Criticism fell into two basic categories, loosely patterned on audience background. For individuals familiar with Balkan folk music, most problematic was the treatment of folk tradition. "Each song was part of this huge tapestry of sounds, and the fact that the songs were not presented in their pure forms was very hard for some people," Briget explains. Others pronounced the production "hard to watch," with those acquainted with Kitka

---

[16] Many of the experiences recounted on stage were drawn from members' personal travel journals.

adding that its unapologetic emotional and physical intensity represented a gross inversion of the ensemble's identity and image. "There were people who felt that *The Rusalka Cycle* wasn't a typical Kitka show because Kitka tends to be very pretty," Briget recalls:

> We were not at *all* pretty—often the opposite—and we did a lot of very dissonant stuff, pushing our vocal ranges well beyond how we normally sing. It strengthened the ensemble because fear would only prohibit that kind of expression. And it could have been a way for our audience to open their eyes as we did—to be exposed to something different and scary and not necessarily pleasant but nonetheless wonderful. But a lot of people just couldn't handle it—they were not ready for Kitka to be ugly.

There are elements of *The Rusalka Cycle* that I agree warrant concern. Like a number of Scene musicians with whom I conversed following the 2008 preview, I am wary of a musical tapestry woven from songs of such varied provenance, particularly as Kitka often performs for individuals who have no awareness of Balkan music or music-culture. Yet what proved initially most disconcerting to me was not that Kitka treated traditional ritual and song creatively but that it did so in telling a story of personal transformation through intercultural exchange. My analysis proceeds from the work's central image, as mirrored in its subtitle, *Songs Between the Worlds.*

Gracing *The Rusalka Cycle*'s promotional poster and companion CD[17] is the figure of a woman, artistically rendered to appear submerged in a crepuscular lake. The woman seems at first glance to lack even the memory of life; her dress wilts from her shoulders, and her hands and feet fall with terminal gravity. Upon further inspection, however, we perceive a face upturned as if to receive its own reflection, which ripples across

---

[17] *The Rusalka Cycle* CD was released in January 2007 and is available at www.kitka. org.

the surface of the water with the whisper of new life. For it would appear that we behold this woman in the stillness preceding some great transfiguration; as one narrative meets and mingles with the other, she is suspended at the threshold of flesh and spirit, and we experience the titillation of ambiguous potential.

By its very ambiguity, this image holds the key to *The Rusalka Cycle*'s symbolic core. As performed, if entirely not as conceived or advertised,[18] *The Rusalka Cycle* is not about *rusalki* nor is it about East European folk material, a reality forged in the process by which the production materialized. Integrating music from multiple traditions and treating a wide subject range, Sadovska precluded *The Rusalka Cycle*'s exclusive identification with a specific body of land or lore, casting the *rusalka* rather more broadly as an emblem of rebirth. As material was collected and compiled, however, a unifying narrative came to the fore, and the story it told was that of a group of twenty-first-century women who journeyed through the *Songs Between the Worlds* into the *World Between the Songs*, inviting the lines distinguishing their lives from life and legend in the Balkans to blur.[19] And this story troubled me in that it resonated beyond Kitka as an allegory for what is perhaps the iconic experience of American Balkan musicians, raising questions with which I continue to grapple in my own intercultural activity: 1) What is the nature of a community built through investment in another culture's expressive forms? 2) How does membership shape individual identity? 3) What is

---

[18] In a follow-up conversation, Briget clarified that Kitka is often intentionally vague in its PR so as not to prefigure assumptions about productions that will inevitably evolve. In this case, program notes were oriented toward the *rusalki* as opposed to their musical and theatrical treatment.

[19] And blur they did. In an interview with RockPaperScissors, Cion quotes Chang as having warned the singers "that when dealing with 'supernatural' subject matter," they "should be prepared for unexpected occurrences in their lives." Cion continues: "The deeper we went into the material, the more intensely we trained, the more bizarre, scary, and miraculous things started to happen. Madness, near-blindness, hallucinatory fevers, heart attacks, broken bones, pregnancies, psychic visions and more all touched the project at various points along the way. We really felt like the Rusalki were there, messing with us, tricking us, and charming us. In forming the piece, we tried to weave all these wild experiences in to the storyboard of the show" (www.rockpaperscissors.biz/index.cfm/fuseaction/current.press_release/keyword_search/rusalka/project_id/339.cfm).

the most honest and respectful approach by which such investment can be sustained? I address these questions as they became relevant to me in discovering Balkan music and the Scene.

As I alluded in Chapter 1, the first time I knowingly heard Balkan music was during my freshman year at the University of Oregon, when I took a class taught by Mark Levy entitled Music in World Cultures. Captivated by the examples Mark presented in his first lecture, I sat at my desk late into the night listening to a Bulgarian choral piece from the course CD, conscious that I—and my experience of the world—had forever changed. The following year, I enrolled in the University of Oregon EEFE, also led by Mark. From the first rehearsal, I hungered for song, savoring each as a fragment of a great tradition that seemed to stretch outward in all directions. Alone or with my fellow singers, I delighted in sending my voice forward and deep, imagining that I did so in communion with the world I glimpsed through melody and text. This music-cultural awakening was accompanied by an academic reorientation, as I shifted my studies from classical musicology to ethnomusicology with a Balkan focus. At some point, however, I began to fear that in my budding enthusiasm I might unintentionally transgress an unspoken line. What qualified me to voice opinions about a body of tradition into which I had only recently begun to delve? Was it right to feel my identity increasingly bound with a world I approached as an outsider?

In the summer of 2006, I was invited to sing with fusion band Tungl Ludo,[20] which performed Led Zeppelin-style arrangements of Balkan and western European folk songs on instruments I associated with rock music. With the exception of our lead vocalist, most members had minimal exposure to Balkan folk music and expressed little desire to engage it beyond what was involved in capturing a specific aesthetic. This was more than could be said for our audience, as our sole performance that summer was at a

---

[20] The name Tungl Ludo is an Icelandic/Bulgarian hybrid that band members translated as "Crazy Moon."

local club with a student clientele. Perched above a small cluster of dancers, each struggling valiantly to find a physical language for music of such foreign meter, I fought to reconcile my vision of Balkan music-culture with the experience of straining to be heard over drum kit and bass while striving to comport myself in a manner I felt would offer reassurance to the club demographic. At the same time, I wondered at the hubris of public representation—of placing ourselves in a position to define and people the Balkans for listeners who lacked the information required to distinguish our material from its immediate context. And we gave them pittance more; aside from brief summaries of translated text,[21] the most explicit music-cultural indicator was our concert poster, which positioned the cryptic amalgam "ElectroEuroVillageRock" as an addendum to our name. But what proportion of club patrons had even perused the bill? For all they knew, Tungl Ludo was the voice of Balkan musical tradition, and my bandmates and I were, if not native Balkan ourselves, at least of Balkan descent.

Performing with Tungl Ludo solidified the definitive conflict in my experience as an aspiring American Balkan musician, as progressive engagement with Balkan music brought sharp recognition that I was far from prepared to treat it as the basis for creative expression, and I came to abhor the idea of continuing to perform until I could better inform my presentation. Here, however, I encountered a formidable challenge. Months before the resumption of the EEFE, I had no concept of where to find resources and felt suddenly helpless and alone. In a moment of desperation, I approached Mark Levy, who handed me a flyer for Mendocino Balkan Camp and invited me to apply. One year later, I did.

As the summer of 2007 approached, my mind inflated Camp to epic proportions, envisioning an unlimited flow of material and the opportunity to immerse myself in its immediate environment with a liberating candor. Anticipating an isolated event

---

[21] Given that our songs referenced traditional village custom, efforts to help listeners decipher the text may have further muddled our fusion sound, generating dissonance between images of primitive pastoralism and modern aesthetic sensibility.

lacking wider infrastructure or community, I failed to consider that the Camp experience might manifest as anything other than Balkan. Yet if Camp had for many years featured native Balkan instructors, it was also clearly the gateway to another music-cultural realm, and in constituents of that realm I distinguished elements of the very conflict with which I grappled. That summer, I observed that my fellow attendees endeavored to play Balkan music as best they could, though some chose to survey several instruments while others sought finesse in one. Individuals in both categories clearly entertained a desire for intimacy with Balkan music-culture, though many seemed content to experience the Balkans only as filtered through Camp and whatever community I now suspected it might feed. Intriguingly, it was among those with greatest firsthand knowledge that I perceived the most acute self-consciousness—the sense that, no matter how thorough or with what intent, immersion in Balkan music could never result in an American Balkan musician becoming in any way Balkan. Still, few seemed to accept that they remained exclusive inhabitants of the world from whence they came. So how to understand the space they inhabited? Did it exist insofar as it was experienced—as a web of influence stretched between the Balkans and the United States? Or were its boundaries more independently defined?

To address these questions, I turn to the work of ethnomusicologist Mark Slobin, whose book, *Subcultural Sounds*, was described in the Introduction. According to Slobin, music-culture is contingent on the affinities and choices of individual music-cultural actors as they practice, perform, and otherwise interact in a variety of configurations and contexts. This requires further distinction across music-cultural lines. For the individual who invests in another culture's tradition, the result is a state of suspension, as identity and activity are thenceforth molded in the image of a world in which that individual is by nature an outsider. When such exchange proceeds contrapuntally, or in conversation between multiple voices, it carries the capacity to give rise to a new music-cultural world. Conducting fieldwork and interacting with Balkan musicians in their native surroundings, Mark Levy could have continued to operate in a space circumscribed by the Balkans. Instead, as he and his fellow American music-cultural intermediaries came together to learn, perform, and teach—increasingly in the United States—their collective investment acquired community, infrastructure, and history, carving out a space constituents would come to term the American Balkan Scene. If American Balkan musicians coalesce around a tradition of Balkan origin, they do so from a world now sufficiently realized to sustain traditions of its own. Briefly, however, it is important to note that the Scene does not maintain a mutualistic relationship with Balkan music-culture. Limited influence may be observed; as mentioned by Dena Bjornlie, American attention has in some places sparked a resurgence of interest in local tradition, a pattern linked to globalization and visible in various forms worldwide. Yet if the Scene is at root contingent on the Balkans, the majority of native Balkan musicians remain unaware of the Scene, and its existence has no direct bearing on their identity or experience.

Contingency and imbalance reframe my stated concerns regarding tradition, representation, and right, traces of which are scattered throughout the narratives of my interviewees. Despite reservations, I find *The Rusalka Cycle* to offer valuable insight. Telling a story that concentrates meaning not in its basic material but in how that material intersects with the lives of participants, the production counsels us to attend to our personal narratives as members of a community formed through intercultural exchange.[22] Instead of debating whether American Balkan musicians have the right to perform Balkan folk music with an innovative or even a traditional approach, this model suggests that the most honest presentation is one that accounts for the channels by which we encountered and were influenced by Balkan musical tradition and continue in our own work to

[22] Here, I draw a parallel with Barz and Cooley's *Shadows in the Field: New Perspectives for Fieldwork in Ethnomusicology*, in which authors argue that the integrity of ethnographic inquiry is best upheld when researchers remain attuned to the consequences of their presence and influence. Bringing my book in a sense full circle, this view suggests that the ethnographer and the intercultural enthusiast engage culture in a similar manner, leaving a comparable footprint in terms of naming and promoting cultural information.

shape its expression.

The model of *The Rusalka Cycle* speaks in addition to inter-cultural responsibility and the impulse to preserve. Eschewing the tendency to dismiss an outside approach as one of inherent limitation, I draw inspiration from Briget's belief that Scene members are ideally poised to bear witness to a cross-section of Balkan traditions, allowing us to approach a broad spectrum of sounds and styles as expressive tools of equal validity and worth. Here, the question is not how but with what knowledge music is engaged, and the responsibility of the musician is to seek and make plain its original context and subsequent pathways of exchange. But what if such efforts fail to signify? Applying the concept of music-cultural worlds to musical and contextual innovation, the following section explores a heretofore unarticulated dimension of generational transition, beginning with a sketch of Briget's experience with intergenerational ensemble Brass Menažeri.

Briget commenced to sing with Brass Menažeri in late 2004. "My first gig with them was the San Francisco Kolo Festival," she recalls:[23]

Peter had contacted me because we really enjoyed playing music together, and he said, "Why don't you sing 'Opa Cupa' with us?" And I was like, "'Opa Cupa'—that's such a scary song!" Because it's really well known, and a few other singers that I really respect had sung it. I felt really intimidated, but I said yes, and I joined them for that tune. After that, Peter kept calling me to do gigs, and a year later, I was officially invited to join. Shortly thereafter, our snare drummer, Tom Farris, moved to Michigan, and Peter asked me to play snare in his absence. I had never played the snare before, though I had studied percussion, but I took one lesson with Tom, practiced some rudiments, and then started playing it in the band. For some reason I could do it, and that was really cool.

---

[23] See footnote 9 on page 86.

In Chapters 3 and 5, Rachel MacFarlane and Peter Jaques speak of performing with Brass Menažeri for eager young dancers in hipster nightclubs and bars. Echoing their assessment, Briget sees these performances as facilitated by a combination of repertoire and the prior experience of young Menažeri musicians, both factors she credits with enabling the ensemble to benefit from a wider trend. "I think brass band music is in general easy to understand," she explains:

> The energy that you get from a bunch of brass instruments playing in your face is undeniable, and that makes it a bit more accessible than Bulgarian *bitov* or Macedonian *izvorno*. Plus, Peter is a total rock star—he's really well known in that scene. And then in San Francisco there are a couple of bookers who are really interested in Balkan music. There's this one guy, Sol Crawford, who books at Amnesia, which has kind of become our home venue. Through that, we've gained popularity and have been invited to play other shows. And Balkan brass music is currently infiltrating popular culture—a lot of American artists are sampling brass band music, using more brass instruments, and even trying Balkan rhythms, especially in the hipster sphere. So there's been a lot of excitement about the music beyond what *we* are. We're really lucky, in that we're kind of riding that wave—some people say we're riding on the coattails of the Balkan Revolution!

Her evident enthusiasm aside, Briget is quick to acknowledge that club performances have introduced a host of challenges, forcing Brass Menažeri to confront the reality of impending generational transition as manifest in its identity and image. "The image thing in particular has been difficult," she notes:

> We started out playing for folk dancers, and we have this image of a band that can play for folk dancers, but today our main audience is really the bar scene in San Francisco. And our band is very diverse in its personnel. Three-quarters of us are younger people with more mainstream musical backgrounds, so we try to play on that image, but then the rest of the people in the band

are older, more folk-oriented people. Having to combine those images and make them one thing has been really challenging.

The politics of generational transition find expression in Brass Menažeri's relationship with Balkan music, as the ensemble works to position itself between shifting demographics at home and abroad. Like Peter, Briget portrays this as an organic and rewarding process that has encouraged the ensemble to cultivate an innovative versatility rooted in sensitivity to a diverse audience. "So far, most people have been really accepting of us," she affirms:

> Peter is very aware of what folk dancers are going to like and what they're not going to like, so when we do a show for folk dancers, we usually program folk dancing stuff, as opposed to the clubs, where we play simpler rhythms and vocal tunes or sometimes a hundred *čočeks* in a row. If you play more than three *čočeks* in a row for folk dancers, they get bored! We're starting to play more original compositions, but the original compositions that we're doing tend to be in one rhythm or one style so that folk dancers can still dance. It's funny, though—we've tried a couple pieces that start off in a *devetorka*—a fast 9/8—and then slow down, and the folk dancers look at us like, "What are you *doing*?"

Having demonstrated clear willingness to accommodate the folk dance audience, Brass Menažeri has gained a following within the Scene. Far exceeding potential incompatibilities between musicians and dancers, however, a significant proportion of first generation Scene members remain averse to the very idea of public engagement:

> The other night, a folk dancer came up to me and asked, "How do you feel about club dancers dancing at your shows?" He was very skeptical of what we do. I said, "They're great—they love our music, and they dance in the way that they know how to dance." And he said, "I just don't know if I could come out to support those shows. I don't know why you're bringing our music to these people."

I find several explanations for this skepticism. From the perspective of veteran folk dancers and folk dancers-turned-musicians who have devoted significant mental and physical energy to the intimate partnership between Balkan music and dance, the prospect of playing for a casual audience seems counterintuitive at best. Further discomfort surrounds the specter of misrepresentation, as the popularity of ensembles like Balkan Beat Box and Gogol Bordello often results in Scene musicians contributing to an image of the Balkans fundamentally dissonant with their values and vision. Still, the above anecdote is for me a strong indication that the picture is not yet complete.

Toward the end of our final interview, Briget drew my attention to a debate that furnishes the missing link. Conducted over the EEFC online discussion listserv after Balkan Camp in 2007, this discourse was initiated when a first-generation Scene member posted a link to a YouTube video entitled *Zurnas at EEFC Music and Dance Workshop 2007, Mendocino, CA*, conveying her gratitude to the young filmographer for making his video available to the Scene population. Filmed on the last day of Camp, the video depicts attendees of all ages and backgrounds dancing and waving colored streamers as they accompany a procession of *zurna* and *tapan* players en route to the student concert. A slew of responses succeeded this post, as the listserv became a forum for contributors to weigh evidence that innovations attributed to the emergent generation were fundamentally changing Camp and the Scene. Conflating the *zurna* parade with remembered activities she felt to betoken a departure from traditional practice, one first-generation folk dancer countered that such lighthearted whimsy—itself a tradition at Camp—had left little lasting effect. "Some of my favorite memories of East Coast Camp include … hearing the *zurnas* (led by Mark Levy) practicing "Wipe Out" in the outback of Buffalo Gap, and getting to dance *pravo trakisko* to it at the evening dance party," and "playing 'The Itsy-Bitsy Spider' (with a Macedonian translation by George Tomov) in *hijaz*, then in the original in classic Occidental mode on the main stage at Ramblewood," she writes. "I think the traditions have survived all that (and much more) … I don't think there's much reason for dismay."[24] In my opinion, however, there is a vital distinction between playing a *hijaz* rendition of "The Itsy-Bitsy Spider" at Balkan Camp and releasing a video of the *zurna* parade via YouTube: if the former represents playful experimentation at the heart of the Scene, the latter effectively exposes that heart to an indeterminate and in all likelihood uninformed public.

The majority of postings confirm that it was not the parade but its online distribution that was perceived as a threat. "Maybe I'm getting old and not with the times, but I'm not sure I'd want anything and everything that happens at camp to be subject to worldwide posting,"[25] one contributor expressed. Some saw this as a matter of personal privacy violation. Others cringed at being publicly linked to what they deemed the unconscionable flippancy displayed. Most penetrating were the words of another first-generation contributor, who elucidates a common subtext. "On the one hand, if more people were exposed to us, we'd probably have an easier time financially, as far as camps and events are concerned," he suggests:

On the other hand, if more people were exposed to us, our dances and outlook might be perverted/corrupted, especially if over time, our present core was outnumbered by new people who didn't know and didn't care about what we've built up for the last 100 years.[26]

Innovation does not by definition annihilate tradition. What we see with the debate over the *zurna* parade is rather an example of friction that stems from the idea that practices believed to originate with the second generation will intensify interface with the public sphere, extending a bridge into a music-cultural world already beset by change. Here, we begin to envision the act of representation itself as an instrument of *approach*, and the root of first-generation anxiety over public engagement becomes clear. By continuing to perform in hipster clubs, will ensembles like Brass Menažeri trigger an

---

[24] See http://archive.iecc.com/article/eefc/20070718022.
[25] See http://archive.iecc.com/article/eefc/20070718025.
[26] See http://archive.iecc.com/article/eefc/20070718015.

upsurge of outside interest not only in Balkan music but in Balkan Camp and the American Balkan community, solidifying the force of generational transition while accelerating—and increasingly internalizing—the restructuring of the Scene?

For Briget, such fear seems largely unfounded. Alluding to a previous quotation, she questions whether the current popularity of Balkan sounds and styles should be viewed as a bona fide "revolution" or something of more fleeting impact; given what she terms the "fickle, money-oriented, and fad-based" proclivities of the American mainstream, she prophesies the latter. Also instructive is an argument pertaining to how popular culture is consumed. "After a show, I often get questions from audience members wanting to know what the music is and where it comes from, and I tell them that it's from Serbia and about the EEFC," Briget states. "But it's hard to say what will happen. Maybe five out of two hundred people will ever go beyond just coming to our shows." Indeed, if Balkan Beat Box and Gogol Bordello have opened new channels for Scene musicians to publicize their work, the resultant visibility has done little to publicize the Scene. This is due in part to the difficulty of direct communication intrinsic to the club environment. Another factor is audience intent, as the majority of patrons attend clubs to dance, and this remains the extent of their desired relationship with the music performed. Yet even for those who develop an interest in playing Balkan music, Scene membership may prove irrelevant. Aided by a growing number of online audio and video recordings released by the aforementioned fusion bands and native musicians alike, it is increasingly feasible for conceivably anyone to emulate Balkan sounds and styles without thought to engaging a world beyond their own.

Though in recent years the EEFC has registered a slight uptick in the youth population at Camp, as of this writing, public engagement has not significantly swollen the ranks of the Scene. As I see it, however, even a tide of new members would do little to alter the Scene's core design. Perhaps exemplified by Briget's narrative, as long as the image of the Scene as a bastion of tradition remains integral to its public appeal, this image is one in which incoming musicians will continue to invest. Inverting this argument, I ask whether existing Scene members might ever recruit young American music-cultural émigrés. For if informed innovation facilitates the outside success of Brass Menažeri and a handful of likeminded ensembles, it is the resultant versatility that makes them unique and beloved within the Scene. Through the sustained involvement of individuals capable of perpetuating a similar versatility, the Scene will remain vital and vibrant.

This is the crux of Briget's response to the *zurna* parade debate, in which she calls on her fellow Scene members to foster an open and welcoming climate receptive to the possibility and even the promise of innovation that arises through intergenerational conversation. "Being a relatively new person in the community, I feel that the knowledge and expertise of the "core" is incredibly valuable and I am so grateful for all of the work that has been done," she writes:

It is inevitable that new people will join the community and I feel that it is very important to give us a chance to learn from all of the work and research that has already been done.

I care very much about the community that has been built over the last 100 years. It has become like a family for me. I think that the only way to ensure that the dances and outlook don't get corrupted is to welcome and teach the new generation without assuming that they don't care. That only alienates people.

I know a lot of young people who are thrilled to become a part of such a wonderful community and tradition. They WANT to learn the music and dances but often feel that they are not welcome to do so. Folk dancing and non western music education was not offered in any of my education so I basically started from scratch after college. I am pretty sure that a lot of my generation (20 somethings) had a similar experience, and once they are exposed to these traditions, they are eager to learn about them. But there is a steep learning curve so patience is very important.

I think it has to be recognized that the new people will become the core someday. If the preservation of the music and dance is at stake, it is of utmost importance that we welcome new people to learn from the knowledge that is already in place while also encouraging them to [go] out to do research and learn for themselves.[27]

As I prepare to conclude Briget's narrative, and with it my portrait of the American Balkan Scene, tensions surrounding the implications of public exposure focus a concern introduced in the previous chapter. Specifically, will generational transition within the Scene siphon attention away from members' focus on the Balkans? My answer is no. In choosing to go beyond dancing to and sampling Balkan music from the comfort of a familiar landscape, individuals who enter the Scene do so because they appreciate its history and values. And in learning from their forebears, these young émigrés necessarily confront the Scene's historical vision of its relationship with the Balkans, adapting it to reflect their own experience and interests. For although this is a vision undeniably marked by romantic ideal, there have always been American Balkan musicians ready to challenge themselves through firsthand exchange, and this, too, is a pattern that appears poised to endure.

Briget does not separate her desire to honor American and native Balkan traditions. "I feel that I have a responsibility to learn as much as I can, and to present it in a way that stays true to the Balkans," she asserts:

Learning and respecting the meaning and purpose of the songs is of utmost importance. There has become a fascination in the United States with Balkan music and culture, and I feel that it is my responsibility to represent it in a way that is true to the culture from which it stems. There is also the feeling of, "Who am I to be presenting this music that I did not grow up with as if it is mine?" Knowing that there is so much to learn about these cultures, I sometimes feel unqualified. It certainly inspires me to travel to the Balkans to

[27] See http://archive.iecc.com/article/eefc/20070718018.

study the roots of this music and to gain a deeper understanding of its context. As the younger generation, we must respect our elders in the Scene, but we also have the responsibility to create a dialogue between the generations—to push the older generation to share with us and to let them know that we are responsible musicians and dancers. Most of the younger musicians that I know *do* respect tradition, but they also take it to the next level. That's the thing about *any* generation and the thing about tradition; no matter how deeply rooted a tradition is, it's *always* changing, and just being aware of the history will keep things real and rooted.

As the boundaries that have historically separated the Scene from its immediate environment begin to break down, young musicians have a unique and powerful ability to reach a wider swath of the American population than Scene founders could have conceived. Like Peter, Briget sees this goal as best fulfilled through activism that is less about tradition than it is about music-cultural—and, ultimately, human—understanding. In her words:

> I feel that people in our culture are scared to get involved in another culture, especially a culture such as those in the Balkans that have experienced so many wars. But social advocacy is definitely a big part of our role. And in general I've been very disappointed in how little advocacy there is in American pop music right now—hardly anyone is talking about the Iraq war, for instance. Music is the universal language, and I feel that as young people we have the responsibility to spread knowledge to other young people in the United States.

Conclusion

In 2007, I began what I envisioned as a year-long thesis project. Never could I have predicted how my inquiry would grow, each idea exposing unforeseen challenges that opened new worlds of possibility and wonder. A critical juncture materialized in the fall of 2008, when I decided to take what was then a series of narrated biographies and weave a broader theoretical narrative. In identifying and exploring such concepts as authenticity and innovation, I grasped how fortunate I was to have chanced upon an assemblage of interviewees whose stories so perfectly capture vital stages in the history of the Scene and equally how similar concepts would likely have surfaced regardless of with whom I spoke. Still, I can state with some certainty that none but Mark Levy could have offered such penetrating insight into the Scene's initial development, that few save Dena Bjornlie could have provided such an astute comparison of the experience of American Balkan instrumentalists and vocalists, that only Rachel MacFarlane could have so intimately charted the evolution of the EEFC, that Eva Salina Primack most profoundly embodies the music-cultural identity engendered by the Scene, that few save Peter Jaques could have illustrated the complexity of balancing generation and culture, and that it was in fact Briget Boyle who prompted my meditation on *The Rusalka Cycle*. Owing to limitations of time and space, other voices are conspicuously absent—voices such as those of Michele Simon, a former actress attuned to the difference between intercultural inspiration and imitation, and Greg Jenkins, a young clarinetist who has assumed responsibility for nurturing a new crop of young Camp musicians. Then again, perhaps no honest ethnography is ever truly complete. Rather, the task of the ethnographer is to illuminate the structure and function of a world into which others may then choose to delve, articulating concepts and/or a general approach applicable to a diversity of contexts.

Just as I could not have anticipated the shape of my intellectual journey, I plunged without design into the living web of the

Scene. Beginning work, I was the newest member of American Balkan band Kef and hoped that I might one day identify as a Scene musician. In 2009, however, tests confirmed that a medical condition had compromised my ability to sing, and I stopped attending Camp. The resultant displacement intensified my fear of becoming the stereotypical researcher who purports to interpret the lived reality of an alien society, and I redoubled efforts to scrutinize my personal assumptions and biases. Then, in 2010, Eva contacted me to inquire where she and Aurelia Shrenker should perform on the Oregon leg of an upcoming tour. In the space of an hour, we hatched a plan to bring their band Ash (Æ) to my hometown of Corvallis, where they gave a breathtaking concert and workshop. The following year, we added workshops with two local choirs, and I felt a new purpose blossom. If singing was no longer an option for me, what better alternative than to share my love of Balkan music and respect for the Balkan region with my community?

Another shift directly implicated the product of my research. When it became clear that I would not meet my thesis deadline, the University of Oregon graciously permitted me to defer, with the expectation that I would undergo a formal defense after graduation. In February 2012, however, I chose to re-imagine my thesis as an independent project, which I tentatively began to refer to as a book. It would be impossible to overstate my gratitude toward my beloved thesis advisor, who offered to accompany me as I altered course. For her generosity and support, I am indebted beyond words. Her tragic death seven months later echoes like an unspeakable temblor in my heart and throughout the academic community. I miss you terribly, Anne Dhu, and I dedicate this book to you.

Parallel to changes in my experience are changes in the life and work of my interviewees, which allow me to trace the evolution of trends portrayed in my analysis of the Scene.

From 2001 to 2008, Mark Levy performed with Trio Slavej, which specialized in traditional village and more

contemporary wedding repertoire. Following his forth-
coming retirement from the University of Oregon, he
looks forward to exploring Tibetan Buddhist pathways to
peace, happiness, and self-acceptance and to reconnecting
with outdoor pursuits such as hiking, cycling, and skiing.

When I spoke with Dena Bjornlie in 2007, she was performing with Verna Druzhina, a village ensemble that struggled
to reach beyond the folk dance demographic. Currently, she
enjoys occasional gigs with *gajda* player Hector Bezanis and
tambura player Dwight Rowe and has played for a group of folk
dancers from the Bulgarian immigrant community. Between
the demand for native musicians and her isolation from Bay
Area innovators, however, she craves a more consistent musical
outlet, ideally one that pairs traditional instruments with broad
demographic appeal.

In addition to her work with Brass Menaẑeri, Rachel
MacFarlane has devoted the past few years to Fanfare Zambaleta,
a vivacious brass band forged at the Zambaleta World Music
and Dance School. A series of developments surrounding
her role with the EEFC will be addressed in the next section.

Since 2007, Eva Salina Primack has collaborated with a
variety of musicians and ensembles. These include Opa Cupa,
an Italian Balkan band with which she toured the United States
in 2008; electronic fusion ensemble Beats Antique, with which
she recorded the Romani song "Nasvalo"; Grammy-nominated
jazz mandolinist Avi Avital; psychedelic American Balkan
keyboard band Choban Elektrik; New York-based American
Balkan brass band Veveritse; Ukrainian vocal trio Zozulka;
French Yiddish singer Miléna Kartowski; and Bosnian concert
accordionist Merima Ključo. In addition, she has contributed to
several musical theater productions, most notably the Chornobyl
Songs Project with Yara Arts Group and Ensemble Hilka, from
which Zozulka was born. In 2010, Eva appeared in a showcase
performance at the Northwest Folklife Festival with Tzvetanka
Varimezova and a handful of women who were instrumental
in bringing Balkan vocal music to the United States. After Ash
(Æ) disbanded in 2011, she founded the Eva Salina band, which

Conclusion   185

debuted at Golden Festival the subsequent January. With this, she intensified her role as a teacher, leading a biannual singing class series in Brooklyn, a youth class at Mendocino Balkan Camp, and workshops with choirs across the United States and Canada. In early 2012, she coached a trio of young Romani singers for the first International Roma Day celebration in New York, a powerful experience that strengthened her commitment to the Romani community. Shortly thereafter, she was selected to participate in the inaugural OneBeat, an extended music residency and tour program intended to foster musical alchemy between talented young innovators from all reaches of the global soundscape. Her first solo album was released in March 2013.

Like Eva, Peter Jaques has invested in a diversity of ensembles and projects. Chief among these are Janam, a group that explores "the sultry rhythms and soul-stirring melodies" of Balkan, Turkish, Romani, Sephardic, and American Roots music; MWE, a high-decibel Turkish and Balkan processional band; Stellamara, an eclectic world folk ensemble with an "otherworldly" aesthetic[1]; Gamelan X, an innovative *gamelan* inspired by "Indonesian, Balkan, African, Indian, and American traditions"[2]; and Orkestar Sali, led by renowned Romani percussionist Rumen Sali Shopov. In 2010, Seattle Folk Festival organizers approached Peter to inquire whether Brass Menažeri would be interested in collaborating with Mr. Lif, a Bay Area hip-hop artist noted for his progressive activism. As my research drew to a close, Peter announced an impending relocation to Greece, where he is currently studying clarinet as the recipient of a prestigious Fulbright grant. To the dismay of audiences within and beyond the Scene, this precipitated the dissolution of Brass Menažeri, which embarked on a bittersweet farewell tour in January 2013.

Until recently, Briget's performance activity remained centered on Brass Menažeri and Kitka. With the latter, she participated in additional musical theater productions, including The Origin and Singing Through Darkness, and relished

[1] See www.stellamara.com.
[2] See www.gamelanx.com/x/?q=node/3.

the opportunity to collaborate with Meredith Monk and Svetlana Spajic. As Brass Menažeri neared the end of its distinguished twelve-year run, she decided to part ways with Kitka and now appears primarily with True Life Trio, an ensemble celebrating the commonalities between Balkan, Cajun, Mexican, South African, and American Roots traditions. I was privileged to host True Life Trio in Corvallis in May 2013.

The stories of my interviewees offer valuable insight into the perpetual unfolding of the Scene. Of contemporary salience are the consequences of public engagement, a phenomenon that has gained significant ground since I began research. The majority of Scene individuals and ensembles I treat have persisted in their journey outward, confronting challenges that necessitate new patterns of vigilance. For although Scene artists stand to gain listeners by adopting the promotional language of popular fusion outfits, there is something inherently disquieting about a concert flyer that lists Brass Menažeri as a featured performer at the "Best Crazed Gypsy Brass Band Dance Party in SF."[3] This particular irony ultimately penetrated Brass Menažeri's self-presentation. Though members identified at brassmenazeri.com as "San Francisco's original & hottest Balkan Romani ("Gypsy") Brass Band," anyone who chose to click on the word "Gypsy" was automatically redirected to a Voice of Roma discussion of entrenched prejudice against the Romani people. For Eva, who works closely with the Romani community, this discourse is somewhat more personal, manifest in efforts to uphold the integrity of society and culture in her own expression and to contribute to the empowerment of the Romani people. Still, she does not hesitate to seize constructive opportunities to interrogate examples of misrepresentation, appropriation, and imbalance in the hipster and American Balkan music-cultural landscapes, as evident in a Facebook post articulating the

---

[3] This disconnect is even more striking given the fact that the event was a benefit for Bread and Cheese Circus, an activist organization that might be expected to prioritize representational integrity over cultural appeal.

Conclusion

inequity of the fact that fusion bands have access to publicity and resources talented young Romani musicians may never enjoy.

The rise of American Balkan musicians in public debate exposes a need to re-evaluate the nature of the Scene. Already clear in the EEFC listserv debate over the Mendocino *zurna* parade, what began as a private gathering of like-minded individuals has transcended its original design. Yet while conflict still accompanies the use of social media, which has increased among members of both generational demographics,[4] for me the main lesson here is that it may be entirely feasible to cultivate a public voice while maintaining a private core. If Brass Menažeri linked to Voice of Roma to distance itself from stereotypes given new thrust in hipster music-culture, it did not link to the EEFC. The question then becomes whether such privacy is desired or even sustainable.

This question was brought to the fore in an impassioned exchange about the future of the EEFC. In late 2011, I received an email sent en masse to listserv subscribers, in which the EEFC board reported having "recognized that if we wanted to support our mission, we needed to expand the scope of our programming, and of our fundraising." As intimated in Chapter 3, the result was the appointment of "a part-time staff member" responsible for overseeing projected developments. "To accommodate this new position, we have had to adjust the EEFC's staffing budget," the message proceeded. "We regret to say that our current General Manager, Rachel MacFarlane, has chosen ... not to continue with the EEFC through the restructuring." Responses flooded in. First came an outpouring of support for Rachel, accompanied by concern that it would be prohibitively difficult to find anyone else with her remarkable skill set. Other contributors protested a lack of transparency, asserting that there had been no sign that such negotiations were underway. Last came fear that restructuring would herald the death of the EEFC. The board highlighted this in a follow-up email sent on the first of December:

---

[4] Conflict surrounding engagement with social media was again on view in a listserv debate following the 2012 Mendocino Balkan Music and Dance Workshops, in which attendees weighed the benefits, risks, and legalities of posting Camp material on Facebook and YouTube.

In talking with our own community ... it became clear over the course of the last two years, that (1) the majority of our community could not afford a tuition hike; (2) the cost of our programs was not going to go down—in fact it was almost certain to rise; (3) our community did not have the experience and expertise needed to drive a volunteer-led, strong, successful, long-term fundraising effort, and (4) we could be doing more to promote the music, dance, and cultures that we all are passionate about, besides just our workshops...

These realizations led us to the conclusion that if we want to keep the workshops alive, we need to engage an experienced Executive Director who can help us raise funds for new programs and direct a long-term vision for the organization, which in turn will help us keep the workshops going strong.

It was a sad realization for us when we had to recognize that granting organizations don't see our organization as a viable candidate for grant money because the audience for our events is limited to only about 500 workshop attendees per year, including teaching staff, administrative staff, and paying campers. That's not to say our workshops aren't wonderful, but arts or music foundations, or any other organizations, are very unlikely to fund any organizations with such a small "client" base. This is a hard truth to hear, but one we must respond to.

We have limited funds. Very limited funds. The economic downturn that impacted so many in our community impacted us as well, and we have fewer people able to pay for the camps and the higher costs associated with running the workshops. Our community is aging, and the younger generation who would like to come often can't for financial reasons.

Far from a hypothetical threat, inherent in the above message is the idea that the EEFC already faced imminent death, indicating that proposed measures had been devised with the explicit intent of promoting its salvation. Here the conversation took a familiar turn, as contributors confronted the possibility that efforts to heighten public interface would irrevocably alter

Conclusion 189

not only the EEFC but the basic fabric of the Scene. "We do need to find ways to expand our reach, to attract new campers, and to bring in more money," one individual expressed. "Let's just be sure that we don't veer away from who we are and what we value." The implications of current practice are captured by a young instrumentalist, who began by disclosing that his own involvement is primarily restricted to Camp. "Throughout the US ... especially in larger cities, there is a great deal of interest in Balkan music amongst the general live-music-going public," he writes:

> Attendance at such events like Kafana Balkan and Golden Festival are in the hundreds and thousands, but I wonder how many of those attendees know about the EEFC ... or of the Camps?

> A typical attendee, who might have heard and liked Balkan music but not know much about it, will have to go through some effort to find out about Balkan camp. First, they'd probably have to talk to a band member after the show about where they learned the music, and they might get a tip to go to the EEFC site and read more details. Then, they might decide that its really interesting, but that it costs a substantial amount of money, happens twice a year only, and happens at a secluded location far away from any population center (perhaps only a few hours of driving if they're lucky to be at the right place ... on the right coast).

> This makes the EEFC (again, to an outsider) and the camps seem like a kind of private event for those "in the know," and generally inaccessible to folks who would enthusiastically attend a Balkan music show and/or want to learn to play/sing/dance to Balkan music locally.

> I think the current reality of EEFC is unfortunately not really aligned with [the] mission statement "to educate the general public", but rather makes it difficult for the general public, even those already interested in Balkan music, to even know of its existence.

On January 11, 2012, a message entitled "Plans for the EEFC" went out to the listserv in addition to email subscribers.

Answering calls for greater transparency, the board directed readers to new Frequently Asked Questions and fiscal analysis pages at www.eefc.org and divulged plans to "publish descriptions of what existing committees do," to "develop a template for monthly updates that track our progress toward the long-term health of the EEFC," and to "use social media to communicate about the EEFC." Subsequent updates alluded to the potential benefits of outreach to ethnic communities and EEFC visibility at regional Balkan music and dance events, topics that generated further tension. Then, in March 2013, Rachel MacFarlane announced that she had officially rejoined the EEFC as Workshop Manager, eliciting palpable relief. There is little doubt that with her loving guidance continuity will balance change.

Urgent debate surrounding the future of Balkan Camp and the EEFC has at least temporarily subsided. Regardless of the steps ultimately taken, however, I firmly believe that Scene members' passion for Balkan music and dance will inspire them to honor the spirit and traditions of their community whatever the state of its formal infrastructure. To echo Mark Levy, once "bitten" there is no turning back. The stories will speak for themselves.

Glossary

Babi: Grandmothers (Slavic). Singular: *baba*.

Bar: Dance (Armenian).

Bitov: Term used to refer to a group of traditional Bulgarian village instruments (*gajda*, *gŭdulka*, *kaval*, *tambura*, and *tapan*) playing together in a manner promoted as the authentic village foundation of twentieth-century orchestral collectives.

Brač: Second-smallest *tamburica* instrument, akin to the western guitar.

Čalgija: Traditional urban Macedonian ensemble music with Ottoman roots and lyrics that depict the passionate struggles of city life. Common instruments include *ut*, *kanun*, *dajre*, *tarabuka*, clarinet, and violin.

Cimbalom: Instrument belonging to the hammered dulcimer family. Popular throughout Central Europe and Greece, where it is known as the *santouri*.

Čoček: Solo or line dance beloved by Romani and Albanian populations of Kosovo, South Serbia, and Macedonia. Characteristic meters include 9/8 (2+2+2+3), 7/8 (3+2+2), and 2/4.

Dajre: Single-headed frame drum with or without metal jingles. Known in English as the tambourine.

Davul: Turkish for *tapan*.

Devetorka: Basic Macedonian dance in 9/8 (2+2+2+3).

Diaphonic: Musical texture characterized by melody and drone. Typical of the Bulgarian Pirin region (known to some as Pirin, Macedonia).

Dumbek: Goblet-shaped hand drum found throughout the Balkans and the Middle East. Known as *tarabuka* or *tarambuka* in Bulgaria and Macedonia.

Frula: Fipple flute traditionally played by shepherds. Known in Bulgaria as the *duduk*.

Gajda: Bulgarian or Macedonian goatskin bagpipe with blowpipe, chanter (melody pipe), and drone pipe. Also transliterated as *gaida*.

Ganga: Two-voiced, drone-based singing characteristic of Bosnia and Herzegovina, in which a leader is joined by a group of vocalist after the first line of text. Lyrics often associated with courtship are presented in a loud and vigorous manner typified by close intervals.

Gamelan: Traditional Indonesian ensemble comprising metallophones, xylophones, percussion, gongs, flute, vocalist, and strings. Originally associated with the royal courts and typically played as part of a dance, puppet play, or ritual performance.

Gǔdulka: Bowed Bulgarian lute. Constructed of three primary strings suspended above multiple sympathetic strings and played in a vertical position.

Heterophonic: Musical texture in which variants of a single melody are sounded together.

Hijaz: Turkish mode featuring an augmented second between the 2nd and 3rd scale degrees. Common throughout former Ottoman areas of the Balkans and Middle East.

Horo: Dance (Bulgarian).

Kafana: Term used throughout the former Yugoslavia and Turkey to refer to a small local cafe featuring alcohol, coffee, and live music.

Kanun: Trapezoidal zither found throughout Central Asia and the Middle East. Plucked with picks or the fingernails.

Kaval: End-blown wooden flute played at an oblique angle and historically associated with shepherds.

Klezmer: Secular genre developed by European Jews and later incorporated by American jazz musicians. Instrumental melodies include imitations of weeping and laughing.

Kolo: Circle, line, or chain dance with elaborate variations. Practiced throughout the former Yugoslavia.

Kopanica: Line dance in 11/16 (2+2+3+2+2).

Lauto: Greek long-necked fretted lute.

Leventikos: Greek dance in 12/8 (3+2+2+3+2) or 16/8 (4+2+3+4+3).

Glossary

Maškoto: Macedonian men's dance in a slow 7/8 (3+2+2).

Monophonic: Musical texture consisting of an unaccompanied melodic line.

Polyphonic: Two or more melodies expressed simultaneously.

Opanci: Traditional footwear of Balkan peasants.

Oyun: Dance (Turkish).

Pravo: Bulgarian line dance in duple meter.

Pravo trakisko: Bulgarian Thracian line dance in duple meter (3+3).

Rembetiko/Rebetiko (plural *rebetika*): Genre of Greek urban folk music that developed in the 1920s and was revived in the 1960s. Lyrics often reflect the harsh reality of people who are marginalized.

Ručenica: Bulgarian dance in 7/16 (2+2+3).

Rusalki: The spirits of women who have died young, in childbirth, or by drowning. Said to venture from their watery homes to lure people to their deaths, particularly during Rusalka Week.

Sabor: Fair (Macedonian).

Sopila (plural *sopile*): Traditional Istrian double-reed woodwind instrument typically played in pairs.

Tambura: Long-necked fretted lute with a distinctive teardrop shape. Found throughout Bulgaria and Macedonia.

Tamburica: Family of long-necked fretted lutes of various sizes commonly found in northern Croatia and Serbia. Typically spelled *tamburitza* by members of Croatian- and Serbian-American communities.

Tapan: Double-headed drum struck with a large mallet and a thin switch to emphasize strong and weak beats.

Tarabuka: Ceramic goblet drum with a skin head. In Macedonia, this instrument is primarily associated with Turkish and Romani minority groups.

Ut: Turkish for *oud*, a fretless short-necked Arabic lute.

Zurla or Zurna: Double-reed aerophone commonly played in pairs and accompanied by *tapan* (*davul*). Associated with Romani and Turkish minority populations.

References

Babin, Barbara. "How the EEFC Board Works." *Kef Times* 8, no. 1 (2002 – 2003): 9.

Barz, Gregory E., and Timothy J. Cooley, eds. *Shadows in the Field: New Perspectives for Fieldwork in Ethnomusicology.* New York: Oxford University Press, 1997.

Benoit, Michelle. "From the EEFC Board." *Kef Times* 8, no. 1 (2002 – 2003): 2.

Bilides, David G., Rachel MacFarlane, and Kathryn Stately. *Macedonian Folk Songs for Voice and Tambura*, Vol. 1. Santa Fe: DaKaRa Music, 1997.

Bilides, David G., and Rachel MacFarlane. *Macedonian Folk Songs for Voice and Tambura*, Vol. 2. Seattle: Izvor Music, 2001.

Buchanan, Donna A. "Dispelling the Mystery: The Commodification of Women and Musical tradition in the Marketing of Le Mystère des Voix Bulgares." *Balkanistica* 9 (1996): 193 – 210.

———. "Metaphors of Power, Metaphors of Truth: The Politics of Music Professionalism in Bulgarian Folk Orchestras." *Ethnomusicology* 39, no. 3 (1995): 381 – 416.

———. *Performing Democracy: Bulgarian Music and Musicians in Transition*. Chicago: The University of Chicago Press, 2006.

Emerson, Robert M., Linda L. Shaw, and Rachel I. Fretz. *Writing Ethnographic Fieldnotes*. Chicago: The University of Chicago Press, 1995.

Forsyth, Martha. *Listen, Daughter, and Remember Well*. Sofia, Bulgaria: St. Kliment University Press, 1996.

Kirshenblatt-Gimblett, Barbara. "Folklore's Crisis." *The Journal of American Folklore* 111, no. 441 (1998): 281 – 327.

Kremenliev, Boris A. *Bulgarian-Macedonian Folk Music*. Berkeley: University of California Press, 1952.

Lancaster, Julie. "Balkan Camp Branches Out: East Coast Camps." *Kef Times* 7, no. 2 (2001 – 2002): 1, 10 – 11, 17.

———. "In Memoriam: Athan Karras." *Kef Times* 15, no. 1 (2010): 20.

———. "Interview with Bob Liebman." *Kef Times* 9, no. 1 (2003 – 2004): 5, 7, 16.

———. "Interview with Carol Silverman." *Kef Times* 7, no. 1 (2001): 10 – 11.

———. "Interview with Lauren Brody." *Kef Times* 11 (2006): 1, 3 – 4, 12.

———. "Interview with Miamon Miller." *Kef Times* 16, no. 1 (2000): 1, 10.

———. "Interview with Polly Tapia Ferber." *Kef Times* 8, no. 2 (2003): 5, 7, 9.

———. "Interview with Sonia Tamar Seeman." *Kef Times* 10 (2004 – 2005): 1, 5, 7, 12.

Laušević, Mirjana, *Balkan Fascination*. New York: Oxford University Press, 2007.

MacFarlane, Rachel. "Delving into the Heart of Brass: Zlatne Uste Goes to Serbia." *Kef Times* 9, no. 1 (2003-2004): 1, 8 – 9, 13.

Parrish, Mike. Review of *All Dressed Up*, by Medna Usta. *Dirty Linen* 42 (1992): 51.

Peppler, Jane. Review of *All Dressed Up*, by Medna Usta. *Sing Out!* 37, no. 4 (1993): 150.

Rice, Timothy. *May it Fill Your Soul: Experiencing Bulgarian Music*. Chicago: The University of Chicago Press, 1994.

———. *Music in Bulgaria: Experiencing Music, Expressing Culture*. New York: Oxford University Press, 2004.

Silverman, Carol. "Bulgarian Wedding Music between Folk and Chalga: Politics, Markets, and Current Directions." *Musicology* 7 (2007): 69 – 97.

———. "'Move Over Madonna': Gender, Representation, and the 'Mystery' of Bulgarian Voices." In *Over the Wall, After the Fall: Post-Communist Cultures through an East-West Gaze*, edited by Sibelan Forrester, Magdalena J. Zaborowska, and Elena Gapova, 212 – 237. Bloomington: Indiana University Press, 2004.

———. "Music and Marginality: Roma (Gypsies) of Bulgaria and Macedonia." In *Retuning Culture: Musical Changes in Central and Eastern Europe*, edited by Mark Slobin, 231 – 253. Durham, N.C.: Duke University Press, 1996.

———. *Romani Routes: Cultural Politics and Balkan Music in Diaspora*. New York: Oxford University Press, 2012.

Slobin, Mark. *Subcultural Sounds: Micromusics of the West*. Hanover, N.H.: Wesleyan University Press, 1987.

Sugarman, Jane C. Review of *May it Fill Your Soul: Experiencing Bulgarian Music*, by Timothy Rice. *Journal of the American Musicological Society* 49, no. 2 (1996): 332 – 343.

Wollter, Kim. "Balkan Village in the Redwoods." *Kef Times* 7, no. 1 (2001): 6 – 7.

Appendix: A Partial List of Bands that Play Balkan Music in the United States and Canada

All years are approximate, as reported to me. Variations in spelling and usage reflect the practice of individual bands.

A Different Village
Hartford, CT
1989 – 2002
International folk dance music

Agapi Mou
San Francisco Bay Area
2009 –
Folk dance music from Greece and beyond
www.agapimoumusic.com

Ala Nar
Eugene, OR
2001 – 2011
Middle Eastern and Turkish music
www.facebook.com/AlaNarMusic

Alchymeia
Seattle, WA
2010 –
East European/Celtic/Jazz/World fusion
www.alchymeia.com

All-Girl Band, The
Boston, MA
Early 2000s –
International folk dance music
www.facone.org/fac/livemusicatourdances.html#allgirlband

AMAN Folk Ensemble
Los Angeles, CA
1963 – 2004
International folk troupe
www.phantomranch.net/folkdanc/perform/aman
www.dancehistoryproject.org/genre/world-arts/a-history-of-the-aman-folk-ensemble-and-the-avaz-international-dance-theatre/

Anoush
San Francisco Bay Area
1993 – 2006
Folk dance music from the Southern Balkans and Armenia

Ansambl Mastika
Brooklyn, NY
2005 – 2011
Balkan-inspired original music
www.ansamblmastika.com

Ash (Eva Salina Primack and Aurelia Shrenker)
Brooklyn, NY
2007 – 2011
Vocal harmonies from the Balkans, Caucasus Georgia, the Appalachians, and Corsica
www.aesings.com

AVAZ International Dance Theatre
Los Angeles, CA
1977 – 2007
International folk troupe
www.phantomranch.net/folkdanc/perform/avaz.htm
Emerged from AMAN Folk Ensemble

B.A.B.E.S. (Bay Area Balkan Ensemble)
San Francisco Bay Area
1990 – 1995
Southern Balkan folk dance music

Balkalicious Fire Drive
San Francisco Bay Area
2012 –
Greek, Romani, and Macedonian party music
www.bfdmusic.com

Appendix

Balkanarama
Seattle, WA
www.balkanarama.com

BALKANIZE!
Richmond, VA
2005 – 2012
Balkan and Anatolian folk and belly dance music
www.facebook.com/pages/Balkanize/26660296591

Balkanizers
New York, NY
1981 – 1987
Balkan folk dance music

Balkanots, The
New Orleans, LA
2012 –
Folk dance music from the Balkans and beyond

Balkantones, The
Eugene, OR
1980s
Balkan village and wedding music

Balkan Appliances, The
Santa Cruz, CA
Early 1990s
Romani music

Balkan Cabaret
Seattle, WA
2001 – 2010
Ballads and dance songs from Eastern Europe

Balkan Fields
Boston Area/East Coast
2010 –
Bulgarian and greater Balkan folk dance music
Contact: turtleledge@charter.net

202   Appendix

Balkan Noyz Boyz
San Jose, CA
1985 – 1993
Romani music

Balladina
Eugene, OR
1989 – 2011
Traditional and contemporary international folk dance music (majority Balkan)
www.balladina.org

BAMCo (Balkan-American Music Company)
Washington, DC Metro Area
1983 – 1996
Wedding music

Barbelfish Balkan Band (formerly New Land Balkan Band)
Denver/Boulder, CO
1998 –
Bulgarian *bitov*, Macedonian, Greek, and other Balkan dance music
http://stevemullinsmusic.com/bands/the-barbelfish-balkan-band

Bekari
Seattle, WA
Early – mid-1980s
Men's Balkan singing

Bez Granica (formerly Family All-Star Band)
CT, MA, and VT
2007 – 2009
Balkan brass and accordion folk dance tunes

Bigfoot Family Band
Humboldt County, CA
1991 – 1995
Balkan folk dance music

Black Bear Combo
Chicago, IL
2002 –
Innovative Balkan brass
www.facebook.com/pages/Black-Bear-Combo/110303262342805

Appendix

Black Sea Hotel
Brooklyn, NY
2007 –
Innovative Balkan vocal harmonies
www.blackseahotelusa.com

Borozan Brass Band
Seattle, WA
Early 1980s
Balkan brass

Boston Folk Ensemble
Boston, MA
Early 1980s
International folk dance music (majority Balkan)

Boulder Folk Dance Orchestra
Boulder, CO
1970s
Balkan folk dance music

Brash Punks
San Francisco Bay Area
2004 – 2007
Balkan brass

Brass Menažeri
San Francisco Bay Area
2000 – 2013
Balkan brass

Brown Bag Band
Ann Arbor, MI
1980 – 1983
International folk dance music

Bucharest Drinking Team
Seattle, WA (with additional members in Oregon and Colorado)
2010 –
String and brass East European folk/pop fusion
www.bucharestdrinkingteam.com

Bury Me Standing
Boston, MA
2010 –
Gypsy dirge-core
www.burymestanding.org

Cambridge Folk Orchestra
Boston, MA
1960s –
International folk dance music (majority Balkan)
http://voluntocracy.org/CFO

Caprice Rouge
Mid-Hudson Valley, NY
2012 –
Balkan, Romani, and klezmer dance tunes
www.capricerouge.com

Choban Elektrik
Brooklyn, NY
2011 –
Traditional psychedelic jazz/rock Balkan folk
www.chobanelektrik.com

Chubritza
Arcata, CA
1993 –
International folk dance music (majority Balkan)
www.chubritza.com

Da! Mozhem (formerly Počti Gotov)
South San Francisco Bay Area
2006 –
Balkan folk dance music

Dave and the Dalmatians
Seattle, WA
1995 –
Men's *klapa* and beyond
www.daveandthedalmatians.com

Appendix

Deli Kanlı
San Francisco Bay Area
2007 – 2009
Turkish and Balkan folk music

Divi Zheni
Boston, MA
2000 –
Women's Bulgarian vocal ensemble
www.divizheni.net
Directed by Tatiana Sarbinska

Djevojke
Durham/Chapel Hill, NC
1984 – 2003
Women's Balkan vocal ensemble

Dolunay
Brooklyn, NY
2011 –
Turkish Rumeli and classical music
www.facebook.com/DolunayNYC

Drita Albanian Folk Orchestra
Los Angeles, CA
1982 –
Albanian folk music
Contact: ianpricebey@hotmail.com

Drómeno
Seattle, WA
2010 –
Greek and Balkan folk dance music
www.kyklosmusic.com/DROMENO

Dromia
San Diego, CA
2008 –
Traditional and modern Balkan and Romani folk dance music
www.facebook.com/DromiaBalkanMusic/info

Družba
Seattle, WA
Mid-1990s –
Bulgarian *bitov*

Družina
New York/New England
2009 –
Traditional and original Balkan folk dance music
Led by Bulgarian accordionist Ivan Milev

Dunava
Seattle, WA
2005 –
Women's Balkan vocal ensemble
www.dunava.org

Duquesne University Tamburitzans, The
Pittsburgh, PA
1937 –
East European folk music
www.duq.edu/life-at-duquesne/tamburitzans
Longest-running multicultural music and dance troupe in the United States

Eastern Exposure
San Diego, CA
2005 –
Traditional Balkan folk dance music
www.facebook.com/EasternExposureFolkDanceBand

Édessa
San Francisco Bay Area (with an additional member in Santa Fe, NM)
Early 1990s –
Balkan, Turkish, and Armenian folk music
www.edessamusic.com

Emperor Norton's Stationary Marching Band
Somerville, MA
2007 –
Avant world fusion
http://www.ensmb.com

Ensemble Sub Masa
Seattle, WA
Late 1990s – 2009
Romanian music
www.submasa.org

Ersatz Kolo
Atlanta, GA
1993 – 1998
International folk dance music (majority Balkan)

Ethnic Connection, The
Ann Arbor, MI
1988 –
Balkan, klezmer, and Yiddish music
www.pasty.net/~dowens/EC.htm

Eurodanceparty USA
Seattle, WA
2013 –
Balkan folkpop-electronica
www.facebook.com/eurodancepartyusa

Eva Salina
Brooklyn, NY
2010 –
Re-imagined songs of Balkan legends
www.evasalina.com

Evo Nas
Boston, MA
1975 – 1990
Bulgarian *bitov* and Macedonian *izvorno*

Fanfare Zambaleta
San Francisco Bay Area
2011 –
Balkan brass
www.fanfarezambaleta.com

208   Appendix

Fetatones, The
Mendocino Balkan Camp
2011 –
Greek Panos Gavalas tribute band

Flying Tomatoes
Boston, MA
1990s
International folk dance music

Free Range Orkestar
Los Angeles, CA
2010 –
Balkan brass/*chalga*
www.freerange.orkestar.net

Galata
Ann Arbor/Lansing, MI
Early 1990s – 1998
Greek, Balkan, and Scandinavian music

Galata Ensemble
Philadelphia, PA
2007 – 2009
Turkish music
www.myspace.com/galataensemble

Gin and Pontic
Portland, OR
2011 –
Pontic folk dance music

Gogofski
Boston, MA
Early 2000s –
Balkan music for dance and concert performance
www.gogofski.com

Gora Gora Orkestar
Denver/Boulder, CO
2009 –
Balkan Brass-Hop
http://goragora.org/

Appendix

Gradina
Sonoma County, CA
2001 –
Balkan folk songs for dance and concert performance
www.traditionalfun.org/gradina.html

Grupa Dunbarov (formerly Trio Dunbarov)
Vancouver, BC
1992 –
Traditional and modern Balkan folk music

Grupa Pubeski
Brooklyn, NY
2006 – 2009
Youth/adolescent Balkan ensemble
www.myspace.com/grupapubeski

Gypsy Cab
New York, NY
1985 – 1998
Electric Macedonian, Albanian, and Greek Romani music
Allegedly the first electric American Balkan folk band in the northeastern
United States

Hajde
Columbus, OH
1992 –
Bulgarian *bitov* and Macedonian *izvorno*
www.robertsnider.com/hajde

Hajduks
Los Angeles, CA
1950s – 1980s
Tamburitza orchestra
First musical accompaniment for AMAN Folk Ensemble

Harmonija
San Diego, CA
Mid-1990s – 2003
Vocal harmonies from the Balkans and beyond

210 Appendix

Harris Brothers Balkan Band
CT
2009 –
Romani music with some pan-Balkan folk

Helios Greek Band
San Francisco Bay Area
2008 –
Traditional Greek folk dance music
www.heliosgreekband.com

Hijaz
Central CT
2003 –
International folk dance music (majority Balkan)
www.alwaysonsunday.us/Hijaz.html

Igramo
Durham/Chapel Hill, NC

Inspector Gadje
San Francisco Bay Area
2011 –
Balkan brass
www.inspectorgadje.com

Interfolk Band
Orange County, CA
1983 –
International folk dance music
Contact: trekkspill@aol.com

International Folk Sounds
Philadelphia, PA
1995 –
International folk dance music (majority Balkan)
www.internationalfolksounds.org

Izgori
New Jersey/New York
1990 – late 2000s
Bulgarian *bitov* and Macedonian *izvorno* (with vocals)

Appendix

Izvor Balkan Orchestra
Seattle, WA
1975 – 1985
Bulgarian, Macedonian, and Romanian dance songs

Janam
San Francisco Bay Area
2008 –
Balkan, Near Eastern, and American roots and originals
www.janamband.com

Jazayer
San Francisco Bay Area
1973 – 2004
Middle Eastern, Balkan, and Armenian music

Kaba Seattle
Seattle, WA
Early 2000s –
Rhodope *gajda* ensemble

Kaba Venče
San Jose, CA
1975 – 1980
Southern Balkan folk dance music

Kadife
Brooklyn, NY
2007 – 2009
Southern Albanian folk music

Kafana Klub
Portland, OR
2001 –
Folk dance music from the Balkans and beyond
www.kafanaklub.com

Kafana Republik
Seattle, WA
2011 –
Ballads and dance songs from Eastern Europe
www.facebook.com/pages/Kafana-Republik/217150774975955?ref=br_tf
Contact: kafanarepublik@gmail.com

Kaladrios
San Francisco Bay Area
2006 – 2008
Eastern Mediterranean folk music

Karamfil
Rochester, NY
1985 – 2010
Bulgarian *bitov* and Macedonian *izvorno*

Karmache
Boulder/Denver, CO
2014 –
Hot Balkan/Flamenco fusion
http://megyork.com/

Karpouzi
Washington, DC Metro Area
1989 – 2010
Traditional folk music from Greece

Kavala Brass Band
New York, NY
Aegean Macedonian music

Kef
Eugene, OR
2006 –
Balkan brass
www.balkanmusic.org

Kefi
Humboldt County, CA
1995 – 2002
Balkan folk dance music with Greek-inspired originals

Kitka
Oakland, CA
1979 –
Traditional and contemporary women's vocal music from Eastern Europe
and beyond
www.kitka.org
Emerged from Westwind International Folk Ensemble

Appendix

KlaPaDooWopella (formerly Klapa Sokoli)
Seattle, WA
Late 1980s –
Men's *klapa* and beyond

Krebsic Orkestar
Portland, OR
2006 –
Balkan brass
www.facebook.com/pages/The-Krebsic-Orkestar/303404906339691

Kudzustvo
Durham/Chapel Hill, NC
1998 – 2005
Balkan folk dance music

Kultur Shock
Seattle, WA
1996 –
Rock/metal/punk arrangements of traditional Balkan folk music
www.kulturshock.com
Led by Bosnian pop singer Srdjan "Gino" Jevdjevic

Laduvane
Boston, MA
1970s
Women's Balkan vocal ensemble
www.facebook.com/pages/laduvane/327173483979373

Lansing Lizards (aka Lansingskite Gushteri)
Lansing, MI
1983 – mid-1990s
Bulgarian *bitov*

Libana
Cambridge, MA
1979 –
Vocal, instrumental, and dance traditions of the world's women
www.libana.com

Lokum
Burlington, VT
2008 –
Balkan, Turkish, Ladino, Armenian, and Arabic folk music
www.facebook.com/groups/51482668119

Lonely Coast, The
Seattle, WA
2010 –
Traditional folk songs from the Balkans and beyond
www.thelonelycoast.com

Longwood University Balkan Band
Farmville, VA
2002 – 2005
Balkan brass

Luk Na Glavata
Washington, DC Metro Area
1990 –
Macedonian *izvorno* (with vocals)
www.larryweiner.com/luknaglavata.htm

Lyuti Chushki
Washington, DC Metro Area
1998 –
Bulgarian *bitov* (with vocals)
www.lyutichushki.com

Mandala Folk Ensemble
Boston, MA
1966 – 2004
International folk dance troupe (majority Balkan and East European repertoire)

Meden Glas
Los Angeles, CA
1978 – 1981
Bulgarian folk music

Appendix   215

Medna Usta
Santa Cruz, CA
1986 – 1992
Bulgarian and Macedonian folk music

Medovina
Durham/Chapel Hill, NC
Early 1990s – 2007
Bulgarian *bitov*

Merak Gypsy Band
Los Angeles, CA
1990 – 1994
Electro-Romani music
Among the first American Balkan bands to emulate Macedonian Romani
electro-turbo

Meraki (formerly Ensemble Aperiskeptos)
Boston, MA
2008 –
Greek village music

Merakli
New York, NY
2008 –
Greek *smyrnaika*

Mixed Bag
Columbus, OH
1990 –
Folk dance music from the Balkans and beyond
http://recfolkdancecolumbus.org/MixedBag/about-us.htm

Mozarab
Nevada County, CA
Early 1980s – 1989
Balkan folk dance music with Turkish and Arabic music for belly dancers

Musaic
Arcata, CA
2007 –
International folk dance music and song (majority Balkan)
www.musaicmusic.com

Musiki Parea
Vancouver, BC
2000 –
Greek *dimotika*, *smyrneika*, *laika*, and Turkish music
www.facebook.com/pages/Musiki-Parea/105323680677

MWE
San Francisco Bay Area
2009 –
Turkish, Balkan, and Middle Eastern folk music
www.mweband.com

My Son the Doctor
Richmond, VA
2006 –
Romani, Yiddish, and klezmer music
www.facebook.com/pages/My-Son-the-Doctor/106839039360158

NAMA Orchestra
Los Angeles, CA
1974 – 1986
Balkan, Yiddish, and klezmer music
Emerged from AMAN Folk Ensemble
www.pasty.net/~dowens/Nama.htm
www.phantomranch.net/folkdanc/perform/aman_nama.htm

Napred
Durham/Chapel Hill, NC
1980 – 1986
International folk dance music

Nedelja
Durham/Chapel Hill, NC
1986 – 1990
International folk dance music

Nevenka
Los Angeles, CA
1976 –
Women's East European vocal ensemble
Emerged from AMAN Folk Ensemble

Appendix

New Orleans Balkan Superband
New Orleans, LA
2013 –
Brass, accordion, and string busking orchestra playing music of the Balkans
and Carpathians

Nišava
San Francisco Bay Area
1983 – 1985
Seattle, WA
1995 – 2001
Southern Balkan and Scandinavian folk dance music
Emerged from Westwind International Folk Ensemble

Niva
Brooklyn, NY
2011 –
Traditional Macedonian village music
www.facebook.com/nivabrooklyn

Novo Selo
Philadelphia, PA
1973 – 1978
Macedonian *izvorno*
First American Balkan ensemble to focus on Macedonian music

Orfeia
Montgomery County, MD
2006 –
Women's East European vocal ensemble
www.orfeia.wordpress.com
Directed by Tatiana Sarbinska

Orkestar Bez Ime
Minneapolis, MN
2002 –
Balkan party music
www.rogaria.com

218   Appendix

Orkestar RTW
Seattle, WA
1987 –
Modern Balkan folk music
www.orkestarrtw.com

Orkestar Šlivovica
Vancouver, BC
2008 –
Balkan brass
www.orkestarslivovica.org

Orkestar Zirkonium
Seattle, WA
2003 –
Balkan-inspired brass with elements of klezmer, Bollywood, jazz, punk, and
hip-hop
www.orkestarzirkonium.com

Orkestra Keyif
Members in Watertown, MA; The Bronx, Brooklyn, and New York, NY;
Santa Fe, NM; Toronto, ON; and Albany, CA
2000 – 2010
Turkish traditional urban folk music
www.myspace.com/orkestrakeyif

OrnâmatiK
Ann Arbor, MI
2010 –
Electric and acoustic Balkan music with a funky twist
www.ornamatik.com
Contact: ornamatik@gmail.com

Ostali Musikaši
Seattle, WA

Pajdaši
Boston, MA
2002 –
Croatian *tamburica* (with vocals)
www.facone.org/fac/livemusicatourdances.html#pajdasi

Palamythi
West Coast
2011 –
Epic Greek songs
www.facebook.com/palamythi

Pangéo
Seattle, WA
1996 – 2010
Greek folk music
www.kyklosmusic.com/PANGEO

Parea
Durham, NC
1993 –
Folk dance music from Greece and Asia Minor
http://people.duke.edu/~ruslan/Parea.html

Partners in Time (formerly Pleasant Peasant Band)
Honolulu, HI
Early 1980s –
Balkan, Near Eastern, and Middle Eastern folk dance music with some jazz
fusion
http://partnersintime.weebly.com

Pasatémpo
Seattle, WA
2005 –
Greek *rebetika*
www.kyklosmusic.com/PASATEMPO

Pennywhistlers, The
New York, NY
1962 – mid-1970s
East European, Yiddish, and American vocal arrangements
First American women's East European vocal ensemble
Directed by Ethel Raim

People's Bizarre
San Francisco Bay Area
2001 – 2006
Balkan/jazz fusion
www.bellowhead.com/music-site/peoplesbizzare.html

Pickled Herring Tamburica Orchestra
NY

Pinewoods Band, The
Boston, MA
1991 –
International folk dance music
www.facone.org/fac/livemusicatourdances.html#pinewoodsband

Pitu Guli
Los Angeles, CA
1970s
Bulgarian *bitov*, Macedonian *izvorno*, and early wedding music
Emerged from AMAN Folk Ensemble

Planina - Songs of Eastern Europe
Denver/ Boulder, CO
1988 –
East European mixed chorus
www.planina.org

Plovdiv Party Bus
San Francisco Bay Area
2013 –
Music from the Balkans and beyond

Pontic Firebird
New York, NY
2008 –
Greek folk dance music from Western Pontos

Prsut
NY

Radost Folk Ensemble
Seattle, WA
1976 –
East European music and dance troupe
www.radost.org

Rakia Brass Band
Los Angeles, CA
2009 –
Balkan Brass
www.rakiabrassband.com

Rakiya
Boston, MA
2003 –
Electric Balkan and Romani dance music
www.rakiya.com

Raya Brass Band
Brooklyn, NY
2009 –
Original and traditional Balkan brass
www.rayabrassband.com

Rebetiki Parea
San Francisco Bay Area
1994 – 1996
Early *rebetika*

Round Mountain
Santa Fe, NM
2002 –
Indie/World folk with strong Balkan influence
www.roundmountainmusic.com

Savina Women's Folk Choir
Berkeley, CA
1980 – 2000
Women's Balkan vocal ensemble
Emerged from Westwind International Folk Ensemble

Sedianka
Seattle, WA
Late 1980s – mid-1990s
Women's Balkan vocal ensemble

Sevda Balkan Music Ensemble, The
New York, NY
1988 – 1998
Traditional folk and urban song and music of the Balkans

Sevdah
San Francisco Bay Area
1986 – 1990
Southern Balkan folk dance music

Sevdah Orchestra
New York area
1984 – 1988
Music from Macedonia, Albania, and beyond

Sherefe (aka Şerefe)
Boulder, CO
1996 –
Greek, Turkish, Balkan, and Arabic music
www.sherefe.org

Sherita
Brooklyn, NY
2011 –
Balkan, Turkish, Sephardic, and original music
www.sheritanyc.com

Shining Moon
Boston, MA
2000 –
International folk dance music (majority Balkan)

Skordalia
Boston, MA

Skorosmrtnica
Boston, MA
2009 –
International folk dance music
www.facebook.com/skorosmrtnica

Sladki Doumi
Rochester, NY
1992 –
Women's Bulgarian and Macedonian vocal ensemble

Slaveya
Washington, DC Metro Area
1984 –
Women's vocal harmonies from the Balkans and Caucasus regions
www.slaveya.org

Slavic Soul Party!
Brooklyn, NY
1999 –
BalkanSoulGypsyFunk
www.slavicsoulparty.com

Smyrneïki Kompania, The
New York, NY
1985 –
1920s and '30s Asia Minor Greek cafe music

Sokalska Grupa
San Diego, CA
1995 – 1997
Bulgarian *bitov*

Stick and Rag Village Orchestra
Boston (Jamaica Plain), MA
2005 – 2007
Traveling street band playing music from circus, Balkan, and klezmer
traditions
http://ganggreenough.home.comcast.net/~ganggreenough/stickandrag

Svila
Portland, OR
2001 – 2011 (on hiatus)
Women's Balkan vocal ensemble

Svirači
South San Francisco Bay Area
1974 –
Bulgarian *bitov* and Macedonian *izvorno*
www.sviraci.persson-little.com
Allegedly the first band to coalesce out of Mendocino Balkan Camp

Svitanya
Philadelphia, PA
2001 –
Women's East European vocal ensemble
www.svitanya.org

Tipsy Oxcart
Brooklyn, NY
2012 –
Wedding music with a rock rhythm section
www.tipsyoxcart.com

Tito's Revenge
Boston, MA
Mid-1990s
Electric Balkan music

Toids, The
San Francisco Bay Area (formerly Los Angeles)
1996 – 2008
Original music in various Balkan styles

Top Dog Run
Oakland, CA
2002 – 2004
Bulgarian, Macedonian, and Romani music with wedding band influence

Tri Devojce
San Francisco Bay Area
1971 – 1974
Balkan vocal trio

Trio Slavej
Eugene, OR
2001 – 2008
Bulgarian village and wedding music

Appendix   225

True Life Trio
San Francisco Bay Area
2010 –
Vocal harmonies from Eastern Europe and the Americas
www.truelifetrio.com

Tungl Ludo
Eugene, OR
2003 – 2005
ElectricEuroVillageRock

Turli Tava
NY/Cleveland, OH
2000 –
Macedonian music

Turlu
San Francisco Bay Area
2003 – 2007
Balkan folk dance music

Tzigany
Pensacola, FL
1972 – 1978
Folk dance jukebox band

Vadni Raca
San Jose/Menlo Park, CA
1974 – 1976
Southern Balkan folk dance music

Vardar
Seattle, WA
Mid-1980s –
Macedonian *izvorno*

Vecherinka
Seattle, WA
Early – late 1980s
Women's Balkan vocal ensemble

226 Appendix

Veelah
Denver/Boulder, CO
2003 –
Hot East European urban folk music
http://megyork.com/

Verna Druzhina
Santa Cruz, CA
2004 – 2011
Bulgarian *bitov*

Veselba
Ann Arbor/Lansing, MI
1998 –
Bulgarian-style *troika* (*tambura*, *kaval*, and *gŭdulka*)
http://ritter.astro.utoledo.edu/~ndm/FD/veselba.html

Veselba
Los Angeles, CA
2002 –
Bulgarian and Macedonian folk dance music
Contact: ianpricebey@hotmail.com

Veveritse Brass Band
Brooklyn, NY
2006 –
Balkan brass
www.facebook.com/pages/Veveritse-Brass-Band/342515906992?ref=br_tf

Vinovana
Boston, MA
1993 – 2001
International folk dance music

Vitosha
San Francisco Bay Area
1976 – 1986
Bulgarian *bitov*

Voluta Vox
Santa Cruz, CA
1996 – 2000
Song and dance from the Bulgarian, Macedonian, and Romani traditions

Appendix

Westwind International Folk Ensemble
San Francisco Bay Area
1959 – 2011
International folk troupe
www.westwind-folk.org

West Philadelphia Orchestra
Philadelphia, PA
2006 –
Avant Balkan brass
www.westphiladelphiaorchestra.com

What Cheer Brigade
Providence, RI
2005 –
Punk brass with Balkan, Bollywood, samba, and hip-hop inspiration
www.whatcheerbrigade.com

Which Way East
Brooklyn, NY
2007 – 2011
Traditional and contemporary Balkan music

World Village Dance Band
Winnipeg, MB
2005 –
International folk dance music (majority East European)

Xopo
Western New England
Late 1990s –
Traditional Balkan folk dance music
www.xopoandfriends.net

Yale Slavic Chorus
New Haven, CT
1969 –
Women's East European vocal ensemble
www.yaleslavicchorus.com
First all-women's group at Yale University

228 Appendix

Yasha!
San Francisco Bay Area
1978 – 1983
Folk dance music from Greece and Turkey

Zagnut Orkestar
Brooklyn, NY
2004 – 2009
Balkan brass
www.zagnut-orkestar.com

Zapadne Lole
San Francisco Bay Area
1988 – 1997
Tamburica music

Zdravets
Boston, MA
1989 –
Bulgarian *bitov* and Macedonian *izvorno*
www.zdravets.com

Zhena Folk Chorus
San Fernando Valley, CA
1984 – 1994
San Pedro, CA
1994 –
Village songs from Central/Eastern Europe and beyond
www.zhena.org
Emerged from AVAZ International Dance Theatre

ZIMZALA
Orange County, CA
2008 –
Traditional and modern international folk dance music
www.musicbypatty.com/zimzala-folk-band.html

Ziyiá
Members in Berkeley, CA; Boston, MA; and Seattle, WA
1990 –
Traditional Greek music
www.ziyia.com

Appendix

Zlatne Uste
New York, NY
1983 –
Balkan brass
www.zlatneuste.org

Zokino Brothers
San Francisco Bay Area
1978 – 1980
Southern Balkan folk dance music
Allegedly the first American Balkan brass band

Zornitsa
Boston, MA
1992 –
Men's Bulgarian and Macedonian vocal music
Directed by Tatiana Sarbinska

Zozulka
Brooklyn, NY
2011 –
Traditional Ukrainian village songs
www.zozulkatrio.wordpress.com

Zurli Drustvo
CT (formerly Boston, MA and New York, NY)
1984 –
Traditional western Macedonian *zurla* dance tunes

Žabe i Babe
Middletown, CT
1991 – 2000
Traditional and popular music from Bosnia and the former Yugoslavia, with
some originals
www.zabeibabe.com
Co-founded by Mirjana Laušević and Tim Eriksen

Ženska Pesna
New York, NY
1970 – early 1990s
Traditional Balkan village songs
First American Balkan vocal ensemble to perform village songs

230   Appendix

Živio Ethnic Arts Ensemble
Salt Lake City, UT
1982 –
Traditional and modern Balkan, East European, and Turkish folk music
www.zivio.org

Živo Bitov Orchestra
Portland, OR
Bulgarian *bitov* and Macedonian *izvorno*

Hasina Cohen completed her bachelor's degree in ethnomusicology at the University of Oregon under Mark Levy and Anne Dhu McLucas. In late 2014, she will embark on an intensive study of classical Chinese medicine and has been thrilled to discover deep commonalities between these seemingly disparate traditions. Her passions include agates, oak trees, color, rhythm, and the fathomless expanse of the human soul.

Made in the USA
Charleston, SC
30 July 2014